GW00368175

CREDIT MANAGEMENT

*how to manage credit effectively
and make a real contribution to profits*

CREDIT MANAGEMENT

*how to manage credit effectively
and make a real contribution to profits*

R.M.V. BASS

Institute of Credit Management
Special Members' Edition

BUSINESS BOOKS
London Melbourne Sydney Auckland Johannesburg

Business Books Ltd
An imprint of the Hutchinson Publishing Group
17-21 Conway Street, London W1P 6JD

Hutchinson Publishing Group (Australia) Pty Ltd
16-22 Church Street, Hawthorn, Melbourne,
Victoria 3122

Hutchinson Group (NZ) Ltd
32-34 View Road, PO Box 40-086, Glenfield, Auckland 10

Hutchinson Group (SA) (Pty) Ltd
PO Box 337, Bergvlei 2012, South Africa

First published 1979
Reprinted 1981
Special edition for the
Institute of Credit Management 1984

© RICHARD M.V. BASS, 1979

All rights reserved. Except for normal review purposes,
no part of this book may be reproduced or utilised in any
form or by any means, electronic or mechanical, including
photocopying, recording, or by any information storage
and retrieval system without permission of the publishers.

Printed and bound in Great Britain by
Anchor Brendon Ltd, Tiptree, Essex

ISBN 0 220 67026 9 (cased)
　　　0 220 67029 3 (paper)

Contents

v

Foreword

by Dennis G.S. Williams
European Credit Manager, Texas Instruments Inc.

I am very pleased to have the opportunity of writing a foreword to this book by my friend and former colleague Richard Bass. Regrettably, the bibliography available to the student of credit management in the United Kingdom is still relatively small, and a significant proportion of it is published in the USA and, therefore, directed to the North American reader rather than to his European counterpart. This volume will, I believe, prove an acceptable and useful addition to the bookshelves of credit managers and others concerned with the management of trade credit in the British Isles.

In commending this work to the intending reader, I am encouraged by the knowledge that Mr Bass is among those practitioners of credit management who recognise it for what it should be, namely comprehensive and professional management of what is frequently one of the largest, if not the largest, asset in the company's balance sheet. The successful running of a business organisation generally involves the co-ordinated management of a group of diverse assets. It is a matter for regret that in many companies which are otherwise capably managed, trade accounts receivable, though representing as much as 30—40 per cent of total asset value, do not receive their proper share of professional attention, but are relegated to a subordinate level of activity often carried out part-time by financial accounting personnel who do not always have the specialised training, or indeed the authority, to perform the function effectively.

The heavy commitment of company funds represented by trade debtors means that the amounts and periods of credit granted, the quality of the resulting accounts receivable and the techniques used to collect them can all affect sales, profitability, liquidity, the security of working capital and the return on investment of the whole enterprise. It follows that the responsibility for overall supervision of the receivables portfolio, particularly in a large company, is a heavy one which, if it is to be discharged effectively, must be entrusted to a well-trained and fully qualified credit manager.

It may be opportune here to outline briefly the qualities which such a person should possess. The key to a successful credit function in any company is primarily the calibre of the individual chosen to head the operation. The role, if fully developed, can be a demanding one. The first requirement, in addition to possession of the technical capability expected of him, is the understanding of marketing objectives and profit goals, coupled with a broad comprehension of the financial aspects of running a business. The credit manager should identify with overall company policies and be a convinced and enthusiastic proponent of the contribution which good credit management can make towards their achievement. He should be, both by nature and by virtue of the responsibility vested in him, a decision-maker whose judgements will be respected and opinions be sought by his directors and fellow-managers. He will be constantly searching for better ways of doing the job. Good interface with people at every level in his own and outside organisations is essential. Effective credit management is usually not achieved without good communication; the credit manager who frequently leaves his desk and visits customers, attends sales meetings and generally uses every opportunity to sell himself and the company's credit policies will (and so, therefore, will his company) always have a head start over the competition in the successful management of the receivables portfolio.

It is to this type of credit manager, profit-oriented, aware of the wider aspects of business, articulate and innovative, and also to the more junior staff who aspire to succeed him, that I believe this book is addressed. I wish it and its readers every success.

Preface

Credit management is an art which has been practised since the earliest days of civilisation. Being an art — and not a precise science — its techniques have constantly changed according to the needs of the business community.

Credit management in the UK has developed a great deal over the last ten years. Yet whilst we may take pride in being ahead of the rest of Europe in recognising its importance, we are still decades behind the USA. This is strikingly illustrated by the fact that the National Association of Credit Management was founded in the USA in 1896, whereas our own Institute of Credit Management did not see the light of day until 1939.

I am conscious of the fact that in the UK today there are many practices and customs in different industries which result in countless differences in the way credit control operates. I can only draw on my personal experience, broadened by contact with credit managers from many industries and many countries over the last twenty years.

Within this limitation, I shall try to focus on the requirements of successful credit management in industry today. Consumer credit is not covered nor do I include any detailed examination of insolvency procedures. The emphasis that will, I hope, emerge is on credit management as a positive function, vital to the protection of assets but also contributing to profitability.

A substantial part of the book is devoted to export credit because comparatively little has been published on a topic which has become of increasing interest to credit people in recent years.

Acknowledgements

First and foremost I must thank my wife and family for their patience during the twelve months this book was in preparation. Secondly, I owe a great deal to Irene who typed (and re-typed) without complaint.

Many friends and colleagues have helped me, especially in the chapters concerned with export credit. I should particularly like to mention Graham Findlay of Grindlay Brandts Ltd, Nigel Allington and others from Credit Insurance Association Ltd, George Volsik of Bank of America, John Gallagher of Dun & Bradstreet Ltd, David Webb of GKN Ltd, Joe Binns of Fenchurch, Credit Insurance Services Ltd, Tom Hewson of Oxy Metal Industries Europe, Richard Evans and others from ECGD and Denzil Devos of Amalgamated Metal Corporation Ltd.

Finally — my thanks to the authors of the many publications I have consulted for information. A list of these is given at the end of the references.

Part One
Credit Management

Chapter 1

The nature and cost of credit

'Credit, like the honour of a female, is of too delicate a nature to be treated with laxity — the slightest hint may inflict an injury which no subsequent effort can repair.' (*The Morning Chronicle*, 1825). There can hardly be a credit man unable to quote from his own experience an example of the truth of this aphorism.

The right to receive trade credit is very often taken for granted, which goes a long way towards explaining the need for tact and diplomacy. Industry and commerce would rapidly come to a halt if goods could only be sold to buyers able to pay cash on delivery, and indeed the whole concept of a mass production economy depends on continuous buying activity. The result of this need to give credit is that a substantial amount of cash is tied up in accounts receivable (otherwise known as debtors or sales ledger). This simple fact is the crux of all credit management problems. Successful business depends on money flowing through the company fast enough to meet all commitments. Profits derive from the efficient use of assets, but if the cash-flow is sluggish, the profits may never be realised.

The cost of credit

The starting point for efficient credit control is recognition of the cost of credit and its potential effects on profit and liquidity.

The cost of money borrowed from the bank is, let us assume, 9 per cent p.a. This gives a cost of 0.75 per cent for money owing for one month. A company selling on 'net monthly' or 'net 30 days' terms should therefore include in its prices at least 0.75 per cent to cover the cost of credit. But this assumes that customers pay on time. If the average debtor period is three months, then this is costing 2.25 per cent.

The only way this can be recognised and properly accounted for is to charge interest for overdue payments — and conversely to give discount for cash-on-delivery. Exhibit 1.1 illustrates this, comparing Company A (giving no credit), Company B (receiving payments on time) and Company C (charging interest). The subject of payment terms, discounts and charges will be returned to in more detail later.

Besides the cost of money, granting credit involves many other costs such as staff, space, equipment, stationery, credit information, debt recovery, etc. In most companies these costs should be readily obtainable but, unlike borrowing costs, they do not increase uniformly according to the length of credit taken. It is suggested, therefore, given the company is selling on credit terms, that these be regarded as part of the total administration cost built into the price structure. When a decision is taken to spend more money on credit management, care must be taken to relate the extra costs to the expected benefits.

Exhibit 1.1

	Company A, £	Company B, £	Company C, £
Annual sales	600,000	600,000	600,000
Debtor level	Nil	50,000[1]	150,000[2]
Net profit (5%) before cost of credit	30,000	30,000	30,000
Less 0.75% discount for COD	(4,500)		
Less 0.75% cost of credit		(4,500)	
Less 2.25% cost of credit			(13,500)
Plus interest at 0.75% per month			9,000
NET PROFIT	£25,500	£25,500	£25,500

[1] = 1 month, [2] = 3 months

4

Exhibit 1.2

£

Before (Year 1)

Sales p.a.	*1,200,000*
Debtor level	*300,000 = 3 months sales*
Cost of financing	*27,000 @ 9% p.a.*

After (Year 2)

Sales p.a.	*1,320,000*
Debtor level	*220,000 = 2 months sales*
Cost of financing	*19,800 @ 9% p.a.*

INTEREST SAVED = £9,900 p.a.

A decision to recruit a credit manager at say £6,000 p.a., giving a total extra cost to the company of around £7,500 p.a., can only be justified if the likely result is to reduce bank interest by more than that through a reduction in the level of debtors — as in Exhibit 1.2.

The cost of credit in terms of bank borrowings can thus be measured fairly easily, but it goes further than this.

The effect of credit on profits

From Exhibit 1.1 it is clear that if Company C does *not* charge interest on its overdue accounts, the net profit of £25,500 (deducting the cost of one month's credit) will be reduced by a further £9,000. This might be counterbalanced by a reduction in stocks or delays in paying creditors but this is irrelevant. The effect of overdue accounts is a direct erosion of profit. Nonetheless, credit is sometimes used to promote sales more especially in export but also in the home market, usually in an endeavour to attract business from competitors. Long credit can have the opposite effect to that intended, however, since the cost of financing a higher level of debtors may outweigh the additional profit. This is illustrated in Exhibit 1.3. United Components Ltd is shown in Column A with a net profit of £4,200. A decision is made to give an extra 30 days' credit in the belief this will bring a 33.3 per cent increase in sales with a consequent increase of profit to £4,400 (Column B). In the event, sales only rise by 25 per cent and the increased profit is outweighed by higher credit costs (Column C). In desperation the company lengthens its terms by a further 30 days and turnover rises 50

Exhibit 1.3

	A	B	C	D
Sales	120,000	160,000	150,000	180,000
Debtors	20,000	40,000	37,500	60,000
Credit, days	60	90	90	120
Net profit (5%) before cost of credit	6,000	8,000	7,500	9,000
Cost of credit (9%)	(1,800)	(3,600)	(3,375)	(5,400)
FINAL NET PROFIT	£4,200	£4,400	£4,125	£3,600

per cent over the original level. The cost of financing 120-day credit, however, is so high that the end result is even worse (Column D).

The effect of credit on liquidity

Liquidity can be defined as the ease and speed with which current assets can be turned into cash sufficient to meet current liabilities. Stocks have to be turned into sales before they can generate cash and it is generally unprofitable to hold large cash balances. Debtors therefore hold the key to liquidity.

Exhibit 1.4 shows the working capital cycle.

In order to meet its regular commitments — wages and salaries, rent and rates, fuel and factory expenses, raw material and components, hire purchase and interest charges — a company depends on cash flowing through the system at a certain pace. If that pace slows down because debtors are out of control we have a 'cash flow' problem. In times of high inflation this problem is severely aggravated. This was vividly illustrated in the automotive industry in the mid-1970s. The near-monopoly suppliers of raw material imposed price increases and expected payment to terms from customers who could not recover the extra costs without protracted negotiations with the vehicle manufacturers.

If debtors are not being turned into cash fast enough, there can be only two reasons. Either credit terms are too long to support the business or there is an overdue situation. Credit terms have already been examined in the context of credit and profits. The problem of collecting — or avoiding — overdue accounts is covered in Chapter 8.

Exhibit 1.4

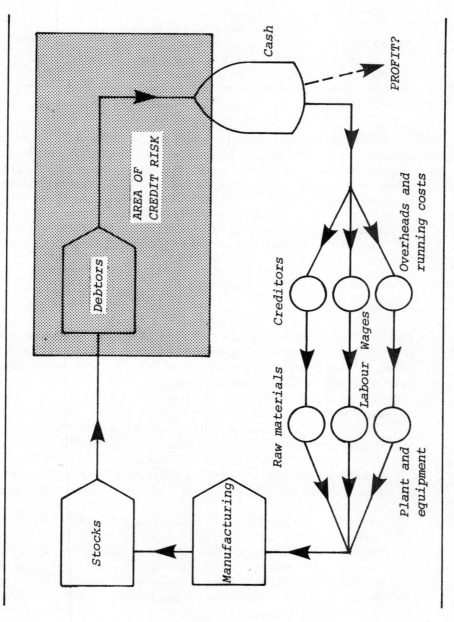

Exhibit 1.5

Current debts are worth	100%
30-day overdue debts are worth	90%
90-day overdue debts are worth	75%
180-day overdue debts are worth	50%
Debts over 12 months old are worth	30%

At this point it is interesting to examine the declining value of overdue accounts (see Exhibit 1.5). This table does not take inflation into account but merely expresses a realistic view of the problems a credit manager must cope with. It is not suggested that 70 per cent of debts over one year old will be 'bad debts' in the usual sense of the words. What is more likely is that the majority of such overdues are in dispute — probably with a large customer — and the end result will be a 'write-off' (hopefully shared) when neither party can prove the other's liability.

Bad debts

Bad debts are often regarded as the most important test of the credit manager's performance. Chapter 19 questions this view and deals with other ways of measuring performance. What needs to be examined here is the effect of bad debts on profits.

When a bad debt occurs it is important to consider what would have happened if that sale had not been made. There are two situations:

1   The factory is working at full capacity and has more orders than it can handle. An order is accepted from Company Y which later goes into liquidation owing 2-3 months' debts. Since business could have been accepted from alternative buyers, the eventual loss must be considered 100 per cent bad — with no mitigating circumstances.

2   The factory is working well below capacity and fixed costs are very high. An order is accepted from Company Z, known to be a 'high risk'. After six months it goes into liquidation. Given that there was no alternative buyer and that several months sales were paid for, it could well have been a correct decision to take the business. The contribution to costs before insolvency occurs could even outweigh the bad debt.

This is a very difficult area for the credit manager. Correct decisions depend on a good knowledge of the company's costing system, and

Exhibit 1.6

	1977	1978
Agriculture	25	29
Manufacturing:		
Food, drink and tobacco	38	40
Chemicals	31	22
Metal and engineering	343	310
Textiles and clothing	239	225
Timber and furniture	128	128
Paper, printing and publishing	136	103
Other manufacturing	264	248
TOTAL MANUFACTURING	*1,179*	*1,076*
Construction	1,004	929
Road haulage	256	229
Wholesaling	476	320
Retailing	788	782
Financial and professional services	723	765
Hotels and restaurants	144	161
Garages	108	119
Other consumer services	506	357
Other industries	622	319
TOTAL COMPANY LIQUIDATIONS IN ENGLAND AND WALES	*5,831*	*5,086*

there may be other factors to consider such as the cost of redundancies if business is refused, or the need to build up a new market.

The actual risks of incurring bad debts vary greatly from industry to industry. Engineering firms producing goods to individual customer specifications incur greater risks than distributors supplying 'off the shelf' as not only has the debt been lost but very probably the value of work-in-progress and even raw materials. Exhibit 1.6 shows the latest statistics on insolvencies in England and Wales in the years 1976-7, broken down by industry (taken from *Trade & Industry*). The question of bad debt reserves is considered in Chapter 19.

Chapter 2

The role of credit management

The purpose of this chapter is to examine the role of the credit manager, to look at his relationships within the company, in particular the sales/credit relationship, and to consider the organisation of the credit department.

In recent years there have been numerous surveys of credit management in British industry, prompted by an increasing awareness of the need for better cash-flow management. That published by the British Institute of Management in 1974 opens with the following statement: 'There is probably no more neglected area of financial management in the UK than credit control and management'.

A striking contrast exists between the USA and the UK on the average collection period, i.e. how quickly debtors are turned into cash. In 1977-78 the level of manufacturers' accounts receivable in the USA was between 41 and 43 days' sales (*Credit & Financial Newsletter*, published by National Association of Credit Management, 475 Park Avenue South, New York 10016). The same source quotes an 'all-time high' of 45 days (in 1970). Whilst information is less readily available on UK industry, approximate figures for quoted and non-quoted companies are believed to be 65 and 70 days.

The cost of credit and its effects on profits and liquidity have been examined. It is clear that uncontrolled credit can rapidly bring disaster. The example of the USA surely indicates that good credit management can help liquidity and profits, since nowhere in the world is the practice of credit management so advanced and its status so recognised.

The first essential is to define the credit manager's job. In many companies there is no such person as credit manager or credit controller. It usually falls to a member of the accounting staff to look after the sales ledger and to organise cash collections. Credit control is not regarded as his principal responsibility and all too often credit work is fitted in when time permits — or when a cash crisis occurs. Many of the companies who do employ a full-time credit manager regard him as a debt-collector of relatively low status in the hierarchy. Ultimately the status of the credit manager can only be improved by a more enlightened attitude by top management, recognising the potential contribution a professional credit manager can give. In the Exeter Survey of 1975, which covered credit management practice in 90 leading UK companies, 37 per cent of credit managers had the status of junior manager.*

Exhibit 2.1 gives a brief job description which should fit most companies' requirements. Most of the other chapters in this book are an attempt to describe how these functions should be carried out and controlled.

To return to the credit manager himself. Many arguments have been fought over his line of responsibility. The most usual arrangement is to report to the chief accountant. The success of this relationship will depend to a great extent on how far the chief accountant holds the traditionally conservative and cautionary views associated with that

Exhibit 2.1 The job of the credit manager

Basic function

Protection of the company's investment in debtors.

Principal objectives

(a) *Assessment of credit standing of both new and existing customers.*
(b) *Establishment of terms, having regard to the risk involved and the potential profit.*
(c) *Maintenance of the sales ledger.*
(d) *Collection of accounts in a manner that produces the optimum cash flow whilst ensuring continuity of business.*

*My thanks to P.R.A. Kirkman for the use of this material — *Author*.

11

position — which will tend to promote the debt-collector image. Less frequently the credit manager is found within the sales/marketing area. This suggests a different view of the credit function, with the accent on granting credit rather than controlling it. There must be a real danger of inadequate control if the credit manager is subject to the immediate authority of the sales director.

There is a case for making the credit manager independent of both finance and marketing, i.e. reporting direct to the managing director.

This is unusual in the UK — more commonly found in the USA — and clearly demands a person of a very high calibre.

The best arrangement is perhaps for the credit department to be an independent unit under the finance director. The credit manager must have a fundamental grasp of and sympathy with both finance and marketing, but his ultimate responsibility must be to the head of finance.

Basis of credit policy

It is essential that a newly appointed credit manager be given clear guidance on company policy towards the granting of credit. A few companies provide a detailed written credit policy but the majority — whether deliberately or by neglect — do not do this, relying instead on the day-to-day relationships between the credit manager and his superior. This avoids the rigidity of a written policy but it can result in areas of doubt and uncertainty. Much will depend on the size of the firm. Generally speaking the bigger the firm the greater the need for some form of written statement, if only to define the credit manager's authority and terms of reference. Guidelines of some kind are very desirable. There are two key questions which must be answered before the credit manager can operate effectively:

1 What level of receivables is regarded as acceptable? What is the nature of the market, i.e. steady or seasonal? The policy of the competition and the current marketing strategy will all have an influence but the decisive factor will be the amount of working capital available.

The credit manager must know what is expected of him and he must be prepared to argue his case if presented with a target which he feels can only be achieved by unduly stringent controls. This point will come up again when credit approval and collections are examined. It is very easy to set rigid standards, to accept only the demonstrably good risks and to demand payment to terms without exception. In the long run a policy of this nature is sure to restrict sales and lose goodwill.

2   Who is responsible for deciding credit limits and terms of payment? Failure to answer this question lies at the root of many bad sales/credit relationships. Too often the credit manager assumes that he has authority when the sales manager has not been consulted and quite naturally resents interference with his customers. According to the Exeter Survey, responsibility for payment terms rests as frequently with sales as it does with credit control, although the questions of risk assessment and acceptance of new customers are more often decided by the credit department. This is hardly logical, since credit limits and payment terms are both different aspects of risk control and should not be determined in isolation from each other.

The best situation is where close liaison exists between credit and sales. Regular meetings between sales and credit departments can produce this. The sales manager will advise the credit manager of a new prospect who he hopes will take a certain volume of goods. The credit manager's job is to check the financial condition of the prospect and try to set a credit limit which will accommodate the expected sales on normal terms. If the maximum credit limit is not sufficient, perhaps a solution can be found in shortening the terms. This theme will be returned to in Chapter 3, but whatever the answer it can only emerge from a close working relationship between sales and credit departments. The final decision should lie with the credit manager, since by training and experience he is better equipped to make a correct judgement. There must always be a 'court of appeal' to which a problem can be referred but this will rarely be used where a good relationship exists.

The sales/credit relationship

The need for this relationship to be positive and close cannot be over-emphasised. It is very easy for the credit manager to be regarded as a negative figure whose purpose is to restrict sales, impose limits, demand money and stop deliveries. Such actions have to be taken — they will only be accepted and recognised as necessary if there exists between sales and credit a climate of confidence. Confidence is bred primarily by good personal relationships. The credit manager who rarely leaves his desk and bombards the marketing department with a stream of procedures, controls and blacklists, must not be surprised if his efforts are greeted by a lack of enthusiasm or even hostility. Written communication is certainly necessary, but how much better if it is preceded by a face-to-face chat or at least a 'phone-call to clear the way.

A more long-term route to confidence is education. The credit manager must ensure that his own staff have some basic product knowledge, as well as detailed information about customers. Of vital importance is the training of new salesmen, who must be taught at the outset the effect on profits of slow payments and insolvencies.

Regular meetings with sales management are another way to promote confidence. Items to be included in monthly credit meetings might be as shown in Exhibit 2.2. The wide range of topics given illustrates the need for a close working relationship with the sales team.

Exhibit 2.2

1	*Minutes of last month's meeting.*
2	*Last month's collection results and debtor figures.*
3	*Discussion on problem accounts.*
4	*Review of outstanding queries.*
5	*Proposed blacklist.*
6	*Changes in distribution network.*
7	*Marketing prospects.*
8	*Cash discounts.*
9	*Should we introduce a reservation of property clause?*
10	*Should we charge interest on overdue accounts?*
11	*Problems in controlling consignment stock.*
12	*Who should be responsible for export documentation?*
13	*Next month's sales conference.*
14	*Next month's programme of customer visits.*

Item 5 — 'Proposed Blacklist' — is a particularly sensitive area over which friction can easily develop. The decision to suspend deliveries as a means of extracting payment and reducing the risk of a bad debt cannot be taken lightly in any company. Some form of early warning system is essential, to alert the sales manager to the situation and give him the opportunity of intervening. In large companies slow payment is often deliberate policy but the firm's buyer may not be aware that important supplies are being jeopardised. A telephone call from the creditor's sales manager warning the buyer of the problem can sometimes accelerate a payment after all approaches to the accountant have failed.

The credit manager has to beware of handing responsibility over to the sales department. It is his job to obtain payment and to use every means at his disposal. This must include liaison with the sales department in the manner suggested above. At the end of the day payment has to be extracted before the profit is wiped out by extended credit.

Organisation of the credit department

In the early days of a firm's life the credit function either begins as part of the accountant's responsibilities or it remains under the personal control of the proprietor. Up to a certain point—determined by the pressures created by a growing business and by the nature of the business — this is perfectly adequate. As a firm grows, its list of buyers becomes longer and what began as an easily managed routine for the accountant develops into a full-time job. What often happens is that the accountant delegates the running of the sales ledger to one of his staff with no knowledge of or training in credit control. Sooner or later management realise that the cash is not flowing as fast as it should or maybe they are hit by a run of bad debts. Ultimately the need for proper credit management is recognised and a new man is appointed — often recruited from outside.

This type of development is typical of UK businesses. Even some of the biggest companies did not employ professional credit people until the 1960s or later. It is comparatively rare for a credit manager to be appointed from the start — although this often happens when American firms set up subsidiary companies in the UK.

A new credit manager is most often faced with the task of creating a credit department from an existing sales ledger organisation, unless he is established outside of the sales ledger with no responsibility for its operation. Opinions differ about which is the better arrangement. My own view is that good credit control is so dependent upon an up-to-date and efficient ledger system that it is essential for the credit manager to be in control. If he is not, then his own operation can be endangered by basic problems such as the timing of statements, the availability of ledgers and the determining of priorities in back-log situations.

Given that the credit manager has the ledger responsibility, the key question to be answered is whether to employ separate people for credit and ledger work. The requirements of a good credit clerk are different from those of a good ledger clerk, and a separation of functions means that credit work is done by specialists whose time and energy is not diluted by ledger work. Ledger work does not demand the ability to talk fluently and persuasively over the telephone, the art of good correspondence or, above all, the capacity to detect problems and to make judgements. Credit work requires a higher level of skill and intelligence. There are nonetheless arguments for uniting the functions. Duplication of work (such as marking-up of payments prior to full reconciliation) is avoided. There is no danger of the credit man being let down because his section of the ledger has not been brought up-to-date. Against this there is the risk that ledger routines will

15

expand to fill most of the day, leaving credit work to be fitted in later. Above all, good ledger clerks do not necessarily make good credit clerks.

A good solution is to organise the department in pairs, one credit clerk with one ledger clerk on the same section of accounts, working together as a team with either one capable in an emergency of doing the other's job.

This kind of organisation should not be regarded as applicable only to big companies with large credit departments. Many small and medium-sized companies could improve their cash-flow by employing, say, two credit clerks and two ledger clerks instead of four ledger clerks who struggle to do the credit job after doing all the ledger routines. It is not unknown to find companies whose collection effort each month covers customers from A to P because time ran out.

The size of the credit operation must depend primarily on the number of active customers. The spread of business is also important. The Exeter Survey found that in 86 out of 98 companies, more than 70 per cent of turnover went to under 30 per cent of the total number of customers. Where this applies, it is worth seeing whether that top layer of customers can be grouped together for special attention, rather than keeping to a straightforward alphabetical division. The following examples illustrate this, as well as giving an indication of total staff required (for both ledger and credit work):

Firm A   Turnover £500,000; 500 active accounts; business evenly spread. One or two clerks should suffice. There should be time for most overdue accounts to be telephoned, the biggest dozen or so being covered personally by the credit manager.

Firm B   Turnover £5,000,000; 1,000 active accounts; 70 per cent of sales going to 50 customers. One experienced clerk or supervisor is needed to deal with the top 50 names. The remainder can be handled by two clerks, one doing ledger work and the other collections.

Every position in the credit department should be clearly defined and carry a written job description. The Institute of Credit Management produced (in January 1978) a series of these covering: Credit Manager, Credit Sanction Manager, Sales Ledger and Collections Manager, Sales Ledger Supervisor and Sales Ledger Clerk.

The bigger a department becomes the more essential it is to have a clear reporting structure within which the responsibilities of clerks, supervisors and managers are positively defined. Exhibit 2.3 illustrates how the credit department of a medium-sized company (say

Exhibit 2.3

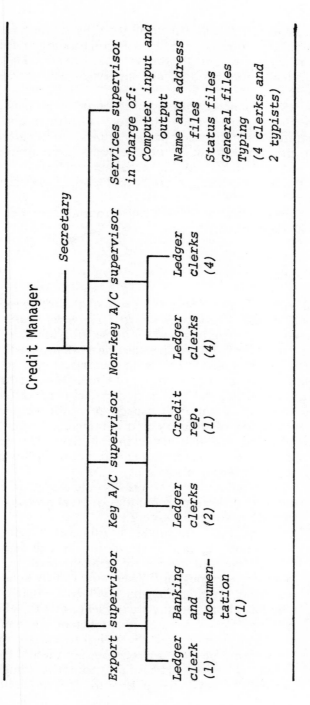

Credit Manager

Secretary

Export supervisor

Ledger clerk (1)
Banking and documentation (1)

Key A/C supervisor

Ledger clerks (2)
Credit rep. (1)

Non-key A/C supervisor

Ledger clerks (4)
Ledger clerks (4)

Services supervisor in charge of:
Computer input and output
Name and address files
Status files
General files
Typing (4 clerks and 2 typists)

17

5,000 accounts, £50,000,000 turnover with 20 per cent export) might be arranged. The features to note in the structure are as follows:

1   Four people report to the credit manager. This is a good manageable number and each supervisor has a precisely defined sphere of authority.
2   The key-account section (say 50 accounts, 60 per cent of turnover) and the export section are both identified and controlled separately, enabling their particular needs to be catered for. Note that the key-account section includes a credit representative whose job is to visit all key accounts regularly.
3   On the non-key section, credit and ledger clerks are working in pairs.
4   The services section covers those routine activities vital to the whole department.

Credit training

External training can involve all or any of the following:
1   *Dun & Bradstreet course in Credit & Financial Analysis*   This is a home-study correspondence course providing a very useful foundation for young people starting work in a credit department and wishing to develop a sound theoretical background.
2   *Credit seminars*   The Institute of Credit Management regularly holds one- or two-day seminars, aimed either at different levels of credit people, at different aspects of credit management or at different parts of industry and commerce. A number of commercial firms are also active in this field. The quality varies considerably and it is recommended that the following points be checked in choosing a seminar:
    a   Exactly what do you want? Specific advice on credit assessment or collection techniques or legal proceedings? Decide first what you are looking for.
    b   Examine closely the subject-headings of the seminars in view. They should be broken down into enough detail for you to see whether your topics are being covered.
    c   Who are the speakers? There are a fairly small number of practising credit managers involved regularly in seminars who have both the direct experience and the ability to communicate. There are also a number of academics who may not be close enough to the action to speak convincingly.
    d   How many speakers and sessions are there? More than four or five sessions in a day usually means that some of the topics can only be covered superficially. It is much better to have

four speakers each talking for 45-60 minutes than seven 30-minute speakers.

e   There should be at least 45 minutes for questions from the floor.

f   There should be detailed notes provided from each speaker.

3   *Membership of the Institute of Credit Management* is essential for anyone intent on a career in credit.

Internal training should always be given to new starters in the credit department and, if possible, should also cater for existing staff. To be of any real value, internal training needs to be carefully planned and a time table worked out, giving the new man a logical progression through the various functions of the department at a reasonable pace. The credit manager or another senior person should regularly review progress — probably at weekly intervals. It is useful if brief sessions can be arranged with other departments so that the credit function can be put into context. Sales, shipping, data processing and accounts are all areas which inter-relate with credit. A period in the bought ledger is very useful in preparing someone for collection work — he can study the techniques employed by both sides.

There are some skills which have to be developed over a period of time and which can only be covered superficially in a training programme. Balance sheet analysis and credit assessment generally fall into this category. The development of sound credit judgement needs the pressure and conflicts of real situations. The credit manager must find time to sit with his staff and discuss current problems, explain why certain decisions were taken or why this customer should be considered a high risk.

Chapter 3

Payment terms and methods

Selection of the appropriate payment terms is a vital step in establishing the supplier/customer relationship, because this together with the credit limit decision will determine not only the required rate of cash-flow but also the volume of sales permissible. For example, a customer with a credit limit of £10,000 will only be able to purchase up to £60,000 annually if terms are net monthly, since the limit will be reached after two months' sales. A decision to give half-monthly terms in return for, say, 1 per cent discount would allow double that sales volume to be made within the same limit. This is illustrated in Exhibits 3.1 and 3.2 from which it is clear that shortening the terms has achieved the following results:

1   Turnover is doubled.
2   Cash-flow is improved (83.3 per cent of sales paid within the sales period, compared to 66.6 per cent).
3   Credit risk is kept at £10,000.

Whilst net profit as a percentage of sales is down by 1 per cent (the cost of a reduction in the payment period), profits in total are substantially increased as a result of the extra sales.

This is a simple illustration of how the credit manager can make a positive contribution to profits through *flexibility* on terms. Most companies have standard terms of payment for home sales, but these should not be regarded as sacrosanct.

Factors influencing settlement terms

Before examining the different terms in use, it is worth listing the factors that influence the choice of terms. These are not given in any order of importance.

1   The normal practice of the trade. It is always very difficult to achieve sales if your terms do not at least match those offered by competitors.
2   The amount of working capital available to finance debtors. These costs have already been discussed.
3   The degree of credit risk. The higher the risk, the shorter the terms must be to achieve the required turnover.
4   The nature of the product. It is usual for quick-selling consumer products, especially perishable goods, to be sold on relatively short terms compared to single expensive items of equipment which may often require stage payments — both before and after delivery.
5   The size of order. Firms selling large quantities of 'off-the-shelf' goods frequently impose a minimum order value if credit terms are required, below which it is uneconomic to supply except on cash-with-order terms.

Credit terms in the UK

Whilst not an exhaustive list, this includes most terms commonly offered.

Net monthly   This is the term most frequently found and requires payment of one month's deliveries — or one month's invoices — to be made at the end of the following month. The chief difficulty here is that while many companies expect to purchase under these terms, all too frequently invoices for the last week's despatches are excluded from the bought ledger's listing on the grounds that the firm's computer has to cut-off by a certain date. The excuse that invoices were received after month-end or just too late for processing is well worn and very hard to counter.

Net 30 days   Another commonly found term, this often ends up being seen as the same as net monthly. In many cases this is unavoidable since on a large account with invoices entered daily, it is unrealistic and impracticable to expect each daily batch of invoices to be covered by a separate payment. Nonetheless, terms of net 30 days are definitely more beneficial to the supplier since he has the right to request

Exhibit 3.1   Company A: monthly terms

Month	Week of sale	Sales volume	Cash payment	Balance
1	1	1,250		1,250
	2	1,250		2,500
	3	1,250		3,750
	4	1,250		5,000
2	5	1,250		6,250
	6	1,250		7,500
	7	1,250		8,750
	8	1,250		10,000
		Payment due	5,000	5,000
3	9	1,250		6,250
	10	1,250		7,500
	11	1,250		8,750
	12	1,250		10,000
		Payment due	5,000	5,000

Sales in 3 months	=	£15,000
Cash flow	=	£10,000
Net profit at 5%	=	£750

payment much sooner (an average of 15 days sooner) than under net monthly terms. High-risk accounts can therefore be controlled far more tightly and, indeed, a higher sales volume can be achieved, as we saw in Exhibit 3.2.

Net 14 days (or any number up to or above 30)   The same principles apply here as for net 30 days. The shorter the period, the tighter the control. A long period, say 45, 60 or 90 days, is usually only found where there is a strong marketing reason. No matter how strong that reason may be, the credit manager has to be very sure that the risk is acceptable before agreeing.

Stage payments   Where expensive plant or equipment is being sold, or where a long 'delivery' period is involved, e.g. in the building trade, it is normal to find stage or progress payments agreed. For machinery requiring a heavy capital outlay and a long manufacturing period,

Exhibit 3.2 Company B: half-monthly terms

Month	Week of sale	Sales volume	Cash payment	Balance
1	1	2,500		2,500
	2	2,500		5,000
	3	2,500		7,500
	4	2,500		10,000
		Payment due	5,000	5,000
2	5	2,500		7,500
	6	2,500		10,000
		Payment due	5,000	5,000
	7	2,500		7,500
	8	2,500		10,000
		Payment due	5,000	5,000
3	9	2,500		7,500
	10	2,500		10,000
		Payment due	5,000	5,000
	11	2,500		7,500
	12	2,500		10,000
		Payment due	5,000	5,000

Sales in 3 months	=	£30,000
Cash flow	=	£25,000
Net profit	=	£1,500
Less 1% discount for shorter terms		(£300)
Adjusted net profit	=	£1,200

there is often a down payment, anything from 10 to 30 per cent, followed either by full payment on delivery or further stage payments at agreed intervals. In the building trade, if the contract is under RIBA rules, a supplier can claim payment at various stages providing he can submit the appropriate certificate.

Where tools are being manufactured, it is common practice for a down payment to be agreed, followed by a percentage on 'sample approval', followed by a final payment on delivery and acceptance. In any of these situations the buyer may require a retention, say 10 per cent of the purchase price, which is withheld for an agreed period or until an agreed event takes place. For example, this could be the agreement of the main contractor's final account or the commissioning of a vessel or a factory.

It is vital for a supplier in these types of business to plan his cash-flow requirements and fix payment terms accordingly. It would be foolish to accept 20 per cent down-payment and the balance on completion in twelve months' time if the suppliers of raw material (which might amount to 50 per cent of the selling price) are going to demand 100 per cent payment by the time manufacture is only half completed.

All the above terms are related to time. There are others related to delivery, which may be used either because the credit risk is unacceptable or because the size of order does not justify the expense of maintaining a credit account.

Cash with order   The most stringent terms. No work is commenced until payment arrives.

Cash before shipment   A little less harsh. Not recommended where goods are being produced to customer specification since non-payment will leave you with unsaleable goods. In any event, cheques should be cleared before goods are despatched. Note: 'pro-forma' terms may mean either cash with order or cash before shipment. To avoid confusion, it is best not to use the term 'pro-forma'.

Cash on delivery   The driver is usually entrusted with obtaining payment before releasing the goods. As well as the danger noted above, there is the added possibility of a cheque being dishonoured.

Load over load   Payment of this delivery has to be received before the next delivery is made. Normally only used in trades involving a regular weekly or monthly delivery.

Letter of Credit   Normally found only in export transactions, Letter of Credit terms are occasionally used for domestic business. The buyer instructs his bank to open a Letter of Credit in favour of the supplier for the value of the order and payment is made by the bank on receipt of the supplier's invoice and/or signed delivery note. Unlike in the export trade, no documents of title are involved. It is merely a way of securing payment by a bank guarantee.

Cash discounts A further group of settlement terms includes the granting of a cash discount in return for payment within an agreed period. In some businesses cash discounts are customary, as for example in the retail trade where such terms as '5% 7 days' ('2% 7 days' in the food trade) and '2½% 14 days' are often encountered.

Settlement terms of 2½ per cent monthly were common in non-retail businesses twenty years ago, but this has largely disappeared. Cash discounts are still prevalent in the USA, particularly terms of ½ or 1 per cent for payment in 10 days with the alternative of paying net in 30 days. Some European countries also make wide use of discounts — notably Germany.

There is considerable misunderstanding of the cost of cash discounts. A discount is a reward for prompt payment and its cost must, therefore, be related to the period of time gained by the supplier on his cash-flow. This presents an immediate difficulty in deciding when a customer would pay if no discount were offered. This will depend primarily on the ability of the supplier to extract payment and on the liquidity of the customer. As an example, let us assume that 90 days' credit (from end of month of invoicing) will be taken if no discount is offered. It is decided to offer 2½ per cent for payment by the end of the first month after the month of invoicing. The true annual cost of this is calculated in Exhibit 3.3.

Unless the borrowing cost of the supplier exceeded 15 per cent p.a., the above would represent an uneconomic rate. Recent surveys indicate a decline in the use of discounts and it is difficult to justify their use (apart from where dictated by custom and practice) on an 'across-the-board' basis. Quite apart from the cost, a major problem is that customers will tend to take discounts even when their payments arrive outside the qualifying period. To allow X days' grace merely pushes the problem further ahead. The inevitable result is either regular 'write-offs' of unearned discounts or a prolonged and often fruitless follow-up procedure — or maybe even both of these.

Discounts can be valuable however if used selectively. A reduction of the payment period also reduces the risk and the use of discounts to increase sales volume on high-risk accounts is recommended.

Exhibit 3.3

Amount of time gained, i.e. 90 days less 30 days = 60 days, divided into 365 to produce the annual rate, multiplied by the rate of discount. Thus

$$\frac{365}{90 - 30} \times 2.5 = 15\% \ approximately$$

At the beginning of this chapter there was an example of this (see Exhibit 3.2). A further illustration is where a customer with a very low credit standing is persuaded to buy on a 'cash before shipment' basis in return for a discount. The discount given should, if possible, equate to the actual cost of money, i.e. if normal bank lending rate is 12 per cent p.a., a discount of $1\frac{1}{2}$ per cent would be fair. A higher discount still must also be regarded as worthwhile if the end result is to produce a substantial increase in sales and profits.

Whenever discount terms are agreed, they must be capable of being used. To offer a discount for payment in 7 or even 10 days is presuming no delays in delivery or postal transit. In practice such short terms are almost unworkable without the use of a personal delivery and cash-collection service.

Interest charges In contrast to discounts, the practice of charging interest on overdue accounts appears to be on the increase. In the 1970s very high interest rates, coupled with periods of strained liquidity, caused many companies to consider interest-charging as a means of accelerating payments. Four main problems have to be faced.

1 Interest on overdue payments may only be charged if it is specifically permitted in the company's Conditions of Sale. If it is decided to amend these conditions to include an appropriate clause on interest, it is advisable for the company to tell its customers about the change, thereby running some slight risk of loss of goodwill or (far worse) retaliatory action from customers who are also suppliers. If the decision is taken, it is prudent to word the amendment in such a way as to leave the company with the *option* of charging interest. At the same time, care must be taken to avoid giving the customer the option of paying to terms or paying late with interest.

2 The effect on business must be considered. If competitors are not charging interest, there is a real danger that some business will be lost. In a very competitive market, a decision to 'go it alone' could be extremely harmful.

3 What rate of interest should be charged? Clearly it must be high enough to avoid being an attractive alternative to payment within terms. On the other hand, to be too high runs the risk of being considered extortionate. A reasonable compromise would be to charge somewhere between 4 and 6 per cent above the Bank of Engand minimum lending rate.

4 What happens if customers refuse to pay interest charges? This is similar to the problem of unearned discount. Unless the supplier

is prepared to go to extreme lengths to enforce payment, there is little point in charging. Ultimately, the strength of the supplier in the market will determine this question.

A serious attempt to introduce and enforce the charging of interest could well be detrimental to customer goodwill, without having any appreciable effect on cash-flow. There is nonetheless some merit in *reserving the right* to charge interest, so that it can be exercised from time to time at the discretion of the credit manager.

In June 1978, the Law Commission report was presented to Parliament. *Inter alia* it recommended that, unless otherwise agreed in the contract of sale, debts should carry the right of interest at a statutory rate of 1 per cent above the average Minimum Lending Rate (MLR) for the previous quarter. Whether legislation will follow remains to be seen. If it does, credit managers would be well advised to urge their companies to amend their Terms of Sale otherwise they may find themselves restricted to the statutory 1 per cent over MLR.

Methods of payment

Having agreed terms with the buyer, the next step should be to determine the manner of payment. In practice this is rarely considered. Payment by cheque or bank transfer is regarded as normal, any other method being exceptional — unless peculiar to a certain trade or business. Nonetheless, the credit manager should be aware not only of the alternatives but also of the pros and cons of all payment methods.

1 Cheque Post-dated cheques should not be accepted, except in exceptional circumstances, since they are an obvious pointer to liquidity problems. The problem of dishonoured cheques will be dealt with in Chapter 9.

2 Bank transfer Some companies prefer to pay all their suppliers by credit transfer. A considerable amount of time is saved by not having to sign cheques but there is a loss of flexibility. Because of this, suppliers who are given the option of being paid by cheque or by credit transfer are probably better off under a cheque system. Individual payments can be released (or withheld) and the customer cannot prevaricate by sending remittance advices ahead of credit transfers, then blaming the banking system for the delay.

3 Direct debit This is a system whereby a supplier is enabled to obtain payment direct from the customer's bank on presentation either of manually prepared direct debit vouchers or of a magnetic tape prepared by a computer. The system can cope with either regular amounts, such as rental charges which are agreed in advance by both parties or, with variable amounts. In the latter case the buyer must have complete trust in the supplier and in practice this system is rarely found except in monopoly or near-monopoly situations where the seller is in a very strong position. Given these conditions, direct debits offer a considerable administrative saving to both buyer and seller.

4 *Bills of Exchange* In domestic trade there has been a revival of interest in bills (sometimes referred to as 'trade bills'). A bill is an unconditional promise to pay the amount stated on a given date. It has to be accepted for payment by the debtor and is payable to the creditor. Bills are normally drawn by the creditor — although they can be raised and accepted by the debtor and then passed to the creditor who signs as drawer. The benefits of using bills are as follows:

a   An accepted bill is better than a promise to send a cheque. No further initiative is required of the customer.
b   An accepted bill is normally presented for payment at the customer's bank. Failure to have sufficient funds to meet the bill will obviously embarrass the customer with his bank. Unless there are no funds at all, the holder of an accepted bill is in a better position than a supplier awaiting a cheque.
c   A supplier can sue on a dishonoured bill, no other evidence of debt being required.
d   An accepted bill can be discounted with a bank if the money is needed before maturity.

Bills are particularly useful to determine a series of payments under a special arrangement. A customer in temporary cash-flow trouble might agree to clear a debt in six instalments. The supplier who holds six accepted bills is in a stronger position than one who depends on six cheques being sent.

When bills are discounted it is most important to keep their value on record against the customer's credit limit. If a discounted bill is dishonoured, the bank has recourse to the drawer, i.e. the supplier. For the same reason, it is illogical for longer credit terms to be extended because a customer is paying by bill rather than by cheque. Whilst the holder of accepted bills is in a better position, nonetheless indolvency will strike equally hard and the ultimate credit risk remains the same. Occasionally, accepted bills are endorsed by a third party, generally the buyer's parent company or possibly a main shareholder or the proprietor. Providing the financial standing of the guarantor is known to be good, this adds very considerably to the strength of a bill. It is seldom found that a UK public company is willing to endorse bills accepted by a subsiary or associate company. Banks do so even less frequently.

5 *Contra accounts* Where firms are both buying from and selling to one another, it is sensible to arrange a regular offset so that one party pays the net balance. Whilst apparently simple, this can be very difficult to run for a number of reasons:

a Disputed items prevent a clean reconciliation and may even lead to both parties claiming a balance in their favour.

b Differences in internal cut-off dates and payment dates can easily cause friction.

c Unless both companies supply each other every month, there will be arguments about when the balance should be paid.

It is essential that any contra arrangement be set out in writing and signed by both parties; otherwise sooner or later problems of the kind indicated above will arise. Also, if one company becomes insolvent, the right of the other to set-off debts will only be admitted by a Receiver or Liquidator if there is clear evidence in writing.

6 *Reservation of property* In recent years many companies have amended their Conditions of Sale in an attempt to strengthen their position as unsecured creditors against a Receiver or Liquidator. Many more companies are still thinking about it. The impetus to this concern with retention of title was provided by the Romalpa case in January 1976. [For full particulars see *Lloyd's Law Reports,* Part 5, Vol. 1, pp 443-4, the editorial by Professor C. Schmitthof in the *Journal of Business Law* (July 1976) and *Conditions of Sale – Retention of Title,* by Dennis Roberts published by the Institute of Chartered Secretaries and Administrators.]

This is not the place to try and restate the complex arguments and problems in law, accountancy, insurance, taxation and banking which have been examined at length by lawyers and accountants. As far as the credit manager is concerned, he has a duty to advise on the best methods of safeguarding his company's accounts receivable. He may feel it prudent merely to point out that in an increasing number of insolvencies, some creditors are achieving a preferential status. The most appropriate wording for a reservation of property clause will depend on the nature of the trade and the product. For some companies a simple clause retaining title until payment is received may be adequate, whereas others may opt for the 'full Romalpa' clause which entitles an unpaid seller not only to repossess unsold goods but also to claim for the proceeds of the sale of those goods to a third party.

Whatever wording is chosen, the subsequent amended Conditions of Sale must be brought to the attention of all customers. It is well established that a Receiver or Liquidator will not entertain a Romalpa claim unless there is clear evidence that proper notice of the introduction of the new conditions has been provided.

Chapter 4

Risk assessment — basic steps

The correct evaluation of credit risk is the most difficult part of the credit manager's job. It is often neglected and sometimes left to the judgement of the sales manager. This tends to happen in companies where the credit manager is regarded primarily (or solely) as a debt collector, with no interest or involvement in a sale until the goods have left the factory. This is 'credit control' as opposed to 'credit management', and it ignores the potential contribution to profits which a trained credit manager can bring.

To select only good risks or safe customers is relatively easy, but the company which follows this policy will not keep its factory busy for long or retain its share of the market. Maximising sales and profits can only be achieved by trading with the marginal accounts — and this demands good credit management.

The credit manager, therefore, has a very positive function. He must assess the degree of risk the company will be exposed to in trading with both existing and potential buyers. Payment terms and credit limits must be established in order to achieve the maximum turnover compatible with that risk. If this is done carefully and with good judgement, the other main part of the credit job — collecting the cash — will be performed that much more effectively. The nature and timing of follow-up procedures should be dictated by the level of risk.

The degree of sympathy or consideration extended to a customer asking for extra time must be determined by knowledge of the financial strength and other resources at his disposal.

It is not only the so-called 'marginal' accounts which need careful assessment. Major buyers with vast amounts of issued capital must be kept under review. Where danger signals are spotted — perhaps by a steady increase in debt financing not accompanied by rising profits — the credit manager must consult with his sales and marketing colleagues so that a positive decision is taken to continue, to restrict or even to cease trading. When such problems arise with major customers, the credit viewpoint should form part of a general business decision, in which the risk of non-payment has to be balanced against other factors such as the stoppage of a production line and the laying-off of workers.

Sources of information

Risk assessment is based on information which is available from a variety of sources. These are detailed in Exhibit 4.1, divided into two sections — basic and depth. The remainder of this chapter is devoted to these basic sources, the depth areas being covered in Chapter 5.

Trade references

The traditional method of credit checking — and sometimes the only one — is to ask for two trade references before an account is opened. If relied upon solely, this is a most unsatisfactory procedure, since it can be assumed that companies will not quote suppliers likely to give a bad

Exhibit 4.1

Basic information sources	In-depth information sources
Trade references	Balance sheet and profit
Bank references	and loss accounts
Agency register	Companies Registry
Agency report	Extel cards
Trade and competitors'	Press reports
opinions	Ledger history
Reference books	Credit visits
Salesmen's reports	Special reports

Exhibit 4.2 Specimen request for references

Attention: Credit Department

I/We request you to open a credit account in the name of:

I/We give below the names and addresses of referees of whom the customary enquiries may be made.

I/We note that payment terms are net 30 days from date of invoice and agree to pay in accordance with these terms.

Expected maximum amount of credit required: £

total/monthly*

*(delete as appropriate)

    Signature _____

    Position _____

Banker's name and address:

Trade referees

(1)   *Name:*   *Address:*

(2)   *Name:*   *Address:*

(NB: Referees should be able to speak for credit figures comparable with that indicated above.)

---

report; some companies go even further and deliberately cultivate good references by selective prompt payment. Nonetheless, references can be helpful, providing they are obtained and checked carefully and they are used to supplement information from other sources.

The request for trade references should be made formally and should incorporate a request for credit terms. This is easily done by using a standard pre-printed form, as in Exhibit 4.2.

Points to note are as follows:

1   The precise name, address and trading style of the buyer is established. A very common problem is to be asked to clear an order from a firm whose name is either misquoted or misspelt. It is essential to get the name absolutely correct when the account is first opened. To this end it is helpful to instruct the sales force to ask for a letterhead when visiting a prospect.

2   Attention is drawn to the standard conditions of payment. The buyer is required to sign his acceptance of these terms. (This document should be filed carefully, as it can prove invaluable to refute subsequent allegations that 'your salesman said we needn't pay for three months'.)

3   The buyer is asked to indicate his expected level of business. This can be a useful guide to the credit limit decision (see Chapter 6) and may be balanced against the natural optimism of the salesman who may be predicting a far higher figure!

4   It is made clear that the references supplied must be able to speak for a similar level of business to that envisaged. There is little point in receiving references which give good experience up to £500 monthly if you want to sell £5,000 per month.

5   It is also made clear to the customer that his account is going to be handled in a business-like manner. For a prospective customer to obtain the impression that anyone can obtain credit merely by placing an order is bad and will not improve the seller's reputation.

Having obtained a completed reference form, the credit manager must contact the referees. Here again, the use of a standard format is recommended, as in Exhibit 4.3.

The questions asked are straightforward and as detailed as necessary to produce helpful answers. What is of equal importance is to whom they are addressed. Some guidelines are as follows. Are the referees reputable companies who can be relied upon to give honest answers? Or does closer examination reveal connections with the potential buyer — either through common directors or an actual legal/financial association? If the amount of credit in view is substantial it may be worth telephoning the credit manager of the referee company. This should certainly be done if the answers on the

Exhibit 4.3   Specimen reference letter

1   *How long have you known*   ....months
    this firm?
                                       ....years

                                       Many years

2   *How much credit do you*   £
    normally allow?

3   *What are your payment terms?*   Pro-forma

                                       Monthly

                                       ....days

4   *Are payments generally made*   To terms
    to your satisfaction?
                                       Up to 1 month
                                         late

                                       More than 1
                                         month late

                                       Very slow/
                                         irregular

5   *Any other relevant information will be appreciated:*

The above information is given in strict
confidence and without responsibility on
my/our part.

Date: _____   *Signed:* _____

forms are contradictory (between two referees) or if any additional comment is given which needs following up. Much can be said over the telephone which is better not put on paper.

A final point on trade references — always send a reply-paid envelope. Credit managers are busy people and small courtesies are appreciated.

Bank references

A bank reference is usually requested at the same time as trade references. The approach to the bank should be as precise as possible, e.g.

> 'Do you consider the above good for trade credit up to £500 a month, on net monthly terms?

Some skill is needed to interpret bank references correctly and the type of reply given to such an enquiry will fall under one of three headings:

a   An unqualified, positive assurance that the risk is good, such as the word 'undoubted'. Not given frequently and therefore of high value.

b   A general indication that the firm in question is operating normally — lacking the positive tenor of *(a)* above. Commonly used references under this heading are 'Respectably constituted private limited company, considered good for its normal engagements', or '. . .we do not think the company would undertake any engagements it could not fulfil'. Such references are of little value.

c   A rather guarded statement whose message lies in what is not said rather than in what is said. Examples of this type are: '. . .their capital appears to be rather fully employed', or (worse) '. . .we regret we are unable to speak for your figures'. Such replies must immediately put the credit manager on his guard.

It is worth telephoning the answering banker to try and obtain a little more information, although more success is likely if the call is made by one's own banker. Banking protocol requires written answers to be given in this way and the request for a reference should, therefore, include a phrase such as

> 'Your reply may, if desired, be sent to our bankers, name and address as follows.'

There is no merit in routing the reference request through one's own bankers. This merely delays the whole procedure. In urgent cases, however, it is a good idea to ask one's banker to telephone the initial request. A great deal depends on the individual bankers as to how much useful information can be obtained in this way. With this in mind, the credit manager should establish a good personal relationship with his company's bank manager, so that the latter is aware of the importance of reference requests and does his best to extract information when asked.

A final point on bank references is that the bank is obliged to state the fact that 'charges are registered' when it is aware of this fact. This tells the enquirer that all or part of the assets of the prospective buyer are pledged as security for a loan. The significance of this will be examined in Chapter 5.

Agency registers

Several credit reporting agencies produce credit rating registers. By far the best known and most widely used is the Dun & Bradstreet Register, which is published annually covering the UK and Northern Ireland in five volumes. Around 200,000 firms are listed geographically under the town where they operate and a single-line entry includes the following:

Name
Trade and address
Date of formation
Nominal and issued capital
The existence of mortgages and charges
Proprietors and associates
Credit rating
Seyd's Extended ratings ⎰ Available only with
Bank code ⎱ the special edition

The vital entry, the credit rating, is an alpha code intended to indicate the *normal (or average) amount of credit* granted to the firm.

This register is an extremely valuable aide to credit assessment, but it should not be used as the sole criterion. Its main value lies in providing a fast reference from which the next step may be immediate order acceptance or further investigation. The fact that an order for £5,000 is outside the rating (of, say, £500) does not mean that the risk is unacceptably high. It is merely an indication that £5,000 is above the normal amount of credit given and that more facts must be obtained before making a decision.

A reference work of this size inevitably becomes out-of-date — although weekly supplements are issued. It is essential that its use is restricted to being a quick guide for smaller-value transactions.

Agency reports

There are in the UK a large number of reporting agencies, some offering a service related to specific trades or industries and others giving a general service. It is worth checking if there is a specialised agency for one's particular industry, since these can frequently offer more detailed information.

The reliability and extent of information vary considerably, not only between agencies, but also between reports from the same agency. In choosing an agency the credit manager should obtain answers to the following questions:

1   Is an experienced employee working continuously (or virtually so) at the Companies Registry? There should be.
2   Does the agency use its own experienced staff to collect local information, or does it rely on agents working for a number of enquiry firms? The former is preferable — but not often found.
3   How long after a report is obtained is it updated? Six months is about the right period. When an updated report is obtained, it should always be compared with the previous one. If there is no evidence of new information the agency should be challenged.
4   Can the agency provide the names of several reputable companies already using its reports? These should be checked and the credit managers asked for their opinion.

The question of cost and speed should not be considered at this stage. Agencies offering low-cost reports are immediately suspect, since worthwhile reports giving up-to-date information cannot be produced cheaply. Speed is, of course, important, but it is very difficult to lay down a minimum reporting period. So much depends on what information is immediately available (at Companies Registry), how long the firm has been trading and how willing the firm is to answer the agency's questions.

The features that should be included in a credit report are as follows:

1   Full name and registered address. Also any trading styles used.
2   Names of proprietors, partners or directors.
3   Amount of authorised and issued capital.
4   Details of any associations with other companies, including associations through common directors. This section should clearly indicate the nature and extent of control exercised by other companies.
5   Brief particulars of the firm's operations, including whereabouts of factories and branches.
6   An extract from (if not the entire) the latest Balance Sheet and Profit and Loss Account. The extract should include details of current assets and current liabilities.

7   A list of secured charges.
8   Details of any County Court judgments recorded within the last twelve months.
9   Name and address of bankers.
10 The recent payment experience of a number of other suppliers (including comments supplied).

Many agencies also indicate the amount of credit they regard as being 'within scope'. Generally any figures given are based on information obtained from other suppliers and are not the result of any attempt at balance sheet analysis. Where a comment is provided such as 'care is recommended' or 'the account should be supervised closely', these again are frequently derived from suppliers' comments, often supplemented by the enquiry agent's own experience in collecting overdue debts.

As with the use of an agency register, a credit report is of most value when it indicates the proposed business to be well within the experience of other suppliers. Failing this, its chief use may be in the balance sheet details — provided these are of recent date.

Trade and competitors' opinions

By trade opinions are meant the opinions of suppliers *not* already quoted as referees. These may include competitors — if the credit manager is free to use this source of information.

Salesmen should be trained to make mental note of other suppliers' names when visiting the factory or the buyer's office. A telephone call between credit managers can be very informative and often leads to a fruitful exchange on other mutual customers.

Where possible this interchange should be developed with other firms in the industry, who may or may not be direct competitors. In a number of UK industries there are credit interchange groups, consisting of anything from 6-30 suppliers who meet regularly and exchange experience and information on common customers. Some go beyond this and co-operate on credit training for their staff. These groups can only succeed if the individual credit managers have complete faith in the integrity of all members. A credit manager who uses membership primarily as a means of obtaining 'inside' or 'advance' information to promote his own company's sales has no place there and will be swiftly found out. The real value is in providing an early warning system about bad payers, in safeguarding each other against potential bad debts and in helping one another on matters of fact, such as the appointment of a new finance director or a change in the internal accounting structure or the invoice passing procedure.

It is advisable that the credit manager should tell his finance director (if not his marketing director) of his intention to join such an interchange group.

Reference books

In addition to credit registers, there are a number of publications of value to the credit manager. The following list is not exhaustive:
1   *Who owns whom* (Dun & Bradstreet). This annual publication identifies membership of groups of companies, both under the parent name and the affiliate or subsidiary.
2   *Key British Enterprises* (Dun & Bradstreet). Issued in two volumes every 18 months, covering 22,000 leading or growing companies, arranged alphabetically, geographically and under SIC headings. Details include names of directors, annual turnover, number of employees and information on products and operations.
3   *Kompass* (published in association with the Confederation of British Industry). Issued in two volumes — Products & Services and Company Information — this is primarily a comprehensive source for procurement. Companies are listed geographically, by county and town. Details include names of directors, bankers' name, share capital, number of employees and product group identity.
Further details of other sources of company information are contained in the *Credit Management Databook*, published by Gower Press.

The salesman's report

Frequently this will be the only first-hand personal information available to the credit manager and potentially it is of high value. But its actual value depends almost entirely on the degree of credit education prevailing in the sales force. A salesman trained in the importance of credit can help in risk-assessment in several different ways by reporting on:
1   The character and competence of the management.
2   The level of activity and the general impression obtained from factory and office.
3   The names of other suppliers who may be useful contacts.
4   Details of the major customers of the client and an assessment of the product.
5   The anticipated level of business.

If the credit manager is able to influence the design and format of the salesman's report, he should be able to stimulate answers to such questions. Regular contact with the salesmen will also help to dispel any impression that his object is merely to control and restrict sales. In all of this, however, the credit manager must never forget that the salesman's primary job is to sell and that glowing opinions of new prospects may be the result of rose-tinted spectacles!

Summary

All the avenues of enquiry detailed in this chapter should be explored, since to rely on one or two sources alone carries the risk that they may be out-of-date or misinformed. A decision based on a credit report which is later found to be inaccurate will deal a severe blow to the credit manager's reputation.

Very often time is too short and a decision has to be made within the day. If the new buyer is listed in the credit register and the amount involved is well within the rating, this can often be sufficient to approve the order. Otherwise the credit manager has to turn to the telephone and here the existence of a credit interchange network is invaluable.

Many credit decisions can be made purely on the information available from the 'basic' sources covered in this chapter. Whenever this information is inadequate or contradictory, or the size of the credit decision demands fuller investigation, the credit manager must proceed to the 'depth' sources covered in the next chapter.

Chapter 5

Risk assessment — in-depth investigation

The most important source of detailed information is the annual accounts. It must be remembered however that a balance sheet is a statement of the company's finances on one day, different the previous day and different the day after. Even if the accounts were examined the day they were completed, this would usually be at least four to six months after the financial year-end. When one adds to this the delays commonly experienced before accounts are lodged at the Companies Registry, the interval between the balance sheet date and the date of analysis is rarely under twelve months and often nearer two years.

The Companies Registry is at Cardiff but a reading room facility is maintained at Companies House in London where the last three years' accounts are recorded on microfilm. Many credit agencies offer a balance sheet service to enquirers not able to visit the Registry. By law (*The Companies Act, 1976*) a public company has to file accounts within seven months of its financial year-end and a private company within ten months. This legislation will eventually be of considerable help to credit analysts but the Registrar of Companies still has a formidable task to bring companies into line.

At the end of 1977 there were approximately 700,000 limited companies in Great Britain, growing at a net annual rate of 10-15,000.

In view of the above it is not surprising that many credit

investigations are hampered by a lack of up-to-date information. To counter this the credit manager should not hesitate to ask the prospect direct for a sight of the latest accounts. He has ample justification for such a request, considering that a bank or finance company would not contemplate an investment without a close examination of the accounts. The trade creditor is also being expected to invest money in the prospect — in the form of goods or services — and moreover he will lack the security commonly afforded to a banker. Another point worth remembering is the dependence customers have on their key suppliers. This gives weight to the request for information.

Whilst there are still companies who resent being asked for their accounts and who refuse on the grounds of privacy — or without giving any reason — there is a general tendency towards a positive response. Sometimes one is even permitted to see management accounts made up to the previous month-end, which, although unaudited, are the nearest thing to a completely up-to-date financial picture. Whenever accounts are produced for examination, it is essential that confidence is respected. The credit manager must not, on his return to the office, promptly circulate, to all and sundry, copies of accounts supplied to him in confidence.

Before examining the various ratios found in the accounts, there are a number of precepts which the credit analyst should learn:

1   Never form an opinion on one year's figures. It is more important to identify trends, preferably over three years or more (or over several months if management accounts are involved).
2   Always be aware of distortions caused by inter-company transactions. More and more companies are linking together in groups for tax advantages, and it is often difficult to assess the financial position of any one company without surveying other members of the group.
3   Remember that it is just as easy for a profitable company to become insolvent as an unprofitable one. Paper profits are of no value unless the rate of cash-flow is fast enough to meet the needs of the business.
4   Try to relate a company's financial performance to the industry in which it operates. Inter Company Comparisons Ltd regularly publish *Industrial Performance Analysis* which gives a three-year detailed comparison of the average performance by over 2,300 companies in 54 different sectors of industry and commerce under various headings including return on capital employed, liquidity, stock turnover and credit period. What one hopes to find is a better performance than the average, if the company is to be regarded as successful.

Analysis of balance sheets and profit and loss accounts

Some idea of the importance of checking the accounts when an important transaction is under review is gained from the following statistics on new company registrations in Great Britain during 1978 (obtained from *Trade & Industry*).

Total number of new companies	62,680
Total authorised capital, £	636,874,000
Total number of companies with capital of £100 or less	39,662
Total capital of '£100 or under' companies, £	Below 4,000,000

A simple calculation shows that 63 per cent of all new companies accounted for under 0.65 per cent of all the authorised capital.

It is clear that a majority of all new businesses start life on very small capital, expecting to be supported to a degree by their suppliers.

The following quotation from 'Business failures in England and Wales' [R. Brough, *Business Ratios*, No. 2 (1967)] is very apt and equally valid over ten years later:

> 'The very small commitment of proprietors' personal capital hardly seems to have prevented them from obtaining credit for an infinitely larger amount. Creditors seem to have been, in fact, the true entrepreneurs in many companies, so far as the risk-bearing function of entrepreneurship is concerned.'

It is interesting to note that in the period 1966-77 the number of compulsory liquidations and creditors' winding-up petitions as a percentage of 'live' companies increased considerably — see Exhibit 5.1.

Exhibit 5.1

	1966	1977	Increase
Number of live companies	*539,400*	*700,000*	*30%*
Number of compulsory liquidations and creditors' winding-up petitions	*2,387*	*5,848*	*145%*

The types of business most prone to failure during 1976-77, as a percentage of the total, were:

Construction	16-17%
Financial and professional services	12-15%
Retailing (non-food)	10-12%

There are many ways of reading a balance sheet, depending on the viewpoint of the reader. The credit manager is trying to assess the ability of the prospect to meet its commitments over a period, sometimes fairly short, i.e. under six months, but often in the context of a long-term relationship. There are three principal aspects of a company's financial standing on which a credit analyst should concentrate:

1 Solvency.
2 Profitability.
3 Capital strength.

Solvency

By solvency is meant the ability of a company to meet its current debts, i.e. those due within one year of balance sheet date, from its current assets (those capable of being turned into cash within one year). The obvious first test of solvency is to compare one with the other. This is known as the current ratio:

$$\frac{\text{Current assets}}{\text{Current liabilities}}$$

The traditional 'good' ratio is 2:1, as is seen in Exhibit 5.2. This 2:1 ratio has become far less commonly seen during the 1970s. Detailed analysis of UK company sources and uses of finance [such as contained in *Modern Credit Management* by P.R.A. Kirkman, George Allen & Unwin (1977)] show a decline in the average current ratio from around 2:1 in the early 1960s to around 1.5:1 in the mid-1970s. The main danger in relying on this ratio as the key to solvency is the inclusion of stocks. A high stock figure may include slow-moving or obsolescent items that may never be sold. To overcome this problem, another ratio is calculated — the quick ratio or 'acid test':

$$\frac{\text{Current assets less stocks}}{\text{Current liabilities}}$$

A 1:1 ratio used to be regarded as a necessary sign of liquidity, but many companies have proved capable of surviving on far thinner ratios than this. A survey of 700 companies' balance sheets showed

Royal Mail Parcels

POSTING DOCKET?

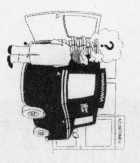

Got It ?

that in 1975 and 1976, 55 and 47 per cent, respectively, of these companies operated on an acid test ratio of 0.8 or less. One reason is that bank overdrafts, whilst often substantial and granted on a short-term basis, are commonly renewed from year to year. Nonetheless the credit analyst should be particularly wary of an adverse quick ratio since UK banks are not slow to safeguard their loans and overdrafts in times of financial strain.

The quality of debtors as a current asset should also be checked. Providing turnover figures are available, the collection period can be calculated to give an idea of the rate of cash-flow.

$$\text{Collection period in days} \quad = \quad \frac{\text{Debtors} \times 365}{\text{Sales}}$$

If receivables are being turned over only three or four times a year compared to an industry average of say 65—70 days, this points to a lack of credit control — which the company may try to compensate for by slow payment of its own suppliers.

In all these calculations, the actual ratios are less important than the trend over a period of years. If this can also be compared with the average for the industry, the analysis becomes more valuable.

To summarise, in examining solvency ratios the credit manager is seeking evidence as to whether or not the company is growing less or more capable of covering current debts with current assets and whether slow payment may be expected because of inadequate credit control.

Exhibit 5.2 XYZ Co. Ltd

Current assets

Stocks	500
Debtors	620
Cash	50
TOTAL CURRENT ASSETS	1,170

Less Current liabilities

Creditors	380
Taxation	200
NET CURRENT ASSETS	590

Profitability

A company that does not make profits will ultimately cease trading since it is not fulfilling its *raison d'être*. In business a company cannot stand still, except for very short periods, and the credit analyst must look for signs of healthy growth or of decline. As in all ratios, trends are all-important and mst be put into context to make sense. If company X has a falling profit record over a five-year period when most companies in that industry were increasing their profits, there is evidently something wrong.

The most widely used measure of profitability is:

$$\frac{\text{Profit}}{\text{Net assets}}$$

which is derived from the following calculations:

$$\frac{\text{Profit}}{\text{Sales}} \times \frac{\text{Sales}}{\text{Net assets}} = \frac{\text{Profit}}{\text{Net assets}}$$

The term 'net assets' in this context is interchangeable with 'capital employed' or 'net worth'. This profusion of terms does not make balance sheet interpretation any easier for the non-accountant, but the underlying concept is the real value of the company — expressed either as a source of funds (capital employed) or as the use of those funds (net assets). Comparing profit to net assets is therefore measuring how effectively the assets are being employed. Even more than liquidity ratios, profit ratios have very little meaning unless compared from year to year, within the industry in question. A refinement preferred by some analysts is to use net *tangible* assets which means excluding items such as goodwill, formation expenses, patent rights and any other intangibles.

Capital strength

This third aspect of a company's finances is concerned with the ratio of risk capital (equity) to loan capital. Many of the £100 companies being formed will have a very high debt ratio — also known as being highly geared. Directors' loans frequently appear in the accounts of these companies, far outweighing the equity capital. In this situation the credit manager must pose a number of questions before making a major credit decision.

Why do the owners not risk more of their own money?

Are the loans secured on the company's assets?

The danger to a highly-geared company running into a liquidity crisis is the appointment of a Receiver by a bank or some other debenture holder, whose primary object is to protect their investment. Trade creditors then find themselves receiving a fraction of their debts, after the holders of secured loans have obtained full restitution.

There is no debt ratio formula that the credit analyst can seize hold of. An analysis produced by J.C. Drury,*Huddersfield Polytechnic, of 700 UK companies for 1975-6 revealed that in both years 80 per cent of surveyed companies had debt capital of less than 80 per cent of shareholders' funds. The smallest level of borrowing occurred in mail order firms, furniture manufacturers and brewers. Very high gearing was found in shipping, the hotel industry and house-builders; 50 per cent of firms in these sectors had debt ratios exceeding 80 per cent. The main point to emerge from this survey, however, was that there is no statistical evidence for a 'normal' debt ratio in any industry.

The above ratios have been selected as 'key ratios'. There are others, but detailed balance sheet analysis can be very time consuming and the credit manager must keep a balance between the need for a quick decision and the desirability of a detailed analysis. He is trying to seek answers — from the evidence of historical trends — to three principal questions:
1   Does the prospect seem capable of paying for the goods or services the company wishes to supply?
2   Does the prospect appear likely to continue in business long enough to justify whatever costs have to be incurred in making a supply decision, e.g. tooling, distribution, or marketing.
3   In the event of a crisis, are the unsecured creditors reasonably well placed?
Exhibits 5.3 and 5.4 set out the basic facts needed for balance sheet analysis.

Companies Registry

As well as revealing the latest filed accounts, a search at the Companies Registry can produce two other pieces of information:
1   Details of all mortgages and other registered charges. The credit investigator is thus fully informed about the existence of secured loans, which must be paid out in full before the claims of unsecured creditors are considered.
2   The names of all directors and shareholders, plus details of other companies with which the directors may be associated.
Each company is identified in the Registry by a unique number. A company can, however, change its name by lodging full particulars with the Registry. A situation can occur (and one is known to the

*My thanks to J.C. Drury for the use of this material — *Author.*

Exhibit 5.3 Balance sheet and profit and loss summary

NAME OF COMPANY			
	Year ended	Year ended	Year ended
Net assets employed			
1 Fixed assets			
2 Investments	⎯⎯	⎯⎯	⎯⎯
	⎯⎯	⎯⎯	⎯⎯
3 Stocks and work-in-progress			
4 Debtors			
5 Other	⎯⎯	⎯⎯	⎯⎯
6 Total current assets	⎯⎯	⎯⎯	⎯⎯
7 Creditors			
8 Bank overdraft			
9 Other	⎯⎯	⎯⎯	⎯⎯
10 Total current liabilities	⎯⎯	⎯⎯	⎯⎯
11 Net current assets	⎯⎯	⎯⎯	⎯⎯
12 Net assets	⎯⎯	⎯⎯	⎯⎯
Sources of finance			
13 Issued capital			
14 Reserves	⎯⎯	⎯⎯	⎯⎯
15 Total shareholders' funds			
16 Loan capital			
17 Other	⎯⎯	⎯⎯	⎯⎯
18 Total capital employed	⎯⎯	⎯⎯	⎯⎯
Profit and loss account			
19 Sales			
20 Purchases			
21 Trading profit			
22 Interest paid			
23 Profit before tax			
24 Profit after tax			
25 Profit retained in the business			

Exhibit 5.4 Balance sheet analysis

NAME OF COMPANY				
Key ratio	Method of calculation*	Year ended	Year ended	Year ended
Current	*6 ÷ 10*			
Quick	*(6 − 3) ÷ 10*			
Coverage of current debt	*10 as % of 12*			
Profit on sales	*23 as % of 19*			
Asset turnover	*19 ÷ 12*			
Return on capital employed	*23 as % of 18*			
Collection period in days	*(4 ÷ 19)/365*			
Stock turnover in days	*(3 ÷ 20)/365 or* *(3 ÷ 19)/365*			
Working capital turnover	*19 ÷ 11*			
Debt ratio	*16 as % of 15*			

NOTES

1 Liquidity is good/bad and improving/steady/worsening.

2 Profitability is improving/steady/worsening.

3 Use of assets is vigorous/slow and improving/steady/ worsening.

4 Debt ratio is rising/steady/dropping.

* The numbers in this column refer to the item numbers in Exhibit 5.3.

writer) where two companies controlled by the same directors and shareholders exchanged names and, in fact, appeared to be what they were not. Company A with issued capital of £2 can become Company B which has £10,000 share capital. Only the registered number cannot be altered and an unsuspecting creditor may be supplying to a 'straw' company, believing it to be one of substance.

A credit problem which can sometimes be created by a visit to the Companies Registry is that of 'agency' or 'management' companies. Many reputable organisations, within their group structure, have companies which, whilst appearing to trade, actually have no assets. Orders are placed, deliveries accepted and payments made, but in fact the supplier is dealing with a 'straw' company which is acting as an agent for another company within the group. It may be argued that it is better to be blissfully ignorant, since if a Registry search reveals this situation the prudent credit manager will be obliged to seek an undertaking or guarantee from the principal company actually utilising the product or service. It is standard practice for many public companies to refuse requests for guarantees. In that event the supplier is left having to decide whether to trust that the parent company would indeed back its subsidiary in the event of a crisis. This point is returned to later under the heading 'Guarantees'.

Historical financial data

Extel Statistical Services Ltd provide a service for credit analysts of public companies and many large private companies. This consists of a summary of balance sheet information for the last three years and details of turnover, profits, taxation, dividends, earnings per share and equity capital for up to ten years. The salient points of the last directors' report are also given. The value of this is that all the information is provided in one or two pages, thus eliminating the need to obtain and search through several sets of accounts.

Press reports

Daily reading of the *Financial Times* is essential, not only to obtain the latest news of and comment on customers' final or half-year accounts, but also to keep abreast of trends and problems in the industry. Articles of this nature usually comment on the performance and standing of leading companies in the field in question, giving invaluable background data to the credit manager.

Most industries have a trade journal, weekly or monthly, which carries snippets of useful information not of sufficient news value to reach the national press.

After being read, all news items and articles should be cut out and filed on a customer status file which will include agency reports, accounts, references and reports of visits and interviews. The importance of keeping press information cannot be over-stressed, since it is often the only material available between annual reports.

Special reports

Most reporting agencies, in addition to producing the standard credit reports referred to in Chapter 4, also have a special reporting service. Assuming sufficient information is available on the subject company, a special report will usually contain detailed balance sheet analysis over several years, a narrative summary of the company's performance and standing, details of all connections with other companies and information on the current directors. The cost of such reports varies according to the volume and accessibility of information and can exceed £100.

Credit visits

Unless the information obtained from the accounts, reporting agencies, banks, credit contacts, etc., is absolutely clear-cut, leaving no reason for hesitation, the credit manager will not make his final decision until he has visited the prospective buyer.

Quite apart from the possibility of obtaining very recent management accounts, a visit gives an opportunity to meet the management, to discuss the likely trading relationship and to look around and gain an overall impression. A joint visit with the sales manager is a good idea, because the buyer is at once made aware of the sales/credit relationship — the fact that the credit manager is an accepted part of the team helping to establish a mutually profitable association. The credit manager is looking for evidence of capable management which can be revealed in many ways. Does the accounting system operate efficiently? Is information up-to-date and immediately available? Are the directors or managers experienced people? Do they have properly thought-out marketing and production plans? Are there any signs of self-interest priorities, such as expensive new cars or regular prolonged business lunches? What is the attitude of the staff to the management? Respectful and cooperative or fearful and down-trodden? A chief executive (whether a sole proprietor or managing director) who holds the reins of power closely to himself, delegating only routine decisions and withholding information from his subordinates, can be a danger to his company and should put the credit manager on his guard.

In addition to good management, the credit manager should also be looking for the outward signs of a well-organised and healthy company. Is the product well-established and in demand? If a new product, what evidence is there of sufficient demand? Are the plant and equipment in good condition? Who are the principal customers?

In short, the purpose of a credit visit is to enable the credit manager to decide to what degree the company and its management inspire confidence. When added to all the other information, does this confidence point to a favourable credit decision? (Further notes on credit visits appear in Chapter 8.)

Guarantees

A mention has already been made of the refusal of many public companies to give guarantees for the payment of debts incurred by subsidiaries. It is important to remember that a parent company has no legal responsibility to the creditors of a subsidiary. The corollary of this is never to make credit decisions based on the strength of the parent company — but nonetheless existence of a prosperous parent cannot be ignored and should increase confidence. If the finances of the subsidiary are weak in relation to the credit being sought, it does no harm to ask for a guarantee. Sometimes the reply is favourable and Exhibit 5.5 shows a recommended format. A refusal can either indicate a lack of confidence coupled with a degree of self-protection, or it may be no more than a policy decision regardless of the particular facts in view.

Equally common is the situation where there is no parent company, but the director and principal shareholder is known to have substantial private means. This often arises when a limited company is recently formed, and creditors suddenly lose the protection they enjoyed in selling to a sole trader or partnership. A request for the personal guarantee of the director in these circumstances is perfectly legitimate. Even better is to seek the joint and several guarantees of the man and his wife, to avoid the danger that all his assets have been put in his wife's name.

Success in obtaining personal guarantees depends in part upon goodwill between the guarantor and the credit manager, and to a greater degree upon the customer's dependence upon the seller. The bigger the company, the more difficult it is to obtain a guarantee

Exhibit 5.5

Dear Sirs,

In consideration of your readiness to comply with our desire that you should supply goods or services to:

(hereinafter referred to as 'the Buyer'), we hereby guarantee the due payment to you of all sums which are now or may hereafter become owing to you by the Buyer.

Our liability shall not in any way be diminished or affected by your giving time or indulgence to the Buyer, nor by any release, agreement not to sue, composition or arrangement of any description granted or entered into by you to or with the Buyer and we shall be liable to you in respect of any obligation accrued hereunder as if we were principal and not surety.

This guarantee shall be a continuing guarantee, subject to our right to give notice of revocation thereof. Any such notice shall be in writing and become effective upon its actual receipt by you at............ but no revocation shall in any way diminish or affect our liability to you in respect of any indebtedness of the Buyer incurred under any contract or obligation entered into between you and the Buyer prior to your receipt of such notice.

Yours faithfully,

Witness to the signature of................

(Signed).....................................

Address..............................Date................

53

because of the need to consult fellow directors and to pass a board resolution.

A guarantee should never be requested and obtained in the belief that it will be enforced. It represents the 'fall-back' position, enabling more credit to be extended than would otherwise be prudent. Further reference to guarantees is made later in this chapter under the heading 'government-controlled companies'.

Sales ledger information

A prime source of information on a customer wishing to increase business should be the sales ledger. Providing it is organised efficiently it should give the credit manager immediate evidence of payment behaviour.

Whilst manual, ledger-card systems give a continuous historical record of payments received and invoices cleared, a simple computer programme can produce a far clearer record. An illustration is given in Chapter 7 (Exhibit 7.4).

A necessary back-up to a computerised receivables system is some kind of manual record, such as a record card which carries full details of follow-up activity, promises received, etc., to augment the bare ouline of payment performance.

Special situations

Most of the analysis techniques covered in this chapter relate to the granting of credit to companies limited by shres, which are the most common form of corporate body. Corporate bodies exist independently from their members and have a legal existence which enables them, *inter alia*, to sue and be sued.

The requirements of the Companies Acts apply also to companies limited by guarantee and to unlimited companies. Both these types of organisation are usually confined to non-trading bodies. As far as credit analysis is concerned, members of a company limited by guarantee are liable up to the amount of their guarantee if the company cannot pay its debts and is declared insolvent. The liability of members of an unlimited company is unlimited.

Other kinds of corporate bodies include corporations created by Charter, such as the BBC, corporations created by Statute such as County Councils, the National Coal Board and the National Enterprise Board, and corporations sole such as a Bishop or the Queen. Credit problems encountered in dealing with some of these are examined later in this chapter.

Unincorporated associations

Under this heading are found several different forms of business organisation, including sole proprietorships, partnerships, clubs, societies, charities (although some charities are companies), trade unions and friendly societies.

The most important aspect of these bodies for the credit manager is the absence of limited liability (apart from registered trade unions and friendly societies). An unpaid creditor looks to the personal assets of the partners, members or the proprietor. While this may sound safer than dealing with a limited company, other problems must be considered. Firstly it is difficult to establish even an approximate idea of the value of those personal assets. Secondly the assets will be open to recourse from other creditors — perhaps supplying other businesses controlled by the same proprietor or partners. Assessment of a partnership or sole trader must follow the same principles as for a company. The analyst is looking for evidence of a stable, profitable business with reasonable liquidity. A particular hazard in dealing with sole traders is, of course, the death of the proprietor which, unless succession plans have been made for competent people to take over, may mean the sudden collapse or gradual stagnation of the firm.

Just because a body is non-profit-making, it does not mean there is no risk in allowing credit. Charities, for example, often depend upon voluntary help for their administration, and accounts are sometimes prepared with the primary objective of concealing operational and administrative costs. Very often, of course, the name and reputation is such that it would not be allowed to collapse and government money would probably be found. This would be small comfort to a supplier deprived of the use of his money for several months. In the case of clubs, societies, etc., if no funds are available to pay creditors, personal liability devolves upon the secretary or other officer placing the order with joint liability on the committee authorising the transaction — if this can be proved from the minutes.

Local Authority bodies – councils, schools, hospitals, etc.

While the risk of a bad debt may appear to be non-existent, the risk of delayed payment is high particularly in times of restricted public expenditure. Many suppliers of schools and, more particularly, of hospitals have traditionally taken a lenient attitude towards slow payment. If they were to stop doing so, our educational and health services would suffer severely. But suppliers must be aware of the danger and the effect on profits. Even the ultimate risk — complete insolvency — could become reality, witness the problems of New York City in the 1970s.

Government-controlled and government-backed companies

There are now (1979) a number of companies effectively under state-control, either directly (such as British Steel Corporation) or through the National Enterprise Board (such as BL). Many of these, had they been under private control, would have collapsed for lack of money. Indeed some of them are under government control *because* they collapsed.

How should the credit analyst view these companies? It is tempting to assume that no risk exists because the government will always provide cash, but this is not a tenable argument. There have been instances of government-backed companies being allowed to crash, and trade creditors, who had given credit in the belief that government support was indefinite, were left with nothing. The classic case is Upper Clyde Shipbuilders Ltd, which was put into liquidation in 1971. Not only did the government hold 48 per cent of the share capital, but it was also a very substantial loan creditor. There is no doubt that suppliers were encouraged to grant credit by the continued close involvement of the government in the management of the company. Attempts to persuade the government to accept some reponsibility towards the creditors, who were owed around £7½ million, came to an end in December 1977.

Another instance was Beagle Aircraft which had a Receiver appointed in December 1969. The company owed over £1.2 million to unsecured creditors who had to a large degree relied on government support; £6 million of public money was lost.

In early 1979 the National Enterprise Board held shares in over 30 companies, of which around two-thirds were minority interests. The amounts of public money so invested ranged from £40 in IRPOR Ltd to around £250 million in BL. The rules governing the activities of the NEB state (Section 10): 'In deciding on their practice in relation to the debts of their subsidiaries, the NEB shall have regard to the practice of companies in the private sector in relation to the debts of their subsidiaries. There will be no government guarantee to the creditors of a subsidiary of the NEB unless the government have undertaken a specific commitment in relation to a Company's debts.' This is clear enough, but although some guarantees have been given to suppliers, they have not been publicised. Suppliers who hesitate to give unsecured credit run the risk of being labelled over-cautious, but the facts do not justify a more liberal approach. For example, in October

1977 the NEB invested £54,000 in Hivent Ltd, a small air pollution equipment company, taking 25.9 per cent of the equity. Within six months the company was declared insolvent and the NEB refused any further financial assistance. Suppliers who had been encouraged to give credit by the sight of government money being injected were left in the lurch.

Apart from companies backed directly by the NEB, there are others whose government support comes from special bodies such as the Scottish and Welsh Development Agencies and the Northern Ireland Department of Commerce. A number of failures occurred in 1977-8 under the umbrella of the SDA — which did not protect creditors. A notable contrast is the case of Harland and Wolff Ltd, which became 100 per cent publicly owned (by the Northern Ireland Department of Commerce) in August 1975. Constant pressure from the British Marine Equipment Council eventually produced an unequivocal statement from the Minister of State, Mr Stanley Orme, in December 1976: 'I wish to confirm that the guarantee given in July 1974 by the Government in respect of the company's liabilities is still in force. It follows therefore that as long as this guarantee remains the position of all creditors, including suppliers, is secured.'

The message is clear. Any supplier required to give a substantial amount of credit to an NEB or otherwise government-controlled company should seek and press vigorously for a guarantee. As regards companies with a minority government holding, from the credit analyst's viewpoint this is best ignored altogether.

Conclusion

This chapter ends with two case-studies, in which only the names have been removed to prevent identification. One illustrates success despite financial problems. The other warns of the danger of acting on insufficient information.

Case study 1 — an engineering group

This case study deals with an engineering group that was within a hair's breadth of failure on several occasions. Accounts are shown for six years in Exhibits 5.6-5.9. Key ratios have been calculated. What do they show?

1 Liquidity This was bad throughout the period. The apparent slight improvement in year 2 was due to the massive increase in the

Exhibit 5.6 Balance sheet and profit and loss summary

NAME OF COMPANY (Case study 1)			
	Year 1 ended £000s	Year 2 ended £000s	Year 3 ended £000s
Net assets employed			
1 Fixed assets	2,507	3,360	3,407
2 Investments	67	83	128
	2,674	3,443	3,535
3 Stocks and work-in-progress	4,555	6,320	7,802
4 Debtors	1,817	4,594	3,661
5 Other	44	76	66
6 Total current assets	6,416	10,990	11,529
7 Creditors	4,340	7,078	7,527
8 Bank overdraft	729	2,189	3,013
9 Other	1,915	1,293	1,253
10 Total current liabilities	6,984	10,560	11,793
11 Net current assets	(568)	430	(264)
12 Net assets	2,006	3,873	3,271
Sources of finance			
13 Issued capital	204	205	205
14 Reserves	1,272	2,209	1,343
15 Total shareholders' funds	1,476	2,414	1,548
16 Loan capital	530	1,459	1,723
17 Other	-	-	-
18 Total capital employed	2,006	3,873	3,271
Profit and loss account			
19 Sales	13,657	16,466	21,610
20 Purchases	-	-	-
21 Trading profit	(71)	1,224	407
22 Interest paid	448	658	1,239
23 Profit before tax	(519)	336	(832)
24 Profit after tax	(451)	307	(758)
25 Profit retained in the business	-	-	-

Exhibit 5.7 Balance sheet analysis

NAME OF COMPANY	(Case study 1)			
Key ratio	Method of calculation*	Year 1 ended	Year 2 ended	Year 3 ended
Current	6 ÷ 10	0.9:1	1:1	1:1
Quick	(6 - 3) ÷ 10	0.3:1	0.4:1	0.3:1
Coverage of current debt	12 ÷ 10	0.3	0.4	0.3
Profit on sales	23 as % of 19	(3.8)	2.0	(3.9)
Asset turnover	19 ÷ 12	6.8	4.3	6.6
Return on capital employed	23 as % of 18	(25.9)	8.7	(25.4)
Collection period in days	(4 ÷ 19)/365	48	102	62
Stock turnover in days	(3 ÷ 20)/365 or			
	(3 ÷ 19)/365	122	140	132
Working capital turnover	19 ÷ 11	–	38.3	–
Debt ratio	16 as % of 15	36	60	111

NOTES

1 Liquidity is good/bad and improving/steady/worsening.

2 Profitability is improving/steady/worsening.

3 Use of assets is vigorous/slow and improving/steady/ worsening.

4 Debt ratio is rising/steady/dropping.

* The numbers in this column refer to the item numbers in Exhibit 5.6.

Exhibit 5.8 Balance sheet and profit and loss summary

NAME OF COMPANY (Case study 1)			
	Year 4 ended £000s	Year 5 ended £000s	Year 6 ended £000s
Net assets employed			
1 Fixed assets	3,197	3,319	5,013
2 Investments	117	104	
	3,314	3,423	5,013
3 Stocks and work-in-progress	6,136	8,989	10,608
4 Debtors	3,181	3,583	3,386
5 Other	110	78	534
6 Total current assets	9,427	12,650	14,528
7 Creditors	5,103	7,805	7,490
8 Bank overdraft	2,391	606	172
9 Other	1,438	273	257
10 Total current liabilities	8,832	8,684	7,919
11 Net current assets	595	3,966	6,609
12 Net assets	3,909	7,389	11,622
Sources of finance			
13 Issued capital	205	205	205
14 Reserves	2,179	4,613	8,023
15 Total shareholders' funds	2,385	4,818	8,228
16 Loan capital	1,325	2,318	2,011
17 Other	199	253	1,383
18 Total capital employed	3,909	7,389	11,622
Profit and loss account			
19 Sales	21,060	22,270	31,088
20 Purchases			
21 Trading profit	1,724	2,894	4,378
22 Interest paid	941	637	437
23 Profit before tax	783	2,257	3,941
24 Profit after tax	799	2,318	2,902
25 Profit retained in the business	928	2,307	3,302

Exhibit 5.9 Balance sheet analysis

NAME OF COMPANY	(Case study 1)			
Key ratios	Method of calculation*	Year 4 ended	Year 5 ended	Year 6 ended
Current	6 ÷ 10	1.1:1	1.5:1	1.8:1
Quick	(6 − 3) ÷ 10	0.4:1	0.4:1	0.5:1
Coverage of current debt	12 ÷ 10	0.4	0.9	1.5
Profit on sales	23 as % of 19	3.7	10.1	12.7
Asset turnover	19 ÷ 12	5.4	3.0	2.7
Return on capital employed	23 as % of 18	20.0	30.5	33.9
Collection period in days	(4 ÷ 19)/365	55	59	40
Stock turnover in days	(3 ÷ 20)/365 or (3 ÷ 19)/365	106	147	125
Working capital turnover	19 ÷ 11	35.4	5.6	4.7
Debt ratio	16 as % of 15	56	53	41

NOTES

1 Liquidity is good/bad and improving/steady/worsening.

2 Profitability is improving/steady/worsening.

3 Use of assets is vigorous/slow and improving/steady/worsening.

4 Debt ratio is rising/steady/dropping.

* The numbers in this column refer to the item numbers in Exhibit 5.8.

collection period. Years 3 and 4 show a small upward trend, more pronounced in the current liabilities/net worth ratio. In a financially strong company, net worth should cover current liabilities several times, indicating that creditors would be reasonably well cushioned in the event of a break-up. In this instance net worth does not approach parity with current liabilities until Year 5. Apart from the peculiar upsurge in debtors in Year 2 (probably caused by a major contract being invoiced at year-end), neither debtors nor stocks show any significant trends.

2 Profitability The level of trading profit fluctuated violently, showing an upward trend in Years 4-6. The turnover of net assets declined, principally because the asset value at the outset was so very low. Return on net assets is extremely high in Years 4, 5 and 6 — but again this is a product of the low asset base coupled with a rising margin on sales.

3 Capital structure The relationship between loan capital and shareholders' funds points to the same conclusion as the other ratios. Year 3 was the nadir of the company's fortunes, when trading profit almost disappeared and loan capital exceeded the equity value. Bank overdraft also reached a maximum, as did interest payable.

The most significant feature of these accounts is what they do *not* show. This company survived, yet a prospective supplier looking at the results of Years 1, 2 and 3 could well assume that it was on the verge of collapse. It was. Survival was primarily due to non-financial factors, including dedicated and determined management, a good product and excellent public relations.

Case study 2 — an international motor factor

In the Spring of 1975 orders were received for automotive components by a number of companies both in the UK and elsewhere in the EEC. The orders came from the London office of a company claiming to be 'international motor factors', with overseas offices in New York, Berlin, Paris and New Zealand.

A reputable reporting agency, after initially advising caution because of insufficient information, produced a revised report which included the following facts:

Number of staff employed	36
Estimated annual turnover	£500,000
Payments	Prompt

In the light of this it would, perhaps, be not unreasonable for credit to be granted. Anyone who did so probably had his fingers burned because within 12 months the company was wound up.

More detailed enquiries would have revealed the following:

1   The company had an issued capital of £2.
2   The company's bankers reported: 'Recently opened account. No experience'.
3   All the overseas addresses given were checked and found to be spurious — no evidence or record of the company was found in any of the areas named.

Direct contact with the company at an early stage revealed nothing. The London office was found to be one room. Telephone enquiries brought the response that the company had a number of export orders. No address was given on the order since the buyer would arrange collection.

It is not known whether the company acted fraudulently, although there was certainly misrepresentation. The significant point is the danger in relying on one source of information — in this case a status report — before granting credit.

Appendix: the Z-score technique

In recent years an increasing amount of research has been made into the possibility of identifying potential business failures. This is frequently known as the 'Z-score' technique. It involves the use of a mathematical formula which utilises a number of financial ratios. Several different versions exist, each with its own proponents. Each one uses a different set of ratios and each ratio is given a different weighting factor.

Z-score formulae generally claim to be able to identify companies which are showing some of the characteristics commonly found to have been displayed by other companies prior to insolvency. Predictions of potential failures are claimed to be possible around two years ahead of the event.

Whilst research into this subject has been conducted for over ten years, there is probably still some way to go before anything like a definitive formula will emerge. Assuming that this does develop, its value to the credit manager must surely be in identifying the buyers which need special care and attention. A company with many hundreds or thousands of volume customers inevitably has a very difficult task in keeping credit limits up-to-date. Any system that facilitates a 'management by exception' approach would be welcome, providing its costs do not outweigh its benefits.

Existing Z-score techniques require programming on a computer, which entails an initial cost and an annual maintenance and running cost. Depending on how reliable the formula has proved to be, the credit manager may have to choose between a human credit analyst and a computer facility!

There can never be an exact, scientific method to guarantee the identification of business failures. A technique that sets off alarm bells and helps to determine priorities can be a very welcome addition to the credit manager's armoury.

Chapter 6

Credit decisions, credit limits and controls

The true function of the credit manager is to contribute to company profits through positive assessment and control. It is not good enough to play safe, to follow a cautious conservative policy towards new business, to deny credit to all but those whose ability to pay is undoubted. There are times when such an approach is justified. If the order book is full, the factory working at full capacity and the demand for goods outstrips the supply, the credit manager can send the doubtful risks to the back of the queue, insist on cash-in-advance or demand security. Such boom periods have been rare and generally short-lived since the 1960s. Instead the credit manager today finds himself in a very different environment in which his ability to turn marginal accounts into good customers is becoming increasingly valuable.

From the information sources examined in Chapters 4 and 5, facts and indications emerge on which credit decisions have to be made. Sometimes the decisions are easy, as when the anticipated level of business is seen to be well within the normal scope of an established company. Others are more difficult and call for examination of balance sheets and perhaps a personal visit.

Other factors affecting credit decisions

There will also be occasions when the final decisions must take into account factors beyond the credit manager's sphere of knowledge or jurisdiction. Examples of this are as follows:

1 Is there an alternative more creditworthy buyer for the product? (This is applicable only for standard goods.)
2 If the goods have already been made to customer specifications and there is only scrap value, does this justify a high risk?
3 Are the goods obsolete stock with a very small book value? If so, a higher risk can be undertaken.
4 Does rejection of the order mean the closing of a production line?
5 Does it mean losing a vital opportunity to gain a foothold in a new market?

The credit manager is not usually in a position to answer these questions, but he must be aware of such implications — which is only possible if he is an accepted member of company management. His job is then to produce an information file which will pass to sales or production for their observations before the final decision is cast at board level.

The time factor

In an ideal world the credit analyst is given lengthy advance notice of new business and has ample time to obtain and evaluate all available data. This does happen — sometimes — depending on how well he has educated the sales manager! More usually, the request for credit clearance comes within days (or even hours) of the despatch or collection date, and there is no time to do anything except use the telephone.

Three or four telephone calls will, given a little luck, produce enough to either refuse or approve an initial order. In order of priority these calls should be made:

a To one or more credit contacts likely to know of the new buyer. Up-to-date experience from a trusted colleague is worth several credit reports.
b To the buyer himself, to ask approval to phone his banker and to ask as much as he will allow about the company.
c To the buyer's banker — if the buyer has authorised his banker to disclose helpful information.
d To a credit agency to see whether there is an up-to-date report on file.

From time to time attempts have been made to reduce the credit decision process to a formula. These vary from the simple rule of not giving more credit than X per cent of the issued capital or the net worth of the buyer, to a complex system of credit scoring calling for detailed information data to be analysed or fed into a computer. Such methods are aimed at removing the guesswork from credit sanctioning and making it more scientific. Their efficiency is very doubtful, because they seek to delete what is often the most important element — human judgement of a total array of facts, impressions and opinions. For example, not many suppliers would have continued giving credit to the company in Case Study 1 (see Chapter 5) had their decisions been based entirely on the financial facts. In actual fact, many suppliers continued in blissful ignorance of these facts, which was probably fortunate for the company.

The basic questions to be considered in any credit decision are 'How much?' and 'For how long?'. The importance of flexible payment terms has been examined in Chapter 3 but the principle bears repeating. If monthly purchases of £5,000 result in an exposure that looks too high — on net monthly terms — the same turnover may be achieved without that degree of risk by reducing the credit period. Apart from the question of terms, a credit decision may be affected by the period of the contract. On the one hand, the credit manager may be encouraged on a doubtful case by the fact that deliveries will be completed within, say, two months, and the chances of the buyer collapsing that quickly should be a lot less than if supplies are to be made over a long period. Against this, however, is the danger that once deliveries are completed, he loses the deterrent of stopping supplies.

In some companies, depending on the average order value, it may be worth operating a 'discretionary limit' or blanket approval system for initial orders. Thus new customers' orders up to, say, £100 could be approved automatically. This policy is clearly beneficial to the marketing department since delays on first orders may mean lost business. Problems can easily occur, however, if careful control is not exercised. Suppose, for example, an initial order for £70 is accepted, an account is opened and an account number is allocated. Unless that account is clearly tagged 'first order only approved' or given some kind of identification, further orders of increasing value may be accepted without question, and within a few months a £500 balance is showing on an account that has had no credit clearance at all.

To avoid this sort of problem — which can rapidly get out of hand — it is suggested that as soon as the initial order is accepted, a letter of the form shown in Exhibit 6.1 is sent by the credit department.

Credit limits

A credit limit should reflect the credit manager's assessment of both the customer's capacity and intentions to pay for a given volume of business.

Exhibit 6.1

Dear Sir,

    We thank you for your recent order, number...
value....
    To avoid any unnecessary delay, this order is
being processed immediately on our standard terms of:

    So that we can handle future orders on credit
terms we ask you to complete the attached form and
return it to us.
    Our Conditions of Sale are printed on the reverse
of this letter. Would you please note that all cheques
should be made payable to... and sent to the following
address:

    ....

    ....

    Thank you for your co-operation.

        Yours faithfully,

Assessment should always be undertaken with a credit limit in mind, and the credit decision should aim at setting a limit high enough to accommodate the expected level of business, having regard also to the terms of payment. For example, an enquiry forecast at £1,000 per month on monthly terms indicates a credit limit requirement of £3,000. This allows for payment to be up to one month late without the credit limit being exceeded. A new buyer predicted to take £500,000 p.a. on net 30-day terms will need a limit of, say, £150,000 — on the same principle of covering three months' sales plus an element of 'rounding-up' to allow for queries.

It follows that credit decisions formed on this basis will result in two distinct types of credit limit:

1   The credit limit which is merely a signpost or guideline to account performance. This may also be called a credit line.
2   The credit limit which is a barrier, which fixes the maximum risk believed to be acceptable.

Credit limits as guidelines occur when the limit needed to

accommodate sales volume is well inside the 'maximum risk' figure. Thus a supplier approached by ICI Ltd on the basis of £10,000 a month can easily establish a credit line of £30,000. It may be argued that there is no point in having a limit at all in this kind of situation, or that the limit should be set at some astronomic figure (perhaps £1 million). The prime reasons for operating guideline limits on 'blue-chip' accounts are that they introduce a discipline into the credit department's routine. Every account which transgresses its limit must be looked at. Maybe sales are increasing — in which case the limit may need increasing. Perhaps payments are slowing down — corrective action is needed. Changing trends in account performance are highlighted, whether they relate to sales volume or payment performance. The next Rolls Royce disaster will never be anticipated if all the 'blue-chip' accounts are ignored or given £1 million limits.

The other type of credit limit is more readily understood but is hopefully used less frequently. If the 'three-month sales' limit requirement is £10,000, but all the available evidence points to £5,000 as being the absolute maximum, then the credit limit of £5,000 is a real limit. Similarly, if £10,000 can be agreed but any more seems dangerous, the limit has to be used as a barrier.

There are, of course, other ways of using credit limits. The limit chosen for each account can represent the maximum amount deemed to be an acceptable risk — regardless of the expected sales volume. In the case of companies of the highest standing, this tends to result in the £1 million limit situation, which has already been discussed. Another method is to set a series of credit limit bands, for example:

£1	—	£500
£500	—	£1,000
£1,000	—	£2,500
£2,500	—	£5,000, etc.

Each customer, having been assessed, is placed into that band whose upper limit represents the maximum acceptable risk. This has the merit of flexibility, but it does not relate the credit limit to the turnover.

The question that no book can answer is under what circumstances do you decide to fix a limit of £5,000 on a buyer who needs £10,000? The experience of other suppliers (apart from referees), the evidence of trends in the accounts, the comments of reporting agencies, the length of time in business, the hazards of the particular industry, the reputation of the company, the impression obtained of the management — all these factors contribute to the decision. The judgement of a credit manager should develop with experience, and not be too easily swayed by the arguments or pressures from the sales department.

It is a good principle to tell customers of their credit limits. This avoids any subsequent embarrassment or misunderstanding if order-acceptance is delayed because of a limit problem. Where the limit is a maximum figure, this must be stated, and conversely where it is no more than a reflection of the customer's needs, this should also be made clear. Problems can arise if an unfavourable credit decision is notified to the customer by the sales office, since the sales staff may not be aware of the reasons for refusal. If it can be arranged, it is better if credit staff have the responsibility for this since it provides an opportunity to explain and discuss the problem. Very often the goodwill of the buyer can be retained if he is persuaded that the reason for the order being refused is the failure of his accountant to pay!

Risk categories

Credit limits which may be either guidelines or barriers can only be used within a system which provides infallible terms of reference. The use of risk categories gives such a framework.

Every customer is placed in a risk category according to the kind of credit limit established. Risk categories can then be used to determine the degree of order-entry control and overdue follow-up. Exhibit 6.2 shows a basic risk-category structure, with three categories: A, B and C. It is possible to use only two categories — to denote the type of credit limit — but this restricts the other uses of the system. On the other hand, the number of categories can be increased at will,

Exhibit 6.2

Risk category	Type of customer	Order referral	Purpose of credit limit
A	*Government and public bodies, hospitals, schools, and large, strong public companies*	*None*	*To indicate a change in payment or buying behaviour*
B	*All others*	*Over £X*	
C	*Customers of doubtful standing and/or persistent bad payment behaviour*	*All orders*	*To indicate maximum balance allowable*

depending on the complexity of the business and the level of sophistication required.

The system illustrated in Exhibit 6.2 operates as follows:

Category A should be reserved for customers with zero or extremely low credit risk. This will include central and local government bodies, hospitals, schools and universities, nationalised undertakings and national or international companies of the highest standing. Since inclusion in this top category means the absence of any form of order-entry control — apart from restrictions imposed because of non-payment — it is essential that a regular check be made on the fortunes of admitted companies. By definition most of these will be public companies whose annual reports are obtainable free and on whom frequent press comment and information appears. The credit limits on Category A customers will all be guidelines, related to the expected maximum balance assuming that sales do not exceed forecast and that payments are arriving within one month of due date. No order referral is necessary since these customers can increase their purchases without giving rise to a significant credit risk.

At the other end of the scale is *Category C* which is used for all customers whose credit limit is a barrier. It should also include any buyers whose payment behaviour demands strict control — whether or not there is a credit limit problem. Order-referral will be 100 per cent for Category C customers, to ensure that credit limits are not exceeded.

Having covered buyers at both end of the risk scale, we are left with the middle range, neither 'blue-chip' nor high-risk, which are placed in *Category B*. For nearly all companies, this is where the majority of customers will be grouped. Credit limits in this category will be guidelines, as in Category A, but a measure of order-entry control is necessary because these companies are not of the highest standing and an unexpected increase in purchasing could push a balance beyond the theoretical maximum. The degree of order-entry control will depend on the type of business and the average order value, but it makes sense to try and relate the referral level to the credit limit. For example, a customer with a £5,000 credit line might require referral of all orders over £2,000 since that figure is more than one month's average purchases. It might be safer — but more difficult to operate — to have all orders in any month referred once a cumulative total of £2,000 has been reached.

Risk categories must be used flexibly, i.e. customers should be moved from category to category according to changes in their risk status or as a result of significant changes in payment performance. It is vital that credit status information files are kept up-to-date and the following system is recommended.

Category A   Annual reports of public companies (obtainable free), plus regular flow of press cuttings and articles. For private companies an annual search if the volume of business warrants it, also press reports, etc. Common sense must be used. If ICI are buying £100 per month, it is not worth the trouble of sending for their annual report.

Category B   As above, plus annual status reports on all private companies.

Category C   As for Category B, with six-monthly up-dating of status information and yearly or half-yearly bank reports on any companies running high balances ('high' balances might mean over £2,000 for some suppliers and over £20,000 for others. Again, common sense must prevail.)

The use of credit contacts to give and receive information should be a continuous process, especially for Category C accounts.

Finally, good use should be made of sales ledger information — as indicated in Chapter 5 — to ensure that trends in sales volume and payment behaviour are easily detected.

Another advantage of a risk-category system is that it facilitates variable follow-up procedures. Thus, where collection letters are used, the timing and frequency can be accelerated for Category C customers, where it is important that overdues are chased immediately, and action to stop shipment be taken sooner than for customers in Categories A and B.

Operating the controls

(a) The basic approach

It is important to use limits and categories in a positive manner. The easy way is to adopt an inflexible attitude, to play safe and always reject orders which would breach the limit. While this may be the right decision on some occasions, the credit manager should always be trying to find ways of accepting marginal business.

Credit limits must not remain static. Most of the problems will arise with Category C customers, on a restrictive, maximum credit limit. Even here, however, a reasonable period (say, six months) of trading with good payments should provide sufficient confidence to increase the limit and gradullay introduce a more liberal attitude.

Other ways of tackling limit problems include switching to a shorter credit period or even offering a cash discount. Discounts that are uneconomic in the strict context of the cost of money may be justifiable if they open the door to an increased sales volume not acceptable on ordinary credit terms.

(b) Order entry

A prerequisite of order-entry is that the credit department has absolute authority over the opening of new accounts, the issuing of account numbers and the maintenance of name and address records.

The first essential is that the correct name and address are recorded when an account is opened. To this end, salesmen and sales office staff should be asked to provide letterheads of new customers and to supply copies of orders where these include instructions to deliver and invoice to different locations. No account should be opened until credit clearance has been given, which will involve the allocation of a credit limit and risk category — unless a discretionary limit is used for initial orders. Credit approval should be in writing, along the lines indicated in Exhibit 6.3.

Preferably the request for a new account should also be in writing, and Exhibit 6.4 illustrates a form suitable for computer systems.

A more detailed examination of customer name and address records is deferred to Chapter 7.

Once an account is opened and a credit limit and category allocated, order referral should be on an exception basis. Thus there is no point in checking orders from Category A customers or from Category B unless the referral limit is exceeded. A sophisticated computer system can very easily cope with this requirement, provided all orders are processed through a central control before being accepted. Such a system can be developed to include checks against the credit limit and even against the payment situation on the ledger. A total order-referral system is illustrated in Exhibit 6.5, each stage either culminating in referral to the credit department or being continued through the computer.

Stage I Customer's order entered on an order-entry form, including the account number (without this it will be rejected automatically). Details are fed into the computer and the risk category is ascertained. Category A status allows the order to move straight to Stage III, while B and C proceed to:

Stage II There is no need for an order-referral level in a computer system. All orders are added to the outstanding balance on the account, to which is added the total value of previously accepted

Exhibit 6.3 Credit referral note

To: From: *Credit Dept*
                                 Date:

    Re:

Enquiry/Order No. _____ dated _____ Value _____

Existing buyer

1 *Order can be accepted*   ☐

2 *Order can be shipped*   ☐

3 *Please refer again before shipment*   ☐

4 *Order cannot be accepted/shipped
   because customer is overdue and/or
   over limit*   ☐

New prospect

1 *Information obtained, details
   attached*   ☐

2 *Business may be accepted*   ☐

3 *Payment terms to be established*   ☐

4 *No information available yet*   ☐

5 *Initial order may be supplied up to*   ☐

   on payment terms of   ☐

6 *Risk category is*   ☐

7 *Temporary credit limit is*   ☐

8 *Other comment*

*A customer code must be applied for in the normal
manner. If a code is not requested within six
months, the above decisions are null and void*

Exhibit 6.4

To: *Credit Dept*   Date:

From:

ADVICE OF NEW CUSTOMER

*The following firm is expected to place/has placed
an enquiry/order with us:*

Trade and bank references obtained:

1

2

3

Likely monthly level of purchases - £ _____

Existing suppliers:

Payment terms sought (if different from net 30 days):

Other information

---

orders not yet shipped. A further adjustment would be to *exclude* that
part of the new order (or of existing orders) which is not scheduled for
delivery for a further month. The grand total is then compared to the
credit limit. Orders which would breach the limit are referred direct to
the credit department, otherwise they move into Stage III.

Stage III For Categories A and B, a check is made whether the
account is more than one month overdue. For Category C the ageing
check looks for an account being more than 10 days overdue. Negative
answers will allow the order to be accepted. Positive answers will lead
to Stage IV.

Exhibit 6.5

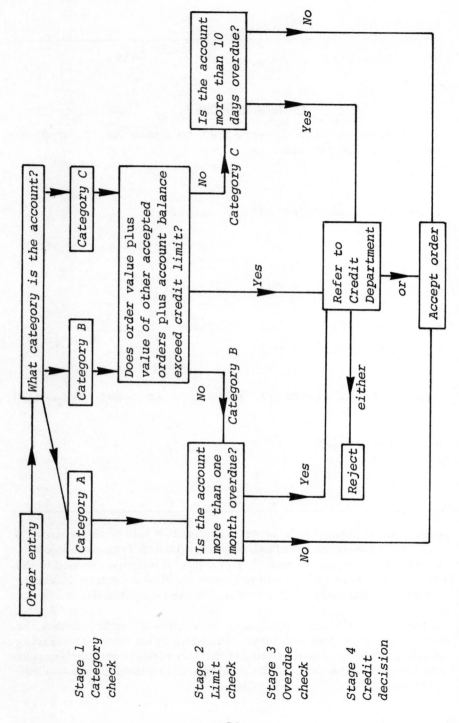

Stage 1
Category
check

Stage 2
Limit
check

Stage 3
Overdue
check

Stage 4
Credit
decision

76

Stage IV The final decision is made — not by the computer but by the credit manager or his trained staff. An additional control which could be built into a computer system and which should take place automatically in any event is to check how long since the credit limit was last reviewed. The above example is most suited to a company selling standard off-the-shelf products to a high volume of customers. Different problems arise where goods are specially made to customer specification, which are looked at below under the heading 'Marginal accounts'.

(c) High credit requests

Requests for credit substantially above the normal buying level usually involve special marketing or production considerations.

Opportunities to make significant increases in sales and profits do not arise every day and invariably there is a price in the shape of a greater credit risk. The credit manager must take care to investigate thoroughly, looking all the while for a way of justifying the additional credit.

The most important step is to determine the reason for the extra volume. Is the customer working on a special contract? If so, with whom and how will it affect his cash-flow? If the end product is going overseas, does he have ECGD cover? If he is looking for extended credit, is this because of the demands of his overseas buyer? Is the rise in purchasing a seasonal event, as when a brewery builds up its stock of kegs ready for summer? If the increased demand is based on no more than a decision to build-up stocks hoping for an up-turn in the market, the credit manager will be a little cautious. In the period 1977-8 many companies anticipated a boom — especially in consumer durables — which did not take place. A common occurrence was for such companies to request extended credit — or just take it — from their suppliers when they found themselves in a cash squeeze. This type of problem is likely to be seen more often, since the cost of reducing the labour-force and the difficulties of so doing continue to increase and firms are pushed towards the alternative of making for stock.

To return to the more usual situation, where the customer has obtained an important contract, it may be possible to secure payment by taking advantage of his own security. For example, a customer is selling an end-product to a buyer in the Middle East on Letter of Credit terms and he needs an exceptional increase in credit. If the risk appears too high, payment may be secured by a back-to-back credit or a transferable credit arrangement. This is examined in more detail in Chapter 12 but in essence it is the establishment of a lien on the customer's payment from his buyer.

Refusal by a customer to give information about his need for higher credit or to supply up-to-date financial information to justify an increased line of credit must inevitably put the credit manager on his guard.

(d) Marginal accounts

All Category C customers should be listed and circulated to sales and shipping departments. Where orders are fulfilled from stock and standard products are involved, the vital control point is the despatch area. The credit manager must make sure the shipping manager and his staff not only operate the controls but understand why. If each order is a special production job, there must be two control points, firstly, in the sales office before manufacture is commenced and, secondly, in despatch. If the production period is lengthy, it is possible that a despatch may have to be withheld because the position on the account has altered since the order was accepted. Where goods to customer specification have been made, there will always be arguments that they may as well be despatched since they are of no value or interest to any other buyer and if they are not shipped they only have scrap value. This proposition should be resisted, principally because if the customer is overdue, to permit further deliveries will be seen as a sign of weakness. Also, any leverage on the customer to pay is given up. A different situation arises where production orders arrive and the customer is over-limit or overdue or both. The sales manager must decide whether to allow production, knowing that despatch will be delayed or prohibited unless the position is put to rights in the meantime.

(e) Stopping supplies

If an effective order-referral system is used, as described above, it may seem superfluous to issue a separate blacklist. This is necessary, however, for the following reasons:
1   A blacklist may include customers from Categories A and B, as well as C.
2   Sales must be told of customers whose orders or desptaches are being held — as opposed to merely being referred for approval.
3   A blacklist should be used in a different way from a referral list. Customers on 'stop' remain so until released by the credit department — whereas all orders from referral customers must be put forward for approval. The *effectiveness* of stopping deliveries is examined in Chapter 8.

78

Chapter 7

The sales ledger and computer systems

Sales ledger management and organisation will be examined under the following headings:
1   Purpose and nature of the sales ledger.
2   Input to the ledger.
3   The name and address file.
4   Statements.
5   Computer aids to credit control.
6   Debit notes.
7   Filing.

The purpose and nature of the sales ledger

The basic purpose of a sales ledger is to record the company's sales to and payments from customers and any adjusting entries in such a manner that each individual transaction can be traced and verified from date of despatch to receipt of payment.

Some companies record cash sales on the ledger; others restrict entries to credit sales — although this might include sales on pro-forma or COD terms.

A consequence of this basic function is the need to balance the ledger every month in the following manner:

Balance at last month-end

Plus Net invoiced sales this month

Less Cash received

Equals New balance plus/minus sundry adjustments.

A failure to balance resulting from duplicate entries, a missing batch of invoices or merely incorrect arithmetic should be of great concern to the credit manager whether or not he is responsible for the ledger. If the difference is substantial, a decision must be made whether to delay the despatch of statements. To do this would be exceptional, since the effect of a small number of statements having to be corrected later is normally less than the risk of customers delaying payments because of late statements.

Ledgers are either 'open-item' or historical. The open-item format is generally associated with a computer system. A new ledger is produced at the end of each month including only those items which are still outstanding or unreconciled. The advantage of this is that the position on each customer's account can be seen at a glance. The historical or 'brought-forward' method involves a continuous ledger to which new items are added each month. For the purpose of statements, it is normal to carry forward the total owing from the previous month and to show individually only the new month's transactions. The drawback of this system is the need for constant manual reconciliations of the previous month's balance. The only benefit of the historical method is that account history, i.e. sales and payment performance, can be obtained immediately from the ledger, whereas an open-item system requires this information to be stored for reference elsewhere. Ways of doing this will be looked at later in this chapter.

Input to the ledger

(a) Internal input The essential requirements of all internally produced entries — invoices, credit notes, contra items and journal items — are that they are given the correct customer account or code number and that their reference numbers are easily identifiable and distinctive. This means taking care that all departments responsible for raising such documents have an up-to-date list of account numbers cross-referenced to names and addresses. The allocation of series of invoice numbers to different divisions or branches must be planned to avoid the possibility of the same numbers being used twice. A simple

way to ensure this is to give each division or branch its own alpha or numerical prefix to invoice numbers.

As well as being entered on the ledger, invoices have to be sent out. Good credit control starts here, because customers who do not receive their invoices within a few days of the dates thereon will use this as a reason to delay payment. This is a particular problem at month-end, when in many companies invoicing rises to a peak. All customers impose 'cut-off' dates, denoting the latest date invoices will be accepted in the period. There are two things the credit manager should do. First, he should constantly try to ensure that all invoices are produced and mailed within two to three days of period-end. Secondly, where many invoices are raised for a small number of very large customers, he may find it worthwhile collecting all these together and making personal delivery of them to the appropriate person.

Invoice design and lay-out are also of interest to the credit manager. There should be a designated space for the customer's order number. The address to which payment is to be sent should be prominently indicated. The terms of payment must be clearly stated. The invoice number, date and customer's account number must be easily identified, not buried amidst a welter of information about job numbers and part numbers. Credit notes should always carry a clear reference to the original invoice and/or customer's debit note.

(b) External input This means customer payments in the form of cheques, bank transfers, direct debits, postal orders or pound notes.

Responsibility for listing, totalling and banking lies with the cashier, but the way each day's receipts are presented to the sales ledger should be dictated by the credit manager. Speed and ease of identification are the key points. A straight alphabetical list is normal, but if this goes beyond, say, 100 items, it will often not be available until mid-day or later. Meanwhile orders are being held and decisions are in suspense. Is it worth having all payments over a certain minimum — £100 or £500 or £5,000 for example — listed separately and given to the credit manager ahead of the main list? In a busy department handling hundreds of remittances daily, this could mean several hours' prior knowledge of all important payments. If cash-allocation is divided alphabetically amongst several clerks, it is sensible to ask the cashier to have the cash-lists typed on separate sheets so that each clerk can have his own. Another responsibility of the cashier is to inform the credit manager *immediately* of any dishonoured cheques — taking care to distinguish between those which are returned by the bank marked 'refer to drawer' and those which are merely marked 'please represent'.

If possible, payments should be reconciled within 24 hours of receipt. Correct allocation of cash is very important, and strict controls should operate to prevent an accumulation of unreconciled payments. This demands discipline in the ledger clerk's job, and the credit manager must not tolerate cash remaining unallocated beyond, say, one month after receipt. 'On account' payments often cannot be avoided and, indeed, are sometimes the only way of maintaining satisfactory cash-flow. A clear distinction must be made between 'on account' payments from major buyers who are temporarily behind in the clearance of invoices through their purchase ledger and 'on account' payments from customers unable to make full settlement. The problem with the former is that if no effort is made to obtain regular reconciliations, the list of potential invoice queries grows ever longer. By the time they come to light, these queries are several months old and more difficult to resolve.

Receipt of an 'on account' payment in place of the full amount requested should sound a warning bell. It is almost invariably a sign of cash shortage and must be followed up immediately.

The name and address file

Control of this should rest with the credit manager and involve the following precautions:
1   Input of new or amended information to be restricted to the credit department.
2   Issue of account numbers to be in the hands of the credit department.

Other departments will need access to the file for shipping addresses, invoicing addresses, account numbers, etc., but only the credit department should be allowed to alter or add to the file. In addition to account number, name, shipping and invoicing addresses, the following information should also be kept on file:
a   Statement address.
b   Credit limit.
c   Risk category.
d   Payment terms.
e   Product code.
f   Regional or branch-office code.

These are merely the principal items that most operations will need to have on file; numerous others can be added to suit individual conditions.

In a manual system, this data is usually kept on a card-index file which, because it is needed by different users, has to be reproduced several times, with great risk of error and lack of control. If it can be put on to computer tape or disk storage, these problems virtually disappear since complete tabulations — either in card form or as a print-out — can be provided to all users simultaneously and control over additions and amendments is easily centralised.

A comprehensive, up-to-date name and address file is an essential basis for operating the sales ledger by computer. The principal ways in which the computer can be used to aid credit management will now be examined.

Statements

Most, if not all, trading companies send statements to their customers, usually monthly. The purpose is to draw attention to unpaid items and to induce payment. So ingrained is this practice that payment will often be refused — or at least delayed — on the grounds that the supplier's statement has not arrived or that it is not agreed. A recent analysis of payments to the author's own company showed that around 16.5 per cent of all payments were made against statements. Some companies who pay on their own remittance advices also attach the statement giving a reconciliation, and many more use statements as a control over their own bought ledger. Demands for payment of old invoices are much easier to verify or challenge if regular statement reconciliation takes place.

The two key features of statements are, first, timing and, secondly, clarity. Statements should be ready for despatch within as few days as possible after month-end. On a manual system where they have to be typed or photocopied, long delays are difficult to avoid compared to a computer operation. In practice the statement run-date will probably be determined by other demands on computer time, since most companies impose a cut-off system for input at month-end.

Clarity of statements demands considerable thought and planning if the end result is to help the customer identify unpaid items and reduce queries to a minimum. Exhibit 7.1 is an example of a computer statement having most of the features and headings normally required.

The main points to note are as follows:

a   The statement is 'open-item' — only uncleared items are shown.

b   Each type of transaction is clearly identified — by an abbreviation rather than a code.

c   Only one value column is used, with 'CR' to denote credit items. This saves valuable space.

d   The use of an item number — generated by the computer — means that the entire line can be identified by that number. This is useful in cash reconcilation.

e   There is a running balance.

Exhibit 7.1

XYZ CO. LTD
5 New Road, Anytown, Wessex

STATEMENT

Telephone: _____
Telegrams: _____
Telex: _____

Account No.

Customer's name and address

Terms - Net 30 days

Cheques to be sent to cashiers dept at heading address. Bank transfers to Barclays Bank Ltd, Anytown, A/C No. 1234567

Document codes

INV - Invoice
C/N - Credit note
D/N - Debit note
CSH - Cash
O/P - Overpayment
U/P - Underpayment
JNL - Journal
CTR - Contra

Page | Period end

Document date	Document code	Product	Document number	Order number	Item number	Due date	Value	CR	Balance

Current	1-30 days overdue
31-60 days overdue	Over 60 days overdue
Debit notes	Unreconciled cash

Total outstanding _____

f   Customer's order number is shown against each item.

g   An aged analysis of the balance is given.

Many companies produce a statement with a tear-off portion on the right, headed 'Remittance Advice'. It is hoped that customers will return this with their cheque, thus assisting in cash reconciliation. In practice the percentage who use this slip is very small, and there is a case for using this part of the statement to give more information — customer order number and due date for payment, for example.

It is generally desirable to show on the statement all items up to the end of the calendar month. This often conflicts with internal cost periods finishing on different dates. If possible, statements should be held over to include calendar month entries falling into the subsequent cost period. This may mean disturbing the arrangements for computer time and requires careful planning with the computer manager.

With a computer system, it is easy to arrange for the statement to be produced in two or more copies — the top copy to go to the customer and the others for internal use. One copy would act as the ledger for the month — the working documents on which incoming payments and reconciliations are recorded.

Computer aids to credit control

Aged analysis

For any credit operation, unless the number of live accounts is below, say, 100, a properly designed aged analysis of the sales ledger is *vital*. Generally produced monthly — but more often if needed — this will provide information on the age of each customer's account, the total balance compared to the credit limit and the amount of cash required to keep it within terms. Exhibit 7.2 shows a typical analysis. Points to note are as follows:

a   Payment terms, credit limit, risk category and area office are all clearly visible.

b   Debit notes and unreconciled cash are not aged but shown in separate columns. This is important since debit notes cannot be regarded as 'collectable' items and should be controlled separately (see below under 'Debit Notes').

c   Customers who have exceeded their limit are highlighted by an asterisk. A better way of identifying over-limit accounts, especially in a large operation, is to have a separate tabulation.

Where different product groups are involved, the analysis can be programmed to print in the required sequence, similarly if analysis under regional offices is desired. Another useful sequence is to have an analysis by risk category.

Exhibit 7.2

CUSTOMER AGE ANALYSIS	Period end 12/77					Page No.			
Customer code and name	Dec	Nov	Oct	Sep	Aug	Jul and prior	D/N	Cash	Total
1120820 Terms net 30 days, ABC Co. Ltd, credit limit £5,000, risk category B, Midlands area:									
Product A	1,000	2,000	500					310	3,190
Product B	400	800	–				163		1,363
Product C	100	530	–						630
TOTAL	1,500	3,330	500				163	310	5,183

Exhibit 7.3

MAJOR ACCOUNT COLLECTION SCHEDULE	Period end 12/77					Page No.	
Customer code and name	Dec	Nov	Oct	Sep and prior	Cash	Total	
1120820 Terms net 30 days, ABC Co. Ltd, Credit limit £5,000, risk category B							*Telephoned –* *Promised –*
TOTAL	1,500	3,330	500		310	5,020	

Exhibit 7.4

ACCOUNT HISTORY	Period end 12/77								
Customer code and name	Period end	Current	1-30	31-60	61-90	90+	D/N	Cash	Total	Sales to date
1120820 Terms net 30 days, ABC Co. Ltd, credit limit £5,000, risk category B, Midlands area	01-77									
	02-77									
	03-77									
	04-77									
	05-77									
	06-77									
	07-77	1,412	2,063	1,841					5,316	
	08-77	925	1,412	2,063					4,400	
	09-77	1,750	925	1,412			163		4,250	
	10-77	500	1,750	925			163		3,338	16,920
	11-77	3,330	500	1,750			163		5,743	20,250
	12-77	1,500	3,330	500			163	310	5,183	21,750

Major account collection (MAC) schedule

In a company with many thousands of accounts, even the aged analysis can become a bulky document which because of its size is not good enough to give the credit manager immediate access to those customers needing priority attention. A further refinement is to have a Major Account Collection (MAC) schedule such as that illustrated in Exhibit 7.3. The MAC schedule only includes customers owing above a certain predetermined figure, chosen to fit the cash collection procedures. Broken down alphabetically, it forms an immediate working collection document for credit clerks. Space is available for cash targets and cash received. Debit notes are excluded altogether.

Payment history

We have already noted the need for access to ledger history, so that trends in payment performance and sales volume can be detected. No visit should be made to a customer — whether the purpose is to collect money or discuss terms — without a prior look at the account history. In an open-item system this information has to be made available on a separate tabulation, as in Exhibit 7.4.

The account history is built up line by line, a month at a time. If desired it can be done on a selective basis, e.g. only category B and C customers, or only customers whose total balance has exceeded a certain minimum. A drawback to this type of payment history is that payments received at the end of a month have the same effect as those arriving at the beginning, and any deterioration in payment behaviour is only identified when the payment is delayed into the next month.

Exhibit 7.5 shows a different type of account history, in which the number of days credit taken is recorded. Payment terms have to be net monthly for this analysis to be of value, since the credit period is measured from the end of the month of invoicing. Sales volume can also be incorporated.

Reminder letters

In the next chapter, reminder letters will be examined in detail. If there are enough small accounts to necessitate reminders, the computer can be programmed to produce them on the required dates during the month based on the age and size of the debt, with further selection possible through the use of risk categories.

The merits of computer reminders are speed and economy. While

Exhibit 7.5

ACCOUNT HISTORY	Period end 12/77											
Customer code and name	Jan	Feb	Mar	Apr	May	Jun	Jul	Aug	Sep	Oct	Nov	Dec
1120820 Terms net 30 days, ABC Co. Ltd, credit limit £5,000, risk category B, Midlands area:												
Sales							1,412	925	1,750	500	3,300	1,500
Credit taken							71	62	65			

the standard of computer printing has improved over the years, computer letters are usually identified as such and given the familiar treatment — into the waste-bin. If the purpose of sending a reminder, however, is primarily to start a collection cycle which only finishes when the customer has paid or is sued, computer reminders are worth using.

If it is decided to use pre-printed letters, typing in the variable details, or to type complete letters, the computer can still give assistance. A programme can be set to identify all customers due to receive a first or second reminder, but instead of printing complete letters, a list of names and addresses is produced. Thus all the tedious and lengthy work of finding the relevant accounts is eliminated.

The key to success in all these operations is to write the programme so that the number of letters produced but not sent is reduced to a minimum. Some points to include in the programme are as follows:

a   Do not add in the value of debit notes to the overdue total.
b   Do not print a first reminder if a second reminder was sent last month for an account which is still unpaid.
c   Do not print letters for overdue accounts if unreconciled cash or credit notes have been entered on the account after the date of overdues.

Order-entry

A computer order-entry program was described in Chapter 6. The advantage and indeed the *raison d'être* of such systems is to allow management by exception. Time is precious and, whenever possible routine checking should be delegated to a machine, leaving the credit manager free to concentrate on the problems which demand judgement.

Real-time systems

A big step forward in recent years has been the development of direct access to computer records through terminals, eliminating the need for written instructions followed by punching. This is often referred to as a VDU (visual display unit) system. While the use of real-time systems is not yet widespread, it is of interest to note the main points and advantages. These can be grouped under three headings:

1   Up-dating of master file   This involves the facility to add or change information held on the name and address file (see above). The new data would be fed in through a typewriter terminal with a display screen showing the amended record.

2 Entry and reconciliation of cash This can be achieved in either one or two stages. If two stages are needed, the first action is to credit the account with the value received. This might be done by the cashier's department, but payments which have to be split between two or more accounts and payments which require intimate knowledge of the ledger before being correctly identified can cause problems. It is probably better to leave the job to the credit department. The second stage involves reconciling the new credit entry with the appropriate debits (and credits). Where large and detailed remittances are involved — especially if debit notes and under- and over-payments have to be put on the account — a certain amount of preparatory paperwork will be necessary before the allocation can proceed. Entry to the account can either be through a keyboard alongside the display or directly onto the screen by using a cursor.

3 Interrogation Unlike up-dating and cash reconciliation, interrogation can be available to a much wider range of users. Sales offices can interrogate the master-file to check a name and address with an account number. Shipping offices can check despatch addresses. The credit manager can telephone a customer and have his account on the screen whilst talking. Controls are necessary to avoid the possibility of the sales manager making his own credit decisions through being able to call up a customer's account on his display terminal. A print facility should be available so that hard copies can be obtained immediately.

The information actually displayed for an account should be a replica of the ledger plus details of credit limit, risk category and, if possible, details of the last payment received and recent payment history.

It is easy to enthuse over computer systems and to aim constantly for improvements and extensions. What has to be borne in mind is whether the cost of enhancements is justified by the benefits. Generally speaking, benefits resulting from computerised credit/ledger systems come under two headings:

a Efficiency and overall credit performance.
b Staff savings.

The first of these is always difficult to prove, particularly when a basic computer system is already operating and the improvements sought after — such as VDUs — involve expensive equipment. A far more convincing case is to indicate a reduction in headcount. In a large department this should certainly be possible where the introduction of real-time systems eliminates a great deal of manual data preparation.

Debit notes

Most manufacturing companies have debit note problems, and these are usually given low priority amongst the routines and procedures of the sales ledger/credit department.

The inevitable consequence of neglect is a gradual build-up of debit notes on the ledger which have to be excluded from cash collections and which are actually a fictitious asset. The credit manager must not ignore the problem but establish controls.

A debit note is defined as a claim for credit made by a customer on a supplier, arising for one of three principal reasons:

1   Goods or services not received (either wholly or in part).
2   Goods or services believed to be incorrectly priced or invoiced.
3   Goods returned.

Clearance of debit notes, either by the issue of credit or proof of customer liability, depends upon action by other departments — production, engineering, quality control, sales, despatch, invoicing — none of whom are ever particularly interested in spending time on these queries. More often than not, the onus will be on the credit manager to activate people outside his control. Controls come under two headings: records and investigation.

Records

Proper records of all debit notes must be kept, preferably within the credit department, in whatever sequence is the most useful — by customer or by product group are common. Customers should be asked to send their debit notes to the person in charge of these files and internal instructions given to ensure that all debit notes are forwarded to the credit department. If the value of debit notes warrants it, it may be necessary to have a separate section within the credit department doing nothing but debit note control.

For large accounts which have a constant high volume of debit notes, it is worthwhile keeping a record card with space to show the history and status of each item. Exhibit 7.6 gives an example of this.

An alternative for a computerised ledger is to have a monthly tabulation of debit notes on each account. Since notes about follow-up and clearance constantly have to be added, a card system may still be preferred.

Investigation

A copy of every incoming debit note should be sent to the appropriate

93

Exhibit 7.6

DEBIT NOTE RECORD												
Date	Debit note no.	Product code	Value	Covered by provision	Copy sent to	Date	Liability accepted Credit note issued			Liability denied		Customer pays	Remarks
							No.	Date	Value	Letter to customer	Customer accepts		

person/department with a request for clearance. This must be followed up regularly. If the complaint is not accepted, a letter of explanation must be written to the customer with a copy to the credit department. Similarly, the issue of part credit should also be covered by a letter.

A common evasion of controls which should be resisted strongly is the practice of free-of-charge replacements. This may seem a quick and inexpensive way of clearing debit notes, but all too often the action needed to cancel the debit note through the customer's purchase ledger is not taken. The apparently unnecessary costs of crediting and re-invoicing are invariably outweighed by the fact that the accounts of both parties are straight.

If, despite these controls, the problem continues to grow, the credit manager should highlight it in his reports to management. Different aspects which can be featured include:

a   The effect on cash-flow. Calculate how many days' sales are accounted for by debit notes.

b   The impact on profits resulting from the need to carry provisions against debit notes.

c   The detrimental effect of uncleared debit notes on customer relations.

One final point on debit notes. Customers who do *not* raise them will cost the company far more than those who do, since it is better to be paid 100 per cent less 5 per cent debit notes than for the whole 100 per cent to be withheld for the sake of 5 per cent credit.

Filing

A well run filing system, while never in the limelight, is nonetheless essential for an efficient credit operation. It is only when filing gets out of hand that its importance is recognised.

Certain documents by their nature can only be filed one way, i.e. correspondence and status files (alphabetically) and invoices (numerically). Other papers, such as remittance advices, need a little thought. Many companies keep all the remittance advices for one month together in date sequence. This may be satisfactory, until something is taken out. A much better system is to file the advices by customer. Big customers will have individual files and others will merely run alphabetically.

A major problem with computer tabulations is space. Microfilm is the answer, providing money is available, but the credit manager must decide which tabulations need to be kept and for how long — apart from the sales ledger print-out which has to be kept for six years.

Chapter 8

Collecting the cash

Effective collections do not just happen. They are the result of planning.

Organisation

The traditional method of follow-up is to start at 'A' and plod through hoping to reach 'Z' before the month has finished. Even where the number of accounts is small or there are sufficient people to ensure 100 per cent coverage, this is a very inefficient system.

Most companies will find that the pattern of their sales ledger follows to a greater or less degree the Pareto principle. This means that 20 per cent of customers account for 80 per cent of sales. Frequently the proportion of high-volume accounts is even smaller. Exhibit 8.1 illustrates this. Given the spread of debt in Exhibit 8.1, it is immediately apparent that priority attention to the 300 largest customers will be more rewarding than an A-Z routine.

This fundamental step of determining how the debt is spread should be the first action of the credit manager in organising collection operations. The advantage of a computer system over a manual ledger is evident in this situation, as a simple program can identify or tabulate the large balances. Depending on the size of the ledger, the number of staff and the degree of sophistication required, other priorities in the collection routine can also be set. Examples of these are as follows:

1 All accounts with items aged over 90 days overdue.
2 All accounts in risk category C exceeding £500.
3 All accounts in risk categories B and C which have exceeded their credit limit.

These suggested priorities lead to another basic principle. To collect regularly current or near-current debts, ignoring long overdue items, is a short-sighted policy that will ultimately bring disaster. Study of the monthly age analysis will reveal areas where debts are stagnating. When these are found they must be brought into the open and reported on until cleared. Most age analyses have an end column on the right-hand side representing the oldest age bracket — perhaps over 90 or 120 days overdue. Neglected overdues fall into this column. A sure sign of bad credit control is a steady increase in this figure — which may go hand-in-hand with collections regularly on target because they are based solely on current sales.

There should be two objectives of a collection programme:

1 To collect sufficient cash to meet the target for the period.
2 To reduce overdues to a minimum, with particular reference to high-risk accounts.

The type of collection procedure will be dictated to a certain extent by the resources, i.e. staff available, but it is normal and good practice for the credit manager and any supervisors or section heads to assume personal responsibility for as many 'special' or problem accounts as can be managed, leaving the others to be followed-up by the credit clerks — subject to whatever priorities are laid down.

There are three methods of follow-up, the techniques of which will

Exhibit 8.1   The Pareto principle in the sales ledger

Group	Number of accounts	Range of balances	Total value, £	Percentage of total number	Percentage of total value
A	1,000	Under £100	50,000	33.3	} 10
B	1,700	£100–£500	425,000	56.7	
C	190	£500–£5,000	860,000	} 10	} 90
D	100	£5,000–£50,000	2,295,000		
E	10	Over £50,000	1,120,000		
TOTAL	3,000		£4,750,000		

be examined in detail later in this chapter. These are:

a Visit.
b Telephone.
c Letter.

Even in the smallest company, the manager responsible for credit (whatever his job-title may be) should find time for an occasional visit to large customers. When the proprietor of a company does his own credit control, personal contact with his major buyers is a basic part of his routine, and this should not be neglected as the firm grows in size.

Big companies often employ credit representatives who spend most of their time visiting customers. But the bulk of follow-up has to be done by telephone or by letter, and the credit manager must decide how much customer chasing can be done by telephone.

A good credit clerk not involved in ledger work will do well to average 20 telephone calls per day. On the basis of 20 working days per month and an average of 2 calls per customer, this indicates a coverage of 200 customers. In practice, because of other demands on his time, the absence of the required contact, etc., this figure should be dropped to 150 maximum. Looking back to the example in Exhibit 8.1, telephone follow-up on the 300 accounts constituting 90 per cent of the debt should be possible with two credit clerks, given that some of the biggest or most difficult accounts will be under the personal control of the credit manager. Thus the lower limit for telephone follow-up might be fixed at £500. By definition all accounts below £500 balance will require follow-up by letter. If, on the other hand, there are only two credit clerks in the department, the manager must lower his sights and put one clerk on telephoning customers owing over £5,000. An alternative is to let both clerks do both telephone and letter follow-up — although more supervision will be required to keep the two activities in the proper balance.

Targets

There is always a big difference between the results of someone 'doing his best' and someone striving to achieve a target. In the credit department every person engaged in collection work needs a personal target, not only to be measured against but more importantly as a self-discipline. Individual targets may be grouped together to give sectional targets which in turn will comprise the departmental target. Fixing the cash target should be a regular monthly routine, and it should be derived from the target or budget level of receivables at which the credit manager is aiming. Thus a receivables budget set in the autumn of Year 1 will set the required debtor level in terms of days', weeks' or months' sales outstanding for the whole of Year 2. This may be a constant objective — 70 days' sales for instance — or a different target may be established for each month-end. This will be looked at again in Chapter 19.

To express a target in cash terms, the following procedure is recommended. At the end of December, a cash target has to be issued which will produce a debtor level of 70 days at the end of January. Total debtors are £5,000,000, December sales £2,400,000 and November sales £2,000,000. The cash target is calculated as shown in Exhibit 8.2.

Exhibit 8.2

Stage I

Target	70 days
LESS number of calendar days in January	(31)
LESS number of calendar days in December	(31)
Balance	8 days

= 27% of November calendar days

Stage II

	£
Cash required is therefore the total debtors at the end of December	5,000,000
LESS (a) All December sales	2,400,000
(b) 27% of November sales	540,000

Therefore the amount required is £2,060,000

As soon as the total cash target is fixed it must be broken down as far as possible. Ideally, as already stated, every individual should have a target. When this smallest unit is reached, the individual or section should consider what has to be done to achieve the target. This will involve some form of listing of major accounts, an example of which is illustrated in Exhibit 8.3.

The use of targets and collection schedules can be further extended to include graphs and charts, so that each section or individual can watch his progress through the month, as actual cash received is plotted alongside the 'cash required' line. While these have great visual impact and can promote a degree of competition, the credit manager should be wary. Some of the time spent in preparing and up-dating such displays might be better used in actually collecting cash, and a row of out-of-date or uncompleted charts is always a dismal sight.

Considerable care is required in the fixing of sectional targets. For example, the export section will almost certainly be running at a higher

Exhibit 8.3 Cash planning form

CASH PLANNING GUIDE – January 1978

Major customers	Credit category and limit		Total now overdue	Total that will be overdue	Promised	Received
AAA & Co. Ltd	A	£10,000	5,491	1,703		
ABC Ltd	B	£10,000	6,339	4,512		
BB & Sons Ltd	A	£50,000	7,906	15,904		
–		–	–	–		
–		–	–	–		
–		–	–	–		
Total major customers			673,913	528,911		
Total unlisted customers			76,895	71,993		
GRAND TOTAL			750,808	600,904		

Target for this month £ _____

debtor level than domestic sections. A section of Ministry accounts, where payment depends on accurate and timely documentation, might be expected to operate at a lower debtor level than a section of local government accounts.

When the month is over and the results against targets are known, not much time should be spent on 'post-mortems'. The actual cash shortfall, if any, will automatically be carried forward into the next month's target and the collectors will know which customers have let them down or are proving difficult to move. In practice, there is often a week or so at the beginning of the month before the new target is fixed. During this early period every effort should be made to collect the late arrivals. This underlines another common sense point which is often forgotten — the collection cycle is continuous and does not start with a blank sheet each month.

Preparation

Collection begins with the invoice, followed by the statement. The importance of both invoices and statements being rendered promptly and clearly has been looked at in Chapter 7. The credit manager should pay special attention to invoices. Is the order number quoted? Most companies have an absolute rule that no invoice can be approved unless it has a valid order number. It would prevent a lot of frustration and wasted effort if the supplier had an equally rigid policy about the despatch of goods and the raising of invoices. Another vital aspect is the name and address on the invoice. Large organisations often have complex procedures for the routing of invoices, often dependent upon which order-number prefix is shown. If these requirements are ignored, there will inevitably be delays before the invoice is passed for payment. A further complication that arises sometimes is that the customer may need to match the invoice with his own goods received note in order to move the invoice into the 'authorisied' file. If the credit department does not normally see customer orders, the sales office will be relied upon to interpret the buyer's instructions for invoicing. In dealing with large customers likely to have special requirements, the credit manager should ensure there is good liaison with the sales office.

A further 'pre-follow-up' point concerns proof of delivery. If goods are delivered by road or rail, there will be a signed delivery note which should find its way back to the transport manager. This person may be first class at organising transport and arranging despatch documents, but he may not be aware of the potential trouble if a careful check is not made that every delivery note is returned, signed and dated, with the receiving company's stamp also shown and, finally, filed in

101

Exhibit 8.4

CUSTOMER RECORD CARD SALES LEDGER	Name and address:	Code No.

Telephone no.

Contacts:

Date	Type	Item number	Value	Remarks	Query passed to	Date

sequence. It is up to the credit manager to prevent problems of this kind. Similarly when customers return goods, the goods receiving procedure should be in good order. If possible, the credit department should be automatically told about goods returned so that the relevant invoice can be tagged and the follow-up routine adjusted. This principle also applies to queries of any kind which are received by the sales office. Education on the need to keep the credit department informed will pay dividends. The lack of good communications will undoubtedly result in customer good-will being lost. Proper record must be kept of all customer follow-up. Despite the use of computer print-outs, there is no substitute for some form of record card. An example is shown in Exhibit 8.4. The card should include certain basic information, such as:

a   Account number.
b   Name and address.
c   Telephone number.
d   Telex number.
e   Names and positions of contacts.

Apart from these details — which are *not* unchanging so should be written in pencil — there has to be adequate space to make brief notes on all follow-up activity. These will include:

1   Amount in question.
2   Date of action.
3   Type of action, i.e. visit, letter, phone.
4   Name of contact if visit or phone call.
5   Result, i.e. 'payment promised in 3 days' or 'see visit report'.

A card is needed for every account — big enough to last at least 12 months. Large customers may warrant a correspondence file of their own and the same principle applies — every call must be recorded. Not only is this a record to check back on before the next follow-up, it also provides a continuous record of relations with each customer.

The final point before we examine the actual collection techniques is the approach to the customer. It is a regrettable fact that in many UK industries it is common practice to ignore payment terms and to take at least an extra month's credit. The golden rule is — do *not* apologise for requesting payment. The customer has ordered and you have supplied goods on certain agreed terms. The contract is not complete until payment is made, and you are entitled to expect payment to be made to terms.

Credit visits

Credit visits for collection purposes (as opposed to assessment) come

under one of two headings:
1   Large companies where the problems are primarily administrative.
2   Companies whose solvency is doubtful or who persistently pay late.

As far as the first category is concerned, there is a growing practice of employing credit representatives whose main function is to visit major customers, not to collect cheques (although this will be done if permitted and convenient), but for two quite different reasons:
1   To establish the best possible personal relationships with key personnel, in order to ensure preferential treatment both in the processing of invoices and the release of payment.
2   To identify queries that will reduce or delay payment and to assist in their clearance.

To be sucessful in these objectives, a credit representative requires many qualities not always found combined. He (or she) must be friendly and sociable and equally at ease whether over a pint with the bought ledger supervisor or entertaining the finance director to a four-star lunch. He requires considerable tact and diplomacy to move between accounts payable and purchasing, helping to lift his company's queries out of the log-jam in the buying office and bringing the cheque to the top of the pile. Apart from these requirements, he needs endless patience and determination, the ability to realise when a fresh approach is needed and to recognise when a particular contact is proving valueless.

Successful credit visits also need proper back-up from the office. Frustration will soon set in if, when the time comes for a return visit, none of the queries brought back last time has been answered.

There are two problems likely to occur with credit representatives. First, because he is constantly dealing with queries and has also to remain on friendly terms with his contacts, he may gradually develop the attitude that his company is always wrong and always be ready to support the customer in his claims for credit and his arguments against having to pay. The second problem is simply that in developing such friendly relationships, the main objective — to be paid — is lost sight of. One partial solution (assuming more than one representative is employed) is to switch them around occasionally. This has the disadvantage that contacts have to be built up again and continuity is lost. The only real solution is for the credit manager to step in before the problems develop and to guide the representative onto the right path.

There is no satisfactory alternative method of controlling large accounts. By 'large' is meant accounts with several hundred open items. Telephone follow-up is not very practicable — apart from chasing a cheque — because of the large number of items that may have to be discussed. Letters are no better, since although these can run to great lengths in detailing outstanding problems, there is no way of ensuring that they are handled within a reasonable period. Long and complicated letters from suppliers tend to remain at the bottom of the pile while the short, easy ones are dealt with. If the company cannot afford a credit representative, then the credit manager must go out himself to do these visits. Indeed it is desirable that he makes visits whether or not representatives are on hand. The credit manager who remains behind his desk every day will rapidly lose touch with both his customers and his staff.

The second kind of customer visit needs a rather different approach. Whilst the basic aim is always the same — how to extract payment quickly and painlessly — the emphasis shifts from a battle with administrative problems to the narrower questions of when will the account be paid and what are the risks of continuing to supply. The decision to visit rather than continue to telephone or write usually depends on the size (or the potential size) of the business. Thus an account of £100 will rarely justify a journey, even though the circumstances, if known, might be as equally deserving as a £10,000 account. Time does not permit many visits in a month, however, and selection has to be on the basis of value to the company, whether the value is seen in terms of a possible bad debt or as profitable sales.

The following procedure is recommended:

1 Make an appointment at the highest level appropriate to the size of the customer. This can range from the proprietor of a small firm through the finance director of a medium-sized concern to the chief accountant of a large company. Very often it is helpful to make the arrangements through your sales manager, in which case the buyer may be the first contact. He can prove a useful ally against his own financial people!

2 Prepare the facts thoroughly before going. A clear summary of the last six months' payments is essential to demonstrate the justice of your case. Details of all orders on hand plus an estimate of future business will be useful. Finally a review should be made of the latest available status information.

3 On arriving at the premises, contrive to see as much as possible of the factory and offices to gain an impression of the level of activity, the amount of stock or finished goods and the general appearance of the firm. If a tour round is offered after talks have finished, always accept and never hesitate to ask questions — even though they may reveal your ignorance!

4 The actual approach when discussions begin will depend on the precise reason for the call. If it is simply to obtain immediate

payment, having already decided that no more business will be accepted, there is little to do beyond being polite but insistent. Give the impression you are prepared to wait all day, but make it clear that the next step will be to instruct solicitors. Never refer to legal action unless you are ready to proceed accordingly and without delay.

If the ability to pay is not in question, it is necessary to find out why the account is outstanding. Reasons generally come under one of three headings:

a Inefficiency.
b Dissatisfaction.
c Deliberate policy.

A brief discussion should reveal which one.

Inefficiency

Causes of inefficiency are legion: 'we are going onto computer', 'we are short of staff', 'we are centralising/decentralising', are common excuses. Sometimes the real reason is not known until persistent probing from a supplier unearths a fault in the system no one had noticed.

It is always worth asking how the invoice-approval procedure works. (This should also be done on the 'administrative visits' described earlier in this chapter.) If there is time, meet the person responsible for handling goods received notes, the clerk who checks the price and order number and the clerk who is finally responsible for moving invoices onto the approved for payment list.

If there really is inefficiency on a big scale, the credit manager has to decide whether to live with it — albeit hoping for some improvement to result from getting himself known to the key people — or to take a tough line and demand that payments be made to terms. Ultimately, a tough line must be taken, but it may be better to accept a transition period and thereby retain goodwill than to insist on immediate action.

Dissatisfaction

There may be a legitimate complaint which has already been voiced but left unresolved. The best answer is to settle the query, which may require a joint visit with the salesman, but if this is impossible the next best thing is to identify and isolate the amount in dispute and to persuade the customer to pay everything else. Thus if a £5,000 invoice is withheld because of a price increase or an alleged shortage, it is reasonable to seek payment less a deduction. Indeed, if the value in query is a very small proportion of the total, it is highly unreasonable of the customer to refuse the whole invoice (or all the month's invoices if a price increase is involved). Nonetheless this is a very common strategem, frequently backed up by an assertion that it is 'company policy' or that 'our system does not allow part payment'. The credit manager's skills of persuasion are at a premium in this situation.

Another fairly common problem is that of 'contra accounts'. If the customer is also supplying goods, it is only natural he will not pay any sooner than he receives payment. The most satisfactory arrangement is either for both parties to exchange cheques at month-end (assuming similar payment terms) or for one side to pay the net difference. This sounds easy, but in practice it often goes wrong because one company or the other receives invoices outside the cost period, or problems of price, delivery, etc., mean that the expected payment or off-set does not work out. Even worse problems develop when the customer is supplying goods not to your company, but to another part of your Group, or when another part of the customer's group is supplying your company. Whether different companies are involved or the buying and selling is between the same two firms, there is no legal right of off-set unless agreed by both parties in writing or evidenced by regular practice. 'Contra' disputes demand a great deal of common sense and goodwill on both sides. Without these ingredients, success can only go to the company in the stronger supply position.

Occasionally a problem only comes to light because of the credit visit. An example known to the author concerned a visit to a slow-paying customer, during which it was discovered that the supplier had been delivering ahead of schedule. The customer was content to store the goods until required, but the accounts department was instructed not to pay until the due date assuming correct delivery. The result of that visit was to improve control in the despatch area of the supplier.

Deliberate policy

There are a minority of companies which set out to take as much credit as they can get away with. Very often such companies neglect their own credit control. This policy is sometimes open and avowed, but at other times it is cloaked by pretexts such as 'all our cheques have to go to head office for counter signature' or 'if you give us a discount we could pay you much quicker'. The credit manager must be able to see through these attempts to hide the fact that his company is being used to provide free working capital. Even when there is no pretence, an attempt may be made to put the credit manager in the wrong — 'all our suppliers give us 90 days' is a common ploy. If this is checked with known suppliers, it usually transpires that 90 days is being taken — but not given.

Absolute refusal to accept such treatment is the correct attitude, but it must sometimes be tempered by the commercial circumstances. The market strength of a customer can result in his being able to dictate terms, especially if orders are scarce and the factory is operating at less than full capacity. The credit manager will only tolerate this after close discussion with sales management, and he should always try to put a time limit on the arrangement. The use of sanctions is examined later in this chapter. The question of customers who *request* extended credit is deferred to Chapter 9.

No visit is complete without a report. The credit manager should insist on a written report within seven days of the visit. The report should clearly state:

a   The names and positions of everyone seen.
b   The purpose of the call.
c   Any relevant background information.
d   Details of any queries discussed.
e   Action to be taken.
f   Recommended follow-up or review date.

Telephone follow-up

The advantage of the telephone over a letter is that of personal contact. A letter can be ignored but a phone call has to be dealt with. The best possible use should therefore be made of this technique. The human voice is capable of immense variation, and the effect produced on the listener depends very much on the tone and the attitude of the caller. The object is to achieve cooperation, to persuade someone to do something he might otherwise defer or not do at all. Too much aggression can easily cause resentment, just as an apologetic half-hearted approach will fail to stimulate any response. The caller must be crisp and business-like, yet ready to pick up a hint of humour or give a sympathetic ear. Women are often very good at telephone work.

There is a good deal of skill in telephone follow-up. Some points to consider are:

1   Preparation   Most calls are aimed solely at obtaining this month's payment, as opposed to the wider scope of a visit. Nonetheless the caller must know something about the customer. If the call is to a bought-ledger clerk or supervisor in a big company, the approach will not be the same if it were to the proprietor of a small company. With the former it is 'the company's money' under discussion, and there is little possibility of personal feelings being involved, as can easily happen when the man at the end of the phone is having to part with his own money! Other necessary preparation includes having the record card on the desk giving details of the last call made and the name and position of the contact, as well as having the up-to-date ledger. If properly kept, the record card will also show the names of other contacts — preferably in ascending order — and some indication of the customer's payment routine.

2 Contact If there is no established contact, it may take more than one call to determine which person to ask for. In some companies the key person is the purchase ledger clerk, without whose cooperation the monthly cheque never exceeds 50 per cent of the required amount. In other firms the bought ledger manager has to be cultivated, to ensure that your cheque is in the first batch for signing and despatch. In any event it is essential to learn the invoice approval and payment release system.

3 Approach Having determined who is the best contact, the object is now to obtain agreement to pay the total amount due. Many companies do not phone until after the account becomes overdue. Unless time does not allow, the first call should be *before* the account is due. In this situation the caller has to be more cautious in his attitude, to avoid giving the impression that debts are being chased before they are due. A useful gambit is — 'Could you please confirm the balance on our account? We are doing our monthly cash-flow forecast, and we want to be sure there are no problems. When will you be sending the cheque?' This kind of approach can be suitably modified if the balance is partly or wholly overdue. The important point is to find out how much is approved. If it is well below the required figure, express surprise and try to check through invoice by invoice. Very often the difference is caused by the customer being 'behind with the ledger', and the caller has to decide whether to accept this or to ask to speak to someone with greater authority. If queries are mentioned, it may be worth trying to settle them over the phone, but more usually this is not feasible. Payment less the amount disputed should then be requested. A common delaying tactic is the request for copy invoices. This is very frustrating, especially when it occurs regularly with the same customers, but copies must always be sent. Send them if possible the same day, marked for the attention of the contact — having first asked him to arrange a special payment as soon as they are authorised.

4 Closing the call Always strive for a firm promise of both date and amount. Only experience will develop judgement whether promises are genuine or just an attempt to fob off. Payments that do not arrive by the date promised — allowing an extra day for postal delays — must be followed up again. Often one is told that 'all the figures are in the computer' and that 'no indication can be given until later in the month'. Find out when the figures will be available and make a point of phoning on that day. Finally, when the payment arrives, if it is less than the amount promised or expected, a return call must be made requesting an immediate further payment to make up the difference. It is not good enough to leave it until next month. The customer must recognise that he is dealing with an efficient supplier who will not be satisfied with less than full settlement.

5   *Danger signals*   There are a number of signs of trouble or potential trouble which telephone collectors should be taught to identify:
a   The customer insists he is buying on extended terms or is entitled to a discount.
b   The customer says he is unable to pay.
c   The customer offers to pay part now and part next month.
d   The customer offers or sends an 'on account' payment.
e   Payment is made later and later each month.
f   Promises are persistently broken.
g   The volume of unsolved queries is having a serious effect on payments.
h   Contra claims are made.
Some of the problems have already been examined, such as queries and contras. The others all indicate an inability or, at best, a determination not to pay within a reasonable period (say within one month of due date at the latest). The credit manager must decide how much responsibility is to be given to the phone collectors in pursuing these customers. Lack of time will certainly mean that some at least of these will have to be passed to the supervisor or manager to deal with, but where possible collectors should be encouraged to follow through. Training of future managers depends a great deal on the experience gained in this way.

Collection letters

Letters are not an efficient means of stimulating payment. Any company whose customers are numbered in thousands rather than hundreds has to use them, however, and they must be used as effectively as possible.
   A reminder letter system should be considered under a number of

headings — purpose, number, content, design and further action.

1 Purpose Letters are sent to provoke a response, preferably payment, but failing that a promise, a plea for time, a prevarication or a reason for non-payment. The 'first reminder' should also set the machinery in motion to ensure that within a reasonable time the account is either paid or credited or under special care of some kind, e.g. legal action or extended credit.

2 Number Having established the purpose as described above, there is little merit in a procedure which involves a long series of letters, each one couched in stronger terms than the last. Two letters should be adequate — a first reminder and a final demand.

3 Frequency and timing Assuming payments are net monthly, the first letter ought to go around the tenth of the first month after due date. This allows for the arrival of payments that just failed to come by month-end and should also give sufficient time for the supplier to have produced his new ledger. It is usual to allow 10-14 days before the second reminder — which should also be the final demand, so that if payment is provoked, there is a reasonable chance it will arrive before the end of the month.

If payment terms are net 30 days, first reminders should really be going out continually through the month depending on invoice dates. This evens out the work-flow but creates other problems. If a customer has one invoice per week, should he be sent four reminders at weekly intervals? A high level of organisation is required to ensure that final letters and first reminders are not sent to the same customer in the same month for different invoices. Whilst a computer programme can be written to cope with these difficulties, the amount of effort required to prevent errors and absurdities is probably not justified by the end result. The majority of companies have a monthly work-cycle — regardless of suppliers' terms — and in most cases the sensible course will be to treat all invoices as falling due at month-end. This does not mean that 30-day terms might as well be monthly account. The benefit of 30-day terms is the additional control given over high-risk accounts, or any accounts running near their credit limit. While no action will normally be taken until after the end of the month following invoicing, customers needing close supervision can be singled out and followed-up as soon as the 30 days have passed.

4 Content Both first and final letters should be brief, polite and to the point. Examples are given in Exhibits 8.5 and 8.6. The first reminder is addressed to the accounts payable manager, since in most

Exhibit 8.5 Specimen first reminder

---

10 June 19..

Attention: <u>*Accounts Payable Manager*</u>

Dear Sirs,

    We have not received payment for your April account value £75.63 which was due at the end of May.
    Your prompt attention to this will be appreciated.

                    Yours faithfully,

Exhibit 8.6 Specimen final letter

Attention: <u>*The Chief Accountant*</u>

Dear Sirs,

<u>*FINAL NOTICE — £75.63*</u>

    We cannot trace any response to our previous reminders about this account.
    We are not aware of any reason why it should not be paid and we must now ask you to arrange full settlement within seven days.
    Failure to pay will result in the account being placed in other hands for collection without further reference to you.

                    Yours faithfully,

Exhibit 8.7 Specimen part-payment reminder

Attention: <u>*Accounts Payable Manager*</u>

Dear Sirs,

    Thank you for your payment of £34.27.
    This clears part of the overdue account referred to in our recent letter, leaving a balance of £41.36.
    Your attention to this will be appreciated and we look forward to receiving a further cheque from you.

                    Yours faithfully,

---

companies he will be the person who decides what response (if any) to make. By contrast the second reminder is addressed to the chief accountant or company secretary, drawing his attention to the prospect of some drastic action. The words 'placed in other hands for collection' are most suitable when both collection agencies and solicitors are used. If only solicitors are used, the wording is better changed to 'put in the hands of our solicitors'.

There is no point in including such phrases as: 'please let us know if you have a query'. If there are problems, the customer will state them without being prompted. Some letters include a disclaimer about payments sent in the last few days. This is a reasonable safeguard worth having if only because of the uncertainty of the postal service.

5 *Design*   There are two opposing schools of thought on the design of reminder letters. The one argues that they should look like individually produced letters because this increases their chances of being answered. The logical extreme of this viewpoint is to have all letters individually typed. The other theory is that since 99 per cent of all reminders go straight into the waste-paper basket, there is no point in spending time and money on them. The object is to produce them quickly and start the conveyor-belt moving. The right answer will depend on several factors:

a   How many typing staff are employed (or could *less* be employed)?
b   What is the average volume of reminders?
c   Can a computer be used either to print the letters or to print a name and address list?

In a situation where several thousand reminders are sent each month, the emphasis must be on speed. If the computer is updating the ledger daily with cash, it should be used to print letters — either in full or merely adding the name and address and account details to a pre-printed form. Since the number of final letters is generally only a small proportion of the first reminders, if possible these should be individually types and mailed for the personal attention of the chief accountant or company secretary.

6 *Further action*   It is a cardinal principle that action threatened must always be carried out. If seven days is the time limit then on day 8 the 'further action' must be taken, whether it be to instruct solicitors, put the account out for collection, stop supplies or just a phone call in a final attempt to avert a crisis. Legal action and the use of collection agents are dealt with in the next chapter. Stopping supplies is examined later in this chapter.

Payments that only clear part of the overdue account must be followed up immediately and brought back into the collection cycle on a revised time-scale. Exhibit 8.7 shows a letter of the type required.

113

Other collection aids

Under this heading there are three different methods which may be used alone or in conjunction with letters or telephone follow-up:

1 Statement stickers These are brightly coloured, eye-catching gummed labels carrying all manner of messages intended to incite payment. They are usually stuck on the monthly statement and try to give the basic message a humorous or snappy approach. Opinions vary on their effectiveness, but they are cheap enough to run a few month's trial. To make a proper test, all accounts should be sent the usual reminder letter, some with and some without stickers on the statement sent prior to the first reminder.

2 Telex A telex message addressed personally to the right person can be very effective, partly because it is a rather unusual method of follow-up and partly because it always carries a sense of urgency. Because of this, it is best reserved for special occasions and not used regularly. Customers are also likely to be annoyed if telexes demanding money are constantly arriving, since their message is open for all to see.

3 Salesmen Some companies make cash collection an integral part of the salesman's job. Others take pains not to involve the sales force. The main argument in favour is the salesman's personal contact with customers, especially with buyers who are often very influential in the payment of suppliers. Against this has to be set the fact that the salesman's primary responsibility is to sell and that he should not be expected to risk damaging his relationships by asking for money.

While both these arguments are strong, the most satisfactory arrangement is for the credit manager to have sufficient resources within his department to do the job. If he knows that he can enlist the aid of a salesman or sales manager when necessary, so much the better. Credit and sales departments should give each other their itineraries for each month so that the best use can be made of customer visits.

Stopping supplies

It is sometimes said that if the credit manager has to stop supplies in order to obtain payment he has failed. This is incorrect. The primary duty of the credit manager is to protect the company's investment, which may occasionally necessitate suspending delivery to minimise a possible bad debt and more frequently to extract payment from a recalcitrant customer.

Earlier in this chapter the reasons for non-payment were discussed under four basic headings:

1 Inability.
2 Inefficiency.
3 Dissatisfaction.
4 Deliberate policy.

If the customer is unable to pay, stopping further supplies is an obvious step to avoid increasing the problem. There are occasions when a customer pleads for a continuation of deliveries on the grounds that the product is essential to the life of the company. Whether this is true or not, the credit manager must be sure not to increase the size of the risk — unless he is convinced that with his company's support the debtor company will survive. This is always very difficult to assess and will be examined in more detail in Chapter 9.

Where inefficiency is delaying payment, stopping supplies should be a last resort, invoked only when it is apparent that no real effort is being made to put matters right.

Non-payment because of dissatisfaction should never result in a stoppage, unless the customer is being totally unreasonable, e.g. withholding £1,000 when only £5 is in dispute.

Customers who do not pay as deliberate policy should be cut off as soon as the condition is recognised. There is often great reluctance by small firms to withhold delivery to large companies because they fear the possibility of losing business. In practice this is unlikely to happen since the small supplier is usually chosen for his ability to supply a particular — often specialist — item which is not readily available from another source. Problems do arise with the supply of a standard off-the-shelf product for which there are always a number of alternative sources. In these situations a delicate balance must be held between losing too much profit on overdue accounts and risking the loss of business through too strict credit control. The advantages of credit interchange are at their greatest at such times. The names of habitual bad-payers who move from one supplier to another become well known. Sensible policies by members of the interchange group can curtail these activities to the benefit of all.

When a decision is made to stop delivery, the first step should be to check whether there are any outstanding orders on hand. If there are, the buyer should be told at once, quoting his order number and other particulars. If there are no orders outstanding, no action should be taken until the next order arrives. To advise a customer that supplies are stopped when no supplies are wanted is an invitation not to pay until the next delivery is required. All communication about stopped orders should be with the buyer. He probably does not know the account is overdue and can be very influential in obtaining payment.

It is not possible to say exactly when supplies should be stopped. Clearly it should be not too quickly after due date, and equally clearly it should not be so late as to give the company a reputation for lax and feeble credit control. For most companies the right moment will be somewhere between the middle of the first and second overdue months. Exceptions to this should be 'high-risk' accounts (Category C on the system recommended in Chapter 6), which demand very tight control because of the credit risk or because of their persistent bad payment record — or both.

Records need to be kept of the dates customers are put on and taken off the stoplist or blacklist. Any customers who have to be stopped so frequently that they are more often on than off the blacklist should be considered for pro-forma terms.

Close liaison with sales is vital in the operation of a blacklist. Prior notice of stop action should be given, either by a list of names or through the sending of a copy of the first or final reminder (depending at what point supplies are to be stopped). If large customers are involved, a briefing with the sales manager is desirable. A phone call to the buyer may be sufficient to avert a crisis.

Overdue accounts

Whilst the above review of collection methods may be said to cover the problem of overdue accounts, it is worth stepping back for a moment to distinguish the wood from the trees.

In Chapter 1 the declining value of overdues was examined in the context of the cost of credit. Sooner or later most companies wake up to an 'overdue problem'. How should this be tackled?

Planning is necessary, if the operation is not to degenerate into an uncoordinated series of panic measures.

Stage I   Identify the problem, both in terms of value, number and age.

Stage II Break it down into controllable units, defining each individual's responsibility.

Stage III Set targets for each person. These should be achievable — just. It may be worthwhile to introduce incentives such as cash bonuses or holidays, but these cannot be maintained forever, and the possibility of a slump in later results must be weighed against the prospects of high achievement early on.

116

Stage IV	Action plan. Draw up guidelines on the use of different techniques — visits, phone calls, reminders.
Stage V	Monitor results. On a monthly basis, giving more points for a reduction in, say, over-90-day overdues than for more current items. Accounts which cannot be collected because of sales or service queries must be highlighted and brought to the notice of the appropriate managers every month until action is taken.

Chapter 9

Debtors in distress, collection agencies, legal action, insolvency and factoring

Debtors in distress

Customers who ask for extended credit as opposed to those who take it deserve more sympathetic consideration. Decisions must be based on the merits of each case, subject to the observance of three cardinal principles:
1   How is the credit risk affected?
2   Will the customer pay the cost of extra credit?
3   What is the impact on cash-flow?

The most important of these criteria is the effect on credit risk. The credit manager relies here on his judgement, having first made sure he has all the available facts. A customer on 30-day terms with a good record of payment, who is well regarded by sales, requests an additional 30 or 60 days' credit for a temporary period of, say, six months. Typical of the reasons advanced for such requests are:

'Rather than reduce production and cut our labour force, we have decided to make for stock in anticipation of an upturn in the market later this year. To help finance this we are asking our major suppliers to give us extended credit for the period. . . .'

'A major export contract has fallen through, giving us a temporary cash-flow problem.'

'We are going to raise additional capital shortly and ask you to bear with us in the meantime.'

'We are reorganising our company/group of companies/capital structure and hope you can. . . .'

'If you want to keep our business you must give longer terms as our other suppliers do.'

All such approaches should be examined carefully and sceptically. A number of questions have to be asked, either directly of the customer or during the analysis.

1   Why are suppliers being asked to help, rather than the bank and/or the parent company?
2   From the latest available accounts, does the company seem to be basically sound and profitable? (Ask for last month's accounts.)
3   What are other companies doing in the same industry? Is this a common problem?
4   What is the attitude of other major suppliers? (Phone them and find out.)
5   How much will the credit limit need to be increased by to accommodate the extra time?

If the risk category system described in Chapter 6 is operating, a customer in Category A or B stands a reasonable chance of a favourable reply — given that the reasons and motive are accepted — whereas a Category C risk by definition will be very hard to approve.

Payment of the cost of extended credit is usually offered by the buyer. If not, it should be requested so that any illusions of free finance are immediately quashed. If business is to be retained (or even increased), the profit level must not be eroded by extra credit costs.

The final point to consider is the effect on cash-flow. If a major customer is involved, there will be a noticeable short-fall during the period before payments are resumed. Can the company stand this? Will it mean a slowing of payments to suppliers? Will discounts be lost?

Behind every request for extended credit there are two possibilities which cause the credit manager sleepless nights. If help is refused and the buyer nonetheless survives (thanks to other suppliers' assistance), will there be an adverse effect? Will the company lose future sales? Clearly consultation with the sales department is important, but fear of a possible sales loss must *never* be allowed to upset a credit risk decision where the facts indicate an unacceptable risk. The other nagging doubt is whether refusal of help may precipitate insolvency. The only answer to this is that if insolvency is that near, the risk is almost certainly too great, and the duty of the credit manager is to minimise the bad debt loss, not increase it.

If the decision is to give assistance, the arrangement should be put in writing. There must be a clear finishing date. It is worth insisting on payment by Bill of Exchange because:

a   Bills can be drawn for the face value of the supplier's statement, thus avoiding the usual shortfall problem.

b   An accepted Bill can be discounted if required.

c   An accepted Bill at the bank is better than waiting for a cheque on the due date.

d   The agreed interest charge can be included in the Bill.

Collection agencies

The intervention of a third party between supplier and customer is generally recognised to be undesirable but effective.

There are two alternative forms of outside help (disregarding factoring which is examined later in this chapter), and many companies use both a collection agency and a solicitor. Since lack of success by the former is usually followed by legal action initiated by the agency, collection agencies may be regarded as no more than an intermediate stage on the road to the Courts. There are also companies who refuse to employ agencies, preferring to go direct to a solicitor or to the Courts. It is worth examining the arguments for and against collection agencies. Before doing this, some definitions are required.

Types of collection agency

In the UK there are hundreds of firms offering to collect debts, some local or restricted to particular trades and others operating on a national basis. Three principal types can be distinguished:

a   Mercantile agencies or trade associations.

b   Voucher agencies.

c   Commercial agencies.

Mercantile agencies are non-profit-making bodies, charging an annual membership fee and a percentage of monies recovered. Voucher agencies sell books of collection vouchers to client companies who are entitled to complete a voucher for any outstanding debt and send it to the agency. A series of collection letters is then started aimed at having the debt paid direct to the supplier. If this is not successful, some voucher agencies offer to continue collection action for a further fee — usually a percentage of the debt.

The most widely used type of agency is the commercial agency which offers to try and collect a debt on the basis of 'no collection — no charge'. The best of these firms follow up by phone after one letter and may even make personal visits. In practice a client company with a reasonable level of regular business to offer can usually negotiate a special arrangement with an agency, designed to dovetail the firm's own follow-up procedures with the agency system.

The case for collection agencies

1   Time otherwise spent in pursuing relatively small amounts is available for other work — such as phoning large customers. In a credit department with strained resources, it makes sense to use the time available to best effect.
2   A good agency is well equipped to trace absconded debtors and verify registered offices. A credit information service is often available, plus the services of solicitors specialising in debt recovery.
3   The alternatives are more expensive:
    a   Employing sufficient staff to do all collection work — whereas an agency is only paid if it collects.
    b   Passing accounts direct to a solicitor at an early stage may well be as effective but at a considerably higher cost than an agency.

The case against agencies

1   Why pay an agency for doing the job of the credit department? Sufficient staff should be employed to do all collection work, and if they do not have time, they should be better trained and organised.
2   The intervention of a third party is bound to upset customer relations. The agency has no long-term interest in maintaining goodwill.
Every credit manager must decide whether to use an agency. In general, a company with a high volume of small accounts can probably benefit.

Tips on choosing an agency

1   Check that the agency is licensed for debt collection under *The Consumer Credit Act, 1974.*

2   Ensure that the agency is financially sound. Run a credit check as if it were a new customer.
3   Obtain the names of several client companies and speak to their credit managers about the agency's performance.
4   Ensure that the agency uses an audited client trust account with its bank.
5   Check that all directors and senior staff are fully bonded.
6   Check that the agency either employs or works very closely with solicitors experienced in debt recovery.
7   Ensure that all cheques received are either passed straight over on receipt or are covered by a monthly (or more frequent) payment, whichever is preferred.
8   Check that the collection procedure will be tailored to form a proper extension to one's own follow-up system. There is no point in sending a further series of letters which merely repeat requests for payment.
9   Check that a regular report is given on all accounts passed over, to avoid the possibility of 'difficult' debts being overlooked or shelved.
10 Ensure that the interest rate charged is competitive. The higher the volume of accounts, the lower the rate should be. Rates vary a great deal. Anything below 5 per cent is exceptional and if offered by a new agency should be regarded as a special offer to attract custom. Rates over 10 per cent should be resisted, but are nonetheless quite common. Many agencies have scale fees reducing in size as the debt value increases.

A final point is that it pays to experiment with several agencies, monitoring their success rate over a period of several months before deciding which offer the best service. A good agency should show a success rate of 70-80 per cent within a month of receiving instructions.

It is important to decide at what stage an account should be passed to an agency. Too early is equivalent to giving money away, since a good proportion of customers are still paying without the need of more drastic efforts. Too late and the agency is given an impossible task. The 'right time' will vary from company to company, but with the majority it should be between the end of the second and the third overdue month.

Dishonoured cheques and bills

A cheque that is returned by the bank to the supplier — often marked 'refer to drawer' — can be taken as a sure indication that the customer is close to insolvency. Immediate action should be taken, generally a demand for cash (*not* another cheque) within seven days. Under no circumstances should the cheque be returned to the customer. The same applies to a Bill of Exchange not honoured at maturity.

By contrast, a cheque may be dishonoured and returned marked 'please represent'. This means that the customer's bank believes that funds will be available and the cheque may be represented over and over again until it is either met or 'referred to drawer'. It is good practice to advise the customer that his cheque has bounced, that it will be represented on a certain future date (not beyond seven days) and that failure to have it met will result in legal action being taken.

Legal action

A number of points need checking before legal proceedings are started:
1   Is it certain that the debt is not disputed? Check thoroughly with the sales office that there are no unanswered queries on price, delivery, etc.
2   Is the name and trading style of the customer verified? The importance of careful checking when an account is first opened now becomes apparent.
3   Is it reasonably certain that the customer has sufficient assets to pay the debt? This is generally more difficult to establish with a sole trader or partnership than with a limited company, but personal assets are available to creditors in the former cases.

As regards a minimum figure which is worth suing for, this depends upon whether or not an outside solicitor is being used and, if not, on how management time is valued. Below £25, say, the cost benefit becomes steadily more slender. Some companies however are willing to sue for any amount to demonstrate they are not a soft touch, or on principle in order to stop debtors 'getting away with it' and moving on to abuse other firms.

Legal action can be taken in one of four different ways:
a   Through the company's own legal department (restricted by definition to large firms).
b   By the solicitor employed by a collection agency.
c   By the credit manager or senior member of his staff working direct with the County Court.
d   Through a solicitor. This is by far the most common method, and care should be taken in the choice of solicitor. There are firms of solicitors specialising in debt collection, but for the majority of solicitors, debt collection and insolvency work is not regarded as a major activity. While the work may not be refused, it will

Exhibit 9.1 High Court procedure

HIGH COURT WRIT

Completed form (2 copies taken or posted to High Court or any District Registry with fees)

(Costs not recoverable unless debt exceeds £150)

Issue

'Case Number' allocated. Court seals one copy and gives to Plaintiff who must prepare copy to serve on Defendant

Service

By post to registered office of a limited company

By personal service on partner or owner by solicitor, enquiry agent or process server

If not served, solicitor or creditor or enquiry agent will attempt to trace debtor

Within 14 days of service

Defendant pays (incl. costs)

OR

Defendant makes offer

OR

Defendant enters an appearance

OR

Plaintiff obtains judgment from Court

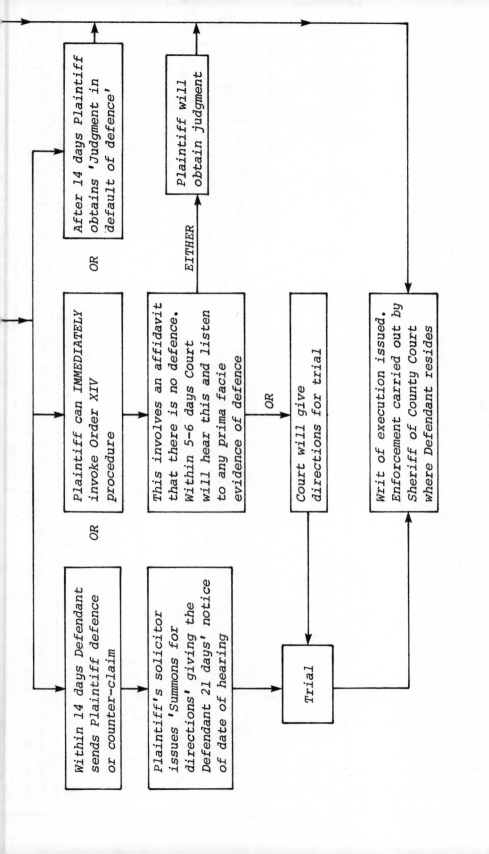

Within 14 days Defendant sends Plaintiff defence or counter-claim

Plaintiff's solicitor issues 'Summons for directions' giving the Defendant 21 days' notice of date of hearing

OR

Plaintiff can *IMMEDIATELY* invoke Order XIV procedure

This involves an affidavit that there is no defence. Within 5–6 days Court will hear this and listen to any prima facie evidence of defence

OR

OR

After 14 days Plaintiff obtains 'Judgment in default of defence'

EITHER

Plaintiff will obtain judgment

Court will give directions for trial

Trial

Writ of execution issued. Enforcement carried out by Sheriff of County Court where Defendant resides

Exhibit 9.2 County Court procedure

Completed praecipe, claim form and fee taken or sent to County Court (normally in Plaintiff's area)

Maximum £2,000

Issue

Plaint number allocated and Summons issued. Plaintiff given Plaint note

Service

By post to registered office of a limited company

By personal delivery to individual, partner or owner by court bailiff, solicitor, enquiry agent or process server

If not served, solicitor or creditor or enquiry agent will attempt to trace debtor

Within 14 days

Defendant pays (including costs)

OR

Defendant asks permission to pay by instalments

Either

Plaintiff agrees and Court enters judgement accordingly

Either

First instalment not paid

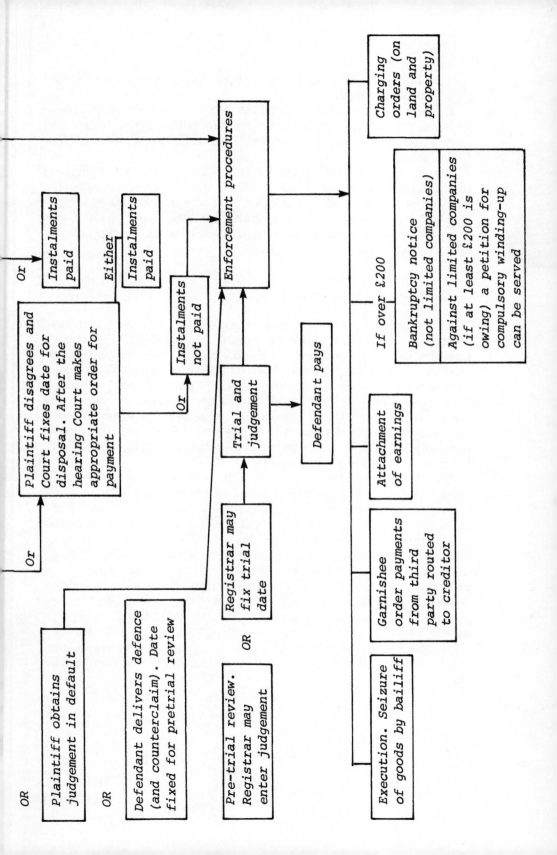

probably not be carried out with the same expertise a specialist firm would apply.

The detailed procedures of legal action are not covered in this book. Exhibits 9.1 and 9.2 illustrate in simple form the various stages and alternative courses which are reached in both County Court and High Court actions.

The choice between County and High Court will be partly dictated by the nature of the debt. A County Court summons may be issued for any amount up to £2,000. A High Court writ may be issued for any amount, but costs are only recoverable for actions over £150. Costs may still be higher than in the County Court but the service is faster and more efficient.

Moratoriums and compositions

In an endeavour to avert legal action, a customer may ask creditors to hold off for a period, to allow a breathing space so that the company's liquidity can improve for the benefit of all. Generally only major creditors will be approached. The alternative to agreeing to such an arrangement — called a moratorium — is to proceed with legal action which may well lead to liquidation. This, in turn, will mean the realisation of assets for less than their 'going concern' value. Where a moratorium proposal appears to be a worthwhile attempt to keep the company afloat and not a strategem to outwit creditors, it is better to accept it than force a winding-up.

A different kind of arrangement with creditors is a composition or deed of arrangement. As with a moratorium, the purpose is to avoid insolvency proceedings, but in a composition all or some of the creditors agree to accept a percentage of their total claim in full settlement. The advantages are that the costs of bankruptcy or liquidation are avoided and the settlement itself should be made fairly quickly. Even if most creditors agree, however, the company is unlikely to be able to resume normal trading because of the understandable reluctance of creditors to risk more money after having given away a portion of their original debt. A deed of arrangement occurs when, as part of the composition, property is assigned to a trustee for division amongst creditors. To be effective, a composition must have the agreement of a majority of creditors both in number and value.

Enforcement procedures

As indicated in Exhibits 9.1 and 9.2 there are a number of ways in which judgement may be enforced, depending on the circumstances. Before any execution costs are incurred, however, the creditor should try to find out whether there are any assets. Obtaining judgement is of no value if the debtor is insolvent.

1   Seizure of goods by the bailiff (County Court) or sheriff's officer (High Court)   This is usually more effective against companies or partnerships where items of value can be found in any office, e.g. typewriters, copying machines and furniture, as compared to a private house in which the wife of the debtor can claim to own all the furniture. In both situations there is the danger that goods are under a hire-purchase agreement. Nonetheless, the threat of seizure often brings results.

2   Attachment of earnings   This is generally unsuccessful, depending in the first instance on the Court deciding how much 'protected earnings' should be and, secondly, on the debtor's employer cooperating fully. Since debtors are not normally in stable employment, the problems of tracing them and enforcing fresh attachment orders are immense. This remedy is only available against individuals in employment.

3   Garnishee order   If the creditor can establish that a third party owes money to the debtor, application can be made for a garnishee order which requires the third party to pay the amount direct to the creditor. The most common method is to garnishee a debtor's bank account.

4   Charging orders   A rarely used method, giving the creditor a charge on land, property or stocks and shares owned by the debtor.

5   Bankruptcy notice (against partnerships or individuals)   The threat of bankruptcy can be very effective, providing the creditor is sure sufficient assets are available and he is confident the debtor will prefer to pay rather than go out of business. However, if the business is near to collapse anyway, there is little advantage in giving the final push since all creditors will be treated equally by the Official Receiver. It is more skilful to find a way of extracting payment without causing bankruptcy. The procedure is as follows:
a   A bankruptcy notice is issued by the Court and served on the debtor *personally*.

129

b   Unless paid or disputed within ten days, an 'act of bankruptcy' has been committed.

c   Providing at least £200 is owed, the creditor (alone, or joined with others) presents a bankruptcy petition (must be within three months of the act of bankruptcy).

d   The Court hears the petition and if satisfied issues a receiving order.

e   The affairs of the debtor then come under the control of the Official Receiver, whose function is to distribute any assets between all creditors in accordance with the following order of precedence:
   (i)   Secured creditors.
   (ii)   Bankruptcy costs.
   (iii) Preferential claims, principally rates, taxes, national insurance and a limited amount of wages and salaries.
   (iv)   Unsecured creditors.
   (v)   Deferred creditors.
   (iv)   The bankrupt.

6 Winding-up petition (against limited companies)   Providing the debt is not below £200, a creditor with an unsatisfied judgement debt may present a winding-up petition to the High Court (or to the County Court if the paid-up capital does not exceed £120,000). The Court hears the petition — and any opposition to it — and decides whether to issue a winding-up order. Several creditors may join in the petition. If a winding-up order is made, the Official Receiver takes charge of all assets as provisional liquidator. His initial duty is to assess the financial condition of the company including the causes of failure and make recommendations about further enquiries. Having prepared a statement to this effect, the Official Receiver then must call a first meeting of creditors. This meeting decides whether to appoint an outside liquidator in place of the Official Receiver and whether to appoint a Committee of Inspection.

The liquidator's task is to realise the assets of the company and distribute them in accordance with the following order of precedence:

1   Secured creditors — *excluding* holders of floating charges.
2   Liquidation costs.
3   Preferential claims (principally rates, taxes, national insurance and a limited amount of wages and salaries).
4   Holders of floating charges.
5   Unsecured creditors.
6   Shareholders.

It is important to note that compulsory winding-up can be initiated in other ways than to enforce a judgement debt.

Under Section 223 of *The Companies Act, 1948*, a creditor owed at least £200 can make a statutory demand for payment — called serving a 21-day notice — since if payment is not paid or disputed within three weeks a winding-up petition can be issued. This method thus by-passes the lengthy procedure of action through the Court, from the issue of a writ to the obtaining of judgement. It is recommended for use against large companies who persistently neglect to pay suppliers. While their ability to pay is rarely in question, often only the threat of a winding-up petition will extract settlement. A winding-up petition must be advertised seven clear days before the Court hearing, both in the *London Gazette* and in a local or London newspaper as appropriate.

The Court is empowered to wind up a company for a number of reasons besides those outlined above. Both of these — enforcement of a judgement debt and the issue of a Section 223 notice — come under the general heading that the company is unable to pay its debts. Other causes include default in delivering the statutory report to the Registrar of Companies or in holding the statutory meeting, failure to commence its business within one year from its incorporation or suspension of business for a whole year, reduction of members below two (private companies) or seven (others), if the Court is of the opinion that winding-up is just and equitable, and, finally, if the company itself passes a special resolution to be compulsorily wound-up.

Other forms of winding-up   A declaration of solvency by a company's directors enables a winding-up to be classed as a Members' voluntary winding-up. The absence of such a declaration produces a Creditors' voluntary winding-up.

A liquidator is appointed by the members in a members' winding-up. In a creditors' winding-up, both creditors and members may nominate a liquidator with the choice of the creditors taking precedence in the event of a disagreement. A committee of inspection to assist the liquidator may be appointed, but it only has statutory powers in a creditors' winding-up. In a members' winding-up, if the liquidator decides that the company is insolvent — despite the declaration of solvency — he must call a meeting of creditors and present them with a statement of affairs.

The detailed proceedings of voluntary liquidations are beyond the scope of this book.

Receiverships   A receiver may be appointed either by the Court (usually to protect property) or by a debenture holder direct (if so empowered). In both cases the appointment is frequently as Receiver and Manager, so he may continue to run the business while fulfilling his primary duty of safeguarding the debenture holder's security.

'Safeguarding' will very often mean realising sufficient assets to produce the value required. In the vast majority of cases, receivership is followed by liquidation since the business is left insolvent.

While running the business, a Receiver and Manager will approach creditors for supplies, often asking for credit on the same terms as the company itself prior to Receivership. Two very important points must be noted in this connection:

1   The Receiver and Manager must specifically accept responsibility for payment of debts so incurred. In recent years there is evidence of a tendency amongst some receivers to limit their liability to a stated amount. Creditors must be wary of this.

2   Orders must not be accepted unless they carry a signature previously advised as authorised by the receiver.

Receivers are usually officers of a firm of auditors or accountants, and they are most frequently appointed by banks whose overriding concern is to get their money out intact.

Trade creditors do not have a voice in the running of a company by a Receiver and Manager, but the Receiver will normally keep creditors informed of the situation. The increasing use of reservation of property clauses in terms of sale in recent years has given a measure of protection to creditors. Providing unpaid goods can be clearly identified, and the existence of a satisfactory retention clause is well documented; a Receiver (and also a liquidator) should allow the goods to be collected or even arrange for payment to be made. In a receivership which leads to liquidation and a final pay-out of a few pence in the pound, creditors who can claim this kind of protection are in an enviable position. What has not yet been resolved is the position of creditors claiming reservation of property on material which has been incorporated or transformed into an end product which is itself the object of a charge or lien by a loan creditor.

Attendance at creditors' meetings is time consuming and therefore costly. Where a substantial debt is involved, however, the credit manager will need to attend, if not personally, then represented by a senior member of his staff and may even wish to join the Committee of Inspection.

Conclusions   A detailed description of insolvency procedures has deliberately been avoided in this book. When this information is needed, an excellent reference book is Sales' *The Law Relating to Bankruptcy, Liquidations and Receiverships.* The sixth edition (January 1977) takes in changes to the law arising from *The Insolvency Act, 1976.*

Factoring

The factoring business has grown steadily in the last ten years or so. At the beginning of 1978 it was estimated by Anthony Thorncroft in an article entitled 'Factoring' (*Financial Times*, 16 January 1978) that turnover had exceeded £800 million, coming from over 1,000 companies. The biggest factoring companies are controlled by the clearing banks, which give both respectability and strength to the industry.

The services of a factor fall under three headings:

1 *Administration of the sales ledger and credit control functions from credit approval to collecting the cash*   The only functions left to the client are the rendering of invoices and the clearance of disputes. The benefits of this include the elimination of credit enquiry and cash collection costs and the use of a sophisticated computerised sales ledger system. The cost of this diminishes as turnover rises and normally ranges between 0.75 and 2.5 per cent of turnover.

2 *Credit insurance*   Most factors cover against bad debts, although there are exceptions. The cost is included in the administration charge.

3 *Finance*   Between 70 and 80 per cent of the value of outstanding debts can be paid ahead of maturity if required. The cost will usually be slightly higher than the client's normal bank borrowing rate. If cash advances are not required, the factor will agree a cash-flow arrangement with the client, usually based on the average credit period experienced. This in itself is very advantageous since cash-flow is predetermined.

Factoring should not be regarded as an alternative to credit management, but as a service that can be of value to companies at a particular stage of development. The majority of clients offer turnover of under £1 million, and most factors prefer to deal with at least £300,000. As a company grows in size, its own accounting systems and staff increase, and a point will be reached where the cost of factoring (based on turnover) outweighs the benefits.

There is no doubt that the professional services provided by a factor in both ledger administration and credit control are of immense value, if only in releasing management time.

Factoring of export turnover can be arranged, either in addition to a domestic service or on its own. This latter course can be attractive to large companies operating their own domestic sales ledger, since they can use the factor's expertise to avoid currency risks, payment difficulties, and language and communication problems.

The success of factoring and its future growth depend on two things

— service and cost. The service offered must be demonstrably first-class — particularly on export business — and a company considering factoring would be well advised to find out which other firms (preferably in the same industry and of a similar size) are already doing it, and to ask in detail about their experience. Presuming the service to be first-class, the cost has to be weighed against the cost of 'in-house' sales ledger/credit administration. Judgements must be made on such questions as:

1 Do we really want credit insurance? Would we have our own policy if we did not use a factor?
2 Would we take advantage of the financial service?
3 How many jobs will be saved at what annual saving?
4 How valuable is it to have a guaranteed regular cash-flow?
5 What would be the cost of employing a credit manager and running a sales ledger operation?
6 Does it matter that a number of decisions on the company's business will be considered and possibly even taken outside the company? The acceptance of new customers, the setting of credit limits and the release of deliveries are all subjects on which the opinion of the factor will be critically important.

Chapter 10

Credit insurance

Domestic credit insurance in the UK receives very little publicity compared to the work of Export Credits Guarantee Department (ECGD), which is examined in Chapter 15. Turnover insured by Trade Indemnity Co. Ltd, which dominates the home market, exceeded £8,150 million in 1977 compared to ECGD's total of over £12,900 million in 1977/78. But while ECGD are insuring over one-third of all UK exports, Trade Indemnity's coverage of domestic sales is under 5 per cent. Comparison with ECGD is perhaps unfair, since the latter offers far more than insolvency cover, but the fact remains that the idea of domestic credit insurance does not find ready acceptance amongst most UK companies. It is generally thought to be expensive, restrictive and unnecessary. Some companies, however, owe their survival to their policies, and many more derive considerable benefit from the protection which, under certain circumstances, cannot be obtained through good credit management alone.

The purpose of credit insurance is to guard against unexpected failures. It is not a substitute for credit management, and it does not provide a licence to sell to any willing buyer. Any company whose sales are unevenly spread among its buyers to such an extent that the failure of one or two major customers would have a serious impact on profits and cash-flow would be well advised to consider the merits of a policy.

The alternatives should also be examined. The final decision will almost certainly be made on a financial basis, influenced by the historical facts of the industry and perhaps also by the economic climate of the day. Thus, since 1970 the building and construction industry has accounted for around 30 per cent of all business failures notified to Trade Indemnity — more than twice as much as that occurring in engineering and metals.

The credit insurance industry

The market consists of underwriters and brokers. The role of the credit insurance broker has been in sharp focus in recent years and a good deal of criticism has been uttered. A broker has two basic functions. Firstly, he obtains business by selling the idea of credit insurance. Second, he liaises between the insurer and the insured, both in the establishment of policy terms and subsequently in the operation of the policy. It is quite possible for the policy holder to work directly with his underwriter. A valuable relationship can develop which brings benefits to both parties, but in practice it is more usual for the broker to act as middleman. This is partly because brokers see this as their job and partly because a close relationship between underwriter and policy holder is only feasible when the latter employs a credit manager of high professional standing.

The broker is paid a commission by the insurer which is part of the premium charged to the policy holder. A good broker's most valuable service occurs at policy renewal, when his knowledge of the insurance business should be used to negotiate the most favourable premium for next year. Depending on the policy holder's degree of professionalism and on the time available, the broker may also handle the day-to-day running of the policy, i.e. the obtaining of limits and the submission of claims. There are only a small number of credit insurance brokers, whose names and addresses are given at the end of this chapter.

The underwriters of domestic credit insurance are employed by two organisations, Trade Indemnity Co. Ltd and Credit and Guarantee Insurance Co. Ltd. The former had paid-up capital of £900,000 and capital and revenue reserves exceeding £5.7 million at the end of 1977. Over 50 per cent of the share capital of Trade Indemnity is held by five major insurance companies, and it is the underlying support of the insurance industry which enables the company to function by means of 'reinsurance' arrangements. The bulk of Trade Indemnity's business is on whole turnover or specific account policies. A small but growing amount of export insurance is undertaken, cover being given against insolvency or protracted default in agreed markets. As for domestic business, export policies may be on whole turnover or specific account. The flexibility with regard to both exclusions and premium rates compares very favourably with ECGD, although, of course, the protection offered by the latter includes political and transfer risk cover. Credit and Guarantee Insurance Co. Ltd, controlled by British, Italian, Dutch and Danish insurance companies with equity of £800,000, specialises in insuring both the pre-delivery and the post-delivery risks on individual contracts.

Pre-shipment risk cover is not usually available from Trade Indemnity. It is more difficult to measure and evaluate, but it can be nearly as critical to a supplier as the post-delivery loss. The insolvency of a buyer just before delivery of a specially made piece of equipment can leave the manufacturer with no alternative customer and the prospect of obtaining only scrap value. Credit and Guarantee also offer a Supplier Default policy, giving protection against consequential loss arising from the insolvency of a supplier.

Trade Indemnity Co. Ltd — establishment and operation of a policy

An explanation of how a policy is agreed and operated is best given by means of a step-by-step examination as follows:

1 Initial review and policy choice Careful assessment is made of the client's credit procedures, and suggestions made where necessary to improve controls. Analysis of sales and receivables reveal the type of risk and generally determine what type of policy is most suitable. Thus a company with 5,000 customers, 1,000 of whom account for 80 per cent of turnover and receivables, may well choose a specific account or 'datum line' policy. With the former, all the insured buyers are identified and approved before the policy begins and new names can be added as needed. On a 'datum line' policy the client decides to insure all buyers whose indebtedness exceeds an agreed figure. This system is growing in popularity at the expense of whole-turnover policies, since many companies are happy not to pay premium on a percentage of their turnover where the individual risks are by definition very small. The whole-turnover alternative will involve the use of a discretionary limit, which is equally if not more demanding on the policy holder's time and money, at a total cost equal to if not higher than that under a datum line arrangement. Trade Indemnity also benefit since they cut down on the volume of small claims. At the other end of the scale, a policy holder may wish to exclude from cover sales to some of his biggest customers on the grounds that the possibility of failure is too remote and why pay premium for nothing? Trade Indemnity will always consider such requests and, on occasions, may be quite happy to exclude certain names because they are already covering a high volume of debt and they are having difficulty in reinsuring or 'laying off the risk'. Very great care and thought needs to be exercised by the policy holder in this situation. Apart from the tragedy of Rolls Royce — which should have deterred credit managers from using the expression 'blue chip' — in recent years the fortunes of British Leyland and Chrysler illustrate the point that no company should be regarded as a perpetual A1 credit risk.

Certain kinds of sale are automatically excluded from cover. These are:

a   Sales to central or local government bodies, nationalised industries, hospitals, schools, etc.
b   Sales to subsidiary or associate companies.
c   Sales on pro-forma terms.
d   Sales to individuals.

These definitions are not always as watertight as they may appear. In the case of companies controlled by the National Enterprise Board, for example, Trade Indemnity may allow clients to choose whether or not to exclude them from cover.

2 Policy terms   Certain terms are standard, such as the definition of insolvency. 'Protracted default' takes place when payment has not been made within 90 days of the due date. The level of indemnity, i.e. the proportion of a sale which is insured, is negotiable but rarely outside the range 75 to 90 per cent. Assuming an indemnity level of 80 per cent and a credit limit of £100,000, if insolvency occurs with £100,000 owing, the policy holder will recover £80,000. If the balance owing is £150,000 he will still only recover £80,000, because the additional £50,000 sales have been made at his own risk and are outside the policy.

3 Premiums   Unlike ECGD there is no 'standard premium'. The rate is negotiable, depending very much on the industry record of business failures, the client's own bad debt experience, the mix of business offered and the effectiveness of the client's credit management. Rates have tended to rise over the years. For a new policy, a rate below 0.2 per cent is unusual and rates over 0.5 per cent are not uncommon.

4 Credit limits   The real test of a policy is whether the policy holder can obtain — over a period — a consistently high proportion (at least 90 per cent) of the limits requested. There will inevitably be refusals, either in the form of a maximum limit below that asked for or a complete rejection. It is here that a close relationship with the underwriter pays dividends. Confidence in the policy holder will result in better limits. The underwriter is able to tap sources of information unavailable to the policy holder, and the more he can learn about his client's business and the performance of the client's customers, the better able he is to make a correct judgement.

In requesting a credit limit, the policy holder (assuming terms are net monthly or 30 days) should calculate a figure representing around three months' sales. This allows for payment to be one month late before the limit is exceeded. To ask for less is imprudent. To ask for more should be unnecessary.

The experience of most policy holders is that Trade Indemnity is reasonably generous on limits. It has to be, since its purpose is not to restrict trade but to encourage it through protection against the unexpected failure. No policy holder should be surprised if a request for £10,000 credit on a company with equity of £100 and net worth of £500 is turned down. On the other hand, if a policy is worth anything it should enable *more* business to be done with the 'middle range' of buyers, because the limits given will be higher than the policy holder would care to risk on his own account.

Most policy holders have come across the situation where a maximum limit is applied on a customer. This may be because the underwriter is unable to agree a higher figure on the information available, or it may be because the underwriter has reached a 'ceiling' of cover available on that buyer in the reinsurance market. It is important that the policy holder finds out which reason is applicable, because if it is the latter he may well decide to trade beyond the maximum limit. This option is, of course, always available, but if a policy holder repeatedly chooses to exceed his credit limits, doubt must be thrown on the value of the policy.

Payment terms will naturally affect credit limits. Any extension beyond the agreed normal terms must be approved by the underwriter, even if no increase in credit limit is required. The reason is that the insurer may see such a request as part of a general approach to other suppliers, with implications that are hidden from individual clients.

Trade Indemnity will take into consideration the ledger history of a customer. If there is evidence of sound and consistent buying and paying, this can help to justify a limit which is difficult because of a lack of up-to-date information.

5 *Controls* Details of unpaid accounts must be declared when three months overdue, and even at this late stage the policy holder may, if he so wishes, put forward a case for continuing to deliver. The underwriter will be aware of overdue reports from other clients. If

139

there is an active relationship with the underwriter, this kind of information is valuable in guiding the supplier to a good decision.

6 Claims Claims arising from insolvency are paid within 30 days of the client's debt being accepted against the insolvent estate. Any money eventually recovered by the policy holder after a claim has been paid must be shared between client and insurer in proportion to the insured and uninsured parts of the original debt.

In cases of protracted default, claims are not paid until six months after the date of default. Since legal action would normally have been taken within this period or the debtor declared insolvent, this type of claim has little real value apart from cases of disappearing debtors.

Trade Indemnity offer a debt collection service to policy holders.

Benefits and alternatives

Protection is against both the effect of bad debt losses on profits and against the temporary loss of cash-flow. Thus, creditors of Rolls Royce Ltd were ultimately repaid in full, but they were denied the use of their money for years. Credit insurance bridges the gap.

Used properly, credit insurance is also a sales aid. Credit limits on many accounts will be higher than the credit manager could agree to without a safety net. When a customer runs into difficulties, the underwriter is usually very reluctant to 'come off cover' until the last possible moment, but policy holders are enabled to continue trading for longer than they would risk if unprotected.

Nonetheless credit insurance costs have to be justified in a tangible way. If premiums are paid over a number of years and the claims experience is very small, management must decide whether the cumulative outlay is still outweighed by the potential losses or whether to put next year's premium into a bad debt reserve. Very few, if any, companies build up bad debt reserves big enough to cover the sort of unexpected losses that credit insurance is aimed at. It would be unrealistic to expect them to do so, except in very high-risk industries such as construction, which demand a high degree of protection.

No kind of insurance policy is taken out with the intention of making a profit from it. Yet, unlike fire or motor insurance, credit insurance is often deemed to be a mistake unless, over a reasonable period, the value of claims paid somewhere near balances the total premium paid. One way of recognising this fact is the operation of a no-claims bonus on premium rates. Trade Indemnity do not like such schemes but occasionally can be persuaded to agree as the alternative to losing a policy. The services of a good broker are invaluable in such negotiations.

140

Members of the UK Credit Insurance Brokers Committee

The following are members of the UK Credit Insurance Brokers Committee:

Bain Dawes Credit Ltd
Chesterfield House, 26/28 Fenchurch Street, London EC3M 3DR.

Credit Insurance Association Ltd
Lloyds Chambers, 9/13 Crutched Friars, London EC3N 2JS.

Credit Insurance Services Ltd
136 Minories, London EC3N 1QN.

Industrial & Mercantile Credit Insurance Ltd
144 Leadenhall Street, London EC3P 3BJ.

John Reynolds & Co. (Credit Insurance) Ltd
21 Quay Street, Manchester M3 3JA.

Sedgwick Forbes Ltd
Sedgwick Forbes House, 33 Aldgate High Street, London EC3N 1AJ.

Stenhouse London Ltd
PO Box 214, Dominion Buildings, South Place, Moorgate, London EC2P 2DX.

Stewart Wrightson Ltd
Kingston Bridge House, Church Grove, Kingston-upon-Thames, Surrey KT1 4AG.

Willis Faber & Dumas Ltd
10 Trinity Square, London EC3

Part Two
EXPORT CREDIT MANAGEMENT

The principles of credit management apply equally to export as to domestic business, but there are a number of significant differences which make export credit both more complex and more interesting.

The supply of goods or services to an overseas buyer introduces a range of factors unknown to the domestic credit manager. These arise from differences in the language, customs, currency, the regulations and the degree of industrial/commercial development found in export markets.

Over 90 percent of all UK exports are made on 'short-term' credit, which means up to 180 days. The chapters which follow on payment terms, letters of credit and cash-flow are written primarily for this majority. Those on risk assessment, ECGD and foreign exchange should be of interest to all exporters. The chapters on export finance and bonds are specifically aimed at those exporters giving longer than six months' credit.

The management of trade credit in the UK has generally been under financial control, even to the extent of making it the accountant's frequently found in the hands of sales and marketing people. Sometimes this is by design, but more often by default because the credit this is by design, but more often by default because the credit controller or accountant does not possess the knowledge necessary to

143

handle export credit problems. Either way the results for the company can be disastrous. While the export sales ledger remains an accounting responsibility, the export sales office is expected to cope with documentation, ECGD and currency. Many companies are realising that this division of functions is not sensible and that the consequences of weak control in export credit are worse than in the home market.

The professional credit manager has a major role to play in exporting. He should be the vital link between sales and finance, providing advice and guidance on payment terms, currency invoicing and market risks. His expertise should ensure good documentation and smooth cash-flow. He should obtain full value from an ECGD policy.

Chapter 11

Export risk assessment

Export risk assessment is divided into two parts — the market or political/exchange risk and the buyer or commercial risk. In any evaluation, the market risk should be considered first, because if it proves unacceptable and unavoidable there is no point in moving on to examine the buyer risk.

Market risk

Several questions need to be asked in assessing market risk:

1 *Is there any likelihood that trade between the UK and the buyer's country may be interrupted by war, revolution or some other political factor?* Recent examples of this kind of problem include Cyprus, Zaire and Iran. Problems of this nature are very difficult to foresee, but caution must always be exercised in dealing with countries whose governments are either unstable or hostile to the UK, or both.

2 *Will there be any difficulty in bringing payment into the UK?* Shortage of foreign exchange has been a severe problem with a number of countries in recent years. Turkey was a classic example of this in

1977-9; other markets suffering similarly at that time (although less severely) included Peru, Zambia, Ghana and Bangladesh.

A country's ability to obtain foreign currency depends on its trading position with other nations and on the way its own economy is performing. A continuous, heavy excess of imports over exports causes higher and higher borrowing from richer nations. Unless steps are taken to control this — which may be political, financial or both — confidence in the country's ability to repay borrowings diminishes. Monetary aid slows down and the government is forced to introduce even more severe controls and restraints. The huge jump in oil prices at the end of 1973 pushed many countries which lacked oil nearer to this situation.

The most frustrating aspect of the problem — from the point of view of both the exporter and the importer — is that the buyer may be a prosperous company which has obtained possession of the goods by paying in local currency. The fact that his bank is unable to buy sterling or whatever currency is needed means that the exporter may cease to supply and the importer suffers through no fault of his own.

Advice on possible exchange problems should always be sought from one's own bank.

3   Are there any regulations or restrictions imposed either by the UK or by the buyer's country which may make trading difficult or virtually impossible? Under this heading come a variety of different situations, including Rhodesia, with whom trade is prohibited by the British government, and a number of markets with very strict import licence requirements.

These various market risks have firstly to be identified. The export credit manager must keep up-to-date on political, economic and financial events in the markets in which his company trades. His principal source of information — apart from the regular perusal of daily and weekly newspapers and journals — is the banks. All the UK clearing banks produce intelligence reports on world markets, and merchant banks do likewise for territories where they are represented. Other more specialised publications exist covering the commercial and foreign exchange regulations of overseas markets. A list of the principal ones is given at the end of the book.

Varying amounts of protection against market risks may be obtained from two sources — the use of secure payment terms and the operation of an ECGD policy. Both these subjects are covered in separate chapters. It is necessary to point out however that these forms of protection may not be available in cases of extreme risk and they should not be regarded as alternatives. If a confirmed Letter of Credit cannot be obtained, it will be very difficult to obtain ECGD cover.

146

Thus for most of 1977-9 ECGD cover for sales to Turkey was only available if sales were made under a confirmed, irrevocable Letter of Credit — which was unobtainable because banks were not willing to confirm Turkish credits.

Buyer risk

As in the home market, proper analysis of buyer risk depends on good information. The quality of information varies immensely, according to the market in view. Not surprisingly, in the developed, industrial nations good information is easier to find than in the third-world countries. But there are also big differences within the industrial nations, most strongly evidenced between the USA and Europe. The reason for this is the comparative weakness and low standing of the credit profession outside the USA. In his survey of European credit information, M. Grandjean states, 'Suppliers have less power in Europe than in the USA. In their negotiations with credit seekers, with banks or with other high-power sources of information, suppliers in Europe are not very well armed. First, most European suppliers have no credit managers. Therefore, they do not even try to obtain information, as they have nobody able to evaluate credit risks. Even in the UK, only a very limited number of suppliers have professional credit men. For this very reason, credit men in Europe have a low level of aspiration in their negotiations to obtain information.' 'A proposal to develop better credit information in Europe', by G. Grandjean; Thesis published by the Credit Research Foundation, New York (1977).]

Information sources on the commercial risk are as follows:
1 Company accounts.
2 Credit reporting agencies.
3 Banks.
4 Official sources.
5 Agents.
6 Credit contacts.

Each of these will be examined in detail.

Company accounts

North America

Balance sheet information in the USA is normally readily available. The credit standing of a company in the eyes of banks and suppliers is a

147

highly prized asset. If a company refuses financial information it is reasonable to assume that there is something to hide — unlike in Europe where firms are not used to being asked to disclose. Accounts can often be obtained directly from a buyer, but they are frequently included in credit agency reports. It is common practice for many corporations to send copies of their quarterly financial statements direct to the reporting bureau. The position is similar, although not so well developed, in Canada.

Europe

Some knowledge of the forms of business organisation found in Europe is helpful, as well as facts about the legal requirements, availability and interpretation of accounts. While the principle of the limited liability company is accepted everywhere, each European nation has developed its own business structure.

Before examining the major countries, it should be noted there are two general principles which, in broad terms, distinguish the understanding of European company accounts from those of the UK:
1   Assets and profits are usually understated because accounts are prepared with the prime objective of minimising taxation.
2   In a number of countries, it is not usual for accounts of companies within a group to be consolidated.

A final point is that in Europe there is no tradition of revealing balance sheets to creditors. A direct approach is unusual and requires tact and diplomacy to have any chance of success.

France   The great majority of French businesses are small, family-controlled enterprises with a strong tradition of secrecy.

There are two forms of limited liability company, the SA (Société Anonyme) and the SARL (Société à responsibilité limitée). A small number of SA are public quoted companies, and these require a minimum capital of F500,000 (which must be fully issued within five years). Non-quoted SAs must have capital of F100,000. The minimum share capital of an SARL is F20,000 (all issued). Unlike in the UK there is no legal requirement for an SA or SARL to show these initials as part of the company name, although it must be indicated somewhere on the company's letter-head. The AGM must be held within six months of year-end, and two copies of the accounts have to be filed with the local court within one month of the AGM. A copy of the accounts has to be filed at the Registry of the local commercial court (where it is available for public inspection). SAs with assets exceeding F10 million must also publish accounts in the BALO (*Bulletin des Annoces Légales Obligatoires*) within 45 days of the AGM.

148

Despite these legal requirements, it is difficult to obtain up-to-date balance sheets in France. Around one-third of all French companies are registered in the Paris area, causing great administrative congestion which is aggravated by the fact that most companies close their accounts on 31 December. Consolidation of accounts is not required, except for newly quoted companies.

A personal visit may be made to the local Registry or photocopies of accounts can be requested through the post (cost in 1978 — F20). *Providing* the accounts are filed, they are usually available between six and 12 months from the balance sheet date. This only applies to SAs. The 'bilans' of SARL companies cannot be obtained from the local Registry.

The address of the Paris Registry is:

> Greffe du Tribunal de Commerce de Paris,
> Bureau No. 6, 1 quai de Corse 75004 PARIS.

A translation of French accounting terms appears in the Appendix to this chapter.

Partnerships are a more common form of business than in the UK. The two principal forms are:

a   *SNC (Société en nom collectif)*   This has a separate legal existence, but partners are both jointly and severally liable for its debts.

b   *SCS (Société en commandité simple)*   This includes sleeping partners whose liability is limited to the amount of contributed capital.

There are no legal requirements for the publication or filing of accounts by partnerships.

One other form of business worthy of mention is the GIE (Groupement d'interest economique). This is a kind of joint venture, having a separate legal existence. Members are jointly and severally liable for the debts of a GIE.

Germany   German industry has a number of distinguishing features. The most important of these is the power exercised by the banks. They have very considerable shareholdings, and management decisions can be vetoed if the bank holds over 25 per cent of the equity.

There are two types of limited company: The AG (Aktiengesellschaft) and the GmbH (Gesellschaft mit beschrankter Haftung). An AG must have a minimum of DM100,000 capital (25 per cent paid-up) and a GmbH DM20,000.

Publication and filing requirements are very lax. Only AGs and large GmbHs have to file their accounts with the Commercial Register without undue delay after the AGM — which must be held within eight months of year-end. Large GmbH companies are those which meet two out of three conditions involving total assets, annual sales and numbers employed.

Accounts are not available to the public at the Commercial Register. Publication (within 12 months of year-end) is in the official newspaper *Bundesanzeiger*. An approach can be made to the *Bundesanzeiger* for a copy of the issue containing the accounts of a particular company, at the following address:

Bundesanzeiger, Verlagsgesellschaft mbH,
Postfach 10 80 06, D5000 Köln 1.

A translation of German accounting terms is given in the Appendix to this chapter. German accounting practice is particularly conservative in its treatment of assets and reserves. Consolidated accounts are legally required but a subsidiary which is itself an AG is not required to publish its accounts.

Another major feature of German industry is the frequent use of partnerships as a form of organisation. There are several different types of partnership, including:

a   *OHG (Offene Handelsgesellschaft)*   Partners are jointly and severally liable.

b   *KG (Kommanditgesellschaft)*   A limited partnership. Only fully liable partners can participate in management.

c   *GmbH & Co. KG*   A partnership in which the wholly liable partner is a GmbH.

No accounts have to be filed by partnerships. Many very large concerns operate in this way.

Because of the strong influence of the banks, German companies do not expect to be asked to disclose their finances to creditors.

Netherlands   Dutch companies are either NV (Naamloze Vennootschap) or BV (Besloten Vennootschap). The former is roughly equivalent to a public limited company and the latter to a private limited company.

NVs must file accounts within eight days of the AGM. BVs are exempt from filing accounts unless their assets exceed FL8 million and they have more than 100 employees. Balance sheets may be obtained by writing to the Chamber of Commerce appropriate to the region where the company is situated.

A translation of Dutch accounting terms is given in the Appendix. Dutch accounting practice is fairly close to that of the UK, and interpretation of balance sheets presents no special problems.

Belgium   A feature of Belgian industry is the power of a small number of holding companies. Consolidated accounts are not required, and it is often difficult to assess a company's worth.

Limited companies are either SA/NV [and also SCA — a form of limited partnership — and SC (Société Cooperative)] have to file their annual accounts (balance sheet, profit and loss account and notes) with the local commercial court (Greffe du Tribunal de Commerce). This information is then sent to the Banque Nationale de Belgique who put it on microfilm. These records are available to the public, either through the post or by personal attendance, as follows:

a   For accounts of SA only up to 31 December 1976:

>   Moniteur Belge,
>   Rue de Louvain 40, B1000 Brussels

b   For accounts of SA, SARL, SCA and SC from 1977 on:

>   Banque Nationale de Belgique,
>   Boulevard de Berlaimont 5, B1000 Brussels

c   Or, according to the registration of the business, the local Greffe du Tribunal de Commerce.

Annual accounts are usually available within 12 months of year-end, but delays in obtaining them from the above bodies are common. They are written in either Flemish or French. While the former is very close to Dutch, there are a number of accounting terms particular to Belgium (in both languages). These are given in the Appendix.

Luxembourg   Business organisations are very similar to those in Belgium, companies being SA or SPRL. Balance sheets and profit and loss accounts for SAs only must be filed at the Tribunal d'Arrondissement within two weeks of the AGM and one month later are available for public inspection. Photocopies can be obtained by writing to:

>   Le Greffier en Chef, Tribunal d'Arrondissement,
>   Boite Postale 15, Luxembourg.

The actual amount of detailed information which has to be published is very limited. It should be brought into line with EEC requirements within a few years.

Italy   Two types of limited company are found — the SpA (Società per Azioni) and the SRL (Società a responsibilità limitata). The former requires a minimum share capital of L1 million and the latter L50,000. Accounts are prepared with the sole object of reducing the incidence of taxation, with the result that assets are frequently undervalued. Italian balance sheets do not always balance and

151

accounts have to be considered unreliable. There is no clear legal distinction between current and fixed assets and the profit and loss account is often given in a condensed form due to the lack of proper accounting principles. A translation of Italian accounting terms is in the Appendix.

Balance sheets of SpAs have to be filed at the local trade registry, where they are available for inspection. Due to the unreliability of the postal service, accounts are best obtained through a bank or reporting agency.

Other forms of business include SNC (general partnership), SAS (limited partnership), SCRL (a cooperative with limited liability) and SCRIL (a cooperative with unlimited liability). None of these organisations have to file accounts.

It is an old joke that if you ask an Italian for his company's balance sheet he will reply, 'which one do you want?' The truth is that in Italy two or even three sets of accounts are maintained — the official one for the tax authority, the real one for the shareholders and perhaps one for the bank. The same practice occurs in Spain and South America.

Denmark   The organisation of Danish industry is relatively similar to that of the UK. Limited companies are either A/S or ApS requiring a minimum capital of KR100,000 and KR30,000, respectively (all subscribed on formation).

Annual accounts must be filed within one month of shareholders' approval and are available for public inspection. An A/S can request exemption from publication, however, which is usually granted. In 1975 around 65 per cent of all A/Ss obtained such exemption. Another relaxation for ApSs is that they are permitted to file a condensed balance sheet if their total assets are below KR2 million.

Forms of partnership in Denmark include I/S (Interessentskab — limited partnership) and KA/S (partnership limited to the extent of contributed shares). No accounts have to be filed.

A translation of Danish accounting terms is in the Appendix.

Copies of A/S and ApS accounts can be obtained (either by visit or through the post) from:

Aktieselskabregistret
Nygade 4, 1164 Copenhagen K.

Sweden   Limited companies are of one type, the AB (Aktiebolag), which has a minimum share capital of SKr5,000. New legislation (1979-80) will increase this minimum to SKr50,000 (all paid in cash).

Annual accounts must be filed with a central registry. Copies can be obtained through the post, address as follows:

Kungl. Patent — och Registreringsverket
Bolagsbyran, Box 6151, 10233 Stockholm.

A translation of Swedish accounting terms is in the Appendix.

Forms of partnership in Sweden include HB (Handelsbolag — general partnership) and KB (Kommanditbolag — limited partnership which must include one unlimited partner). No accounts have to be filed.

Switzerland Limited companies follow the German/French pattern, according to which part of Switzerland is involved. Thus the AG/SA require a minimum capital of SFr50,000 and GmbH/SARL SFr20,000.

Only quoted companies, banks and insurance companies are required to file or publish accounts. Accounts are available to shareholders only, and there is no central or local commercial registry from which details can be obtained.

Spain In the summer of 1978 a *Financial Times* survey stated that 'financial information about companies in Spain is still primitive, unreliable and frequently fraudulent'.

It should be of more comfort to credit managers, however, that over 40 per cent of Spanish industry is owned by the banks, which means that companies in trouble are often supported to a far greater degree than would otherwise be expected — simply because the banks have to protect their investments.

There are two types of limited company in Spain — the SA (Sociedad anonima) and the SRL (Sociedad de responsabilidad limitada). The latter is restricted to firms with under 50 million pesetas capital.

Publication of accounts is a legal requirement on publicly owned companies only, i.e. some SAs. There is no central place where accounts may be inspected, but each province has its own registry.

Austria Forms of business organisations are very similar to those in Germany, limited companies being either AG or GmbH. Only AG are required to publish accounts, and these appear in the official newspaper, *Wiener Zeitung*. Photocopies of company accounts may be obtained direct from:

Wiener Zeitung, Bilanzabteilung,
Rennweg 16, A1030 Wien.

or from:

Compass-Verlag, Abt. Finanz-Compass,
Wipplingerstrasse 32, A 1013 Wien.

Accounts are generally available within twelve months of balance sheet date.

Finland   Every business organisation whose turnover exceeds FMk2 million or whose balance sheet exceeds FMk1 million has to file its balance sheet and profit and loss account at the Commercial Register, address as follows:

Patentti — ja Rekisterihallitus, Kaupparekisteri,
Bulevardi 21, 00120 Helsinki 12.

Copies of balance sheets can be obtained either by personal visit or through the post (*only* within Finland). Accounts have to be filed within six months of financial year-end, but delays of up to one year in obtaining information may be experienced.

While Finnish companies often publish accounts in Swedish or German, some Finnish accounting terms are given in the Appendix.

Norway   Balance sheet information on Norwegian companies is difficult to obtain because of the lack of legal requirements. New legislation covering joint-stock companies (A/S) is expected to enforce the filing of annual accounts from 1979 onwards with the local office of the 'Handelsregisteret', although the Ministry of Commerce is empowered to exempt a company from filing.

A translation of Norwegian accounting terms is given in the Appendix.

Greece   Limited companies (indicated by the suffix 'AE' or 'EPE') are required to publish balance sheets and profit and loss accounts in the government *Gazette*. While it is possible to obtain the relevant issue of the *Gazette* it is easier to enquire through a bank or reporting agency.

Portugal   Limited companies (SARL) and nationalised undertakings (EP) must publish their annual accounts in the official newspaper, the *Gazette*, immediately after the AGM. Copies of SARL accounts can be obtained from the *Gazette* up to twelve months later, but it is usually easier to use a reporting agency.

Partnerships ('Limitada') are exempt from filing their accounts. A translation of some Portuguese accounting terms is in the Appendix.

Other markets

This embraces Australia, New Zealand, South Africa, Japan, where company accounts are obtainable reasonably easily, and all the 'developing' nations of South America, Africa and Asia, where balance sheets are generally hard to find. Even when they do come to hand, the credit analyst must not place too much reliance on them for two reasons. Firstly, as in many European countries, accounts are prepared because the law demands them and this becomes a tax-avoidance exercise. Secondly, the standards of accountancy and auditing fall far below those of Western nations.

Reporting agencies

Many UK credit reporting agencies offer a service on overseas markets. A few are good and many are poor. Successful overseas reporting is a very expensive business, since an agency must take pains to ensure that its contacts and agents all over the world are working actively to obtain up-to-date information. Only experience will tell a credit manager which agencies give good value. What must be borne in mind is the availability of financial information, which varies from market to market.

It is good practice to use two or three different agencies, rather than to rely on one. Most West European countries have their own credit reporting businesses, and it can be worthwhile to obtain reports direct on the local markets. Some overseas agencies will provide English language reports (usually but not always at an additional charge). These will generally be considerably cheaper than reports on the same market from a UK agency.

Most UK and European agencies offer two types of report: the 'normal' and the 'special'. The normal report at best runs to two or three pages, including particulars of directors, partners, company operations, etc., and (if available) the latest financial information. Where the subject of a report does not have to publish accounts (especially common in Germany), the financial information is extremely limited. Another common form of normal report is a pre-printed matrix of categories and values, on which the appropriate answers are ticked. 'Special' reports are much longer (and quite expensive), but of questionable value if no financial data is available. Direct approaches by reporting agencies to a company, asking for financial information, are rarely successful outside the USA or the UK, because there is no tradition of exchanging or supplying information.

By contrast, credit reports in the USA are full of information, often including complete balance sheets for the last three years, lengthy biographical notes on executives and up-to-date payment reports from existing suppliers.

Credit reporting outside the industrial nations, i.e. Africa, South America, the Near and Far East and the Indian sub-continent, is very difficult. Problems in obtaining balance sheets have already been referred to. Direct approaches to companies in these markets for financial information are not often successful, partly because of fears that any information given will somehow find its way to the tax authorities. Often all that can be achieved is a report on the local reputation and scale of business of the subject.

Banks

American banks, inside and outside the USA, are good sources of credit information, because the need to establish a sound credit reputation is recognised in the USA, and banks are allowed more discretion in divulging information.

By contrast, European banks are far more reticent about their customers' finances, but even so they are more helpful than UK banks. In most countries there is a recognised code of practice which prevents a banker from releasing balance sheet information or details of a precise nature about clients' accounts, unless the client authorises it. This leaves the bank freedom to provide background information about a client's business and reputation.

When seeking help from a bank, the credit manager should take pains to phrase his question as specifically as possible, e.g. 'Do you consider XYZ GmbH a good risk for up to DM50,000 credit on net 60-day terms?'

Official sources

Official sources include the commercial offices of UK embassies and consulates abroad and the Export Intelligence Service operated by the British Overseas Trade Board. The information provided is not financial but commercial, covering the local reputation and scope of a company's business, coupled with background data on local trading conditions and regulations. This service is of more value in the developing markets. Even if business is to be conducted on secure terms it is necessary to find out whether a buyer has a genuine, established business.

Agents

A firm's own agent, whether he covers one territory or many different markets, should be a prime source of information. He will often be the only person with direct contact with the customer, so his opinion and assessment of the buyer's ability to pay on due date are important. The opportunities for credit people to visit overseas customers are rare, so the credit manager must make sure, firstly, that it is a recognised part of an agent's job to obtain whatever financial information is available and, secondly, that he has an opportunity to brief the agent on what to look for and what questions to ask.

Credit contacts

As in the home market, a network of trusted credit contacts is invaluable. These are more difficult to establish because of language and distance, but there are two organisations through which export credit information can be exchanged.

1 Institute of Credit Management (12 Queen Square, Brighton) An Export Committee exists for the purpose of assisting members with export credit problems. In 1977 an Export Forum was held and was so successful that it is now a twice-yearly event. A panel of experienced people (generally including representatives from ECGD and the clearing banks) lead discussions on members' questions which have been received beforehand and sorted into an agenda. The emphasis is on informal participation.

2 Finance, Credit and International Business (known as FCIB: the European branch of the National Association of Credit Management; 475 Park Avenue South, New York 10016) Membership of FCIB is by company (as opposed to the ICM of whom membership is individual). Three meetings a year are held in different European cities, the format and objectives being identical to the ICM Export Forum. FCIB started these conferences in 1967, and they provide a meeting place for credit and financial managers from all over the Western world.

While the emphasis in both ICM and FCIB meetings is on market risk and the published transcripts rarely refer to companies by name, of equal if not greater value are the informal talks between credit people on all aspects of credit management.

Public buyers

The credit manager dealing with 'Public Sector' buyers in the UK rarely has a problem — providing his documentation is perfect — but this is not the case in many overseas markets. While government buyers in the industrial nations (and in Comecon countries) can generally be regarded as safe, outside these areas the position is quite different.

The fact that the buyer is a government ministry or department by no means eliminates the possibility of payment problems. Quite apart from political or transfer risks, there is the danger that the individuals negotiating a contract may not have authority to commit their government to expenditure. Another department's approval may be needed before finance is allocated. Further aspects of public buyer risk are examined in Chapter 17.

Conclusion

Some of the most valuable information files are only available to companies who have decided to pay for risk protection, either through insurance with ECGD or Trade Indemnity or through factoring. Where none of these can be approached, the credit manager has to reach a decision from the facts derived from the sources described in this chapter. Time is always against him. It is rare for reliable up-to-date information to be obtained in under two weeks, unless the prospect is a major concern in an industrial market. Credit decisions often cannot wait that long. In the next two chapters terms of sale will be examined, and it will be seen that some of these give the partial or complete security which must be sought when large amounts are to be risked with unknown faraway buyers. Chapter 14 examines export credit decisions in the light of risk assessment and payment terms.

APPENDIX: accounting terminology used in overseas balance sheets

These lists are not exhaustive, but include all the most commonly found terms in company accounts. Where terms are entirely or virtually the same in English as in the local language they are omitted, e.g. 'Réserve légale" in French.

FRENCH-ENGLISH

French	English
BILAN	*BALANCE SHEET*
MONTANT BRUT	GROSS AMOUNT
AMORTISSEMENTS OU PROVISIONS POUR DÉPRÉCIATION	DEPRECIATION
MONTANT NET	NET TOTAL
ACTIF	ASSETS
FRAIS D'ÉTABLISSEMENT	FORMATION EXPENSES
IMMOBILISATIONS	FIXED ASSETS
TERRAINS	LAND
CONSTRUCTIONS	BUILDINGS
MATÉRIEL ET OUTILLAGE	MACHINERY AND TOOLS
MOBILIER ET MATÉRIEL DE BUREAU	FURNITURE AND FITTINGS
MATERIEL DE TRANSPORT	VEHICLES
IMMOBILISATIONS INCOR-PORELLES	INTANGIBLES (i.e. goodwill, etc.)
AUTRES VALEURS IMMOBULISÉES	OTHER 'NON-CURRENT' ASSETS
PRÊTS (*or* CRÉANCES) À PLUS D'UN AN	LONG-TERM RECEIVABLES
TITRES DE PARTICIPATION	INVESTMENTS
DÉPÔTS ET CAUTIONNE-MENTS	GUARANTEE DEPOSITS
VALEURS D'EXPLOITATION	STOCKS
MATIÈRES PREMIÈRES ET FOURNITURES	RAW MATERIALS AND SUPPLIES
PRODUITS SEMI-OUVRÉS	WORK-IN-PROGRESS
PRODUITS FINIS	FINISHED GOODS
VALEURS REALISABLES À COURT TERME OU DISPONIBLES	CURRENT ASSETS
FOURNISSEURS — AVANCES	ADVANCE PAYMENTS TO SUPPLIERS
CLIENTS	DEBTORS
IMPÔTS ET TAXES	TAXES
COMPTES D'ASSOCIÉS	ASSOCIATE COMPANY DEBTORS
SOCIÉTÉS MÈRES ET FILIALES	PARENT AND SUBSIDIARY COMPANY DEBTORS

COMPTES DE RÉGULARIS-ATION — ACTIF	PRE-PAID EXPENSES
EFFETS À RECEVOIR	BILLS RECEIVABLE
TITRES DE PLACEMENT ET BONS	MARKETABLE SECURITIES AND BONDS
BANQUES ET CHEQUES POSTAUX	CASH AT BANK
CAISSES	CASH IN HAND
PERTE DE L'EXERCICE	LOSS FOR THE YEAR
PASSIF	*LIABILITIES*
CAPITAUX PROPRE ET RÉSERVES	CAPITAL AND RESERVES
CAPITAL SOCIAL OU PERSONNEL	CAPITAL
PRIMES D'ÉMISSION D'ACTIONS	SHARE PREMIUM
REPORT À NOUVEAU	BROUGHT FORWARD
SITUATION NETTE (AVANT RÉSULTATS DE L'EXERCICE)	TOTAL CAPITAL AND RESERVES (BEFORE THIS YEAR'S RESULTS)
SUBVENTIONS D'ÉQUIPE-MENT	PLANT SUBSIDIES
PROVISIONS POUR PERTES ET CHARGES	PROVISIONS FOR LOSSES AND EXPENSES
DETTES À COURT TERME	CURRENT LIABILITIES
FOURNISSEURS	CREDITORS
CLIENTS — AVANCES	ADVANCE PAYMENTS FROM CUSTOMERS
PERSONNEL	DEBTS DUE TO STAFF
IMPÔTS ET TAXES	TAXES AND DUTIES
AUTRES CRÉANCIERS	OTHER DEBTORS
OBLIGATIONS ET EMPRUNTS À MOINS D'UN AN	OBLIGATIONS AND LOANS DUE WITHIN ONE YEAR
EFFETS À PAYER	BILLS PAYABLE
BANQUES	OWING TO BANK
BÉNÉFICE DE L'EXERCICE	PROFIT FOR THE YEAR
COMPTE DE PERTES ET PROFITS	*PROFIT AND LOSS ACCOUNT*
PERTE (BÉNÉFICE) D'EXPLOITATION	OPERATING LOSS (PROFIT)
PERTES (BÉNÉFICES) EXCEPTIONNELLES	EXCEPTIONAL LOSS (PROFITS)

IMPÔTS SUR LES BÉNÉFICES	TAX ON PROFITS
PERTE (BÉNÉFICE) NETTE (NET) COMPTABLE	NET LOSS (PROFIT)
COMPTE D'EXPLOITATION GÉNÉRALE	TRADING ACCOUNT
STOCK AU DEBUT DE L'EXERCICE	OPENING STOCK
ACHATS	PURCHASES
FRAIS DE PERSONNEL	WAGES AND SALARIES
TRAVAUX, FOURNITURES ET SERVICES EXTERIEURS	SUPPLIES AND SERVICES
FRAIS DIVERS DE GESTION	ADMINISTRATIVE EXPENSES
FRAIS FINANCIERS	INTEREST CHARGES
DOTATION	DEPRECIATION
STOCKS À LA FIN DE L'EXERCICE	CLOSING STOCK
CHIFFRE D'AFFAIRES	TURNOVER
VENTES	SALES
VENTES DE DÉCHETS	SALE OF SCRAP
RISTOURNES, RABAIS ET REMISES OBTENUS	DISCOUNTS AND ALLOWANCES

Notes

1   French companies use a pre-printed set of documents — the *Bilan*.
2   Stocks are not included under the heading 'Current Assets', but are shown separately.
3   Because of the common practice of paying by bill of exchange, the total creditors have to be obtained by adding '*Fournisseurs*' to '*Effets a payer*'. Similarly trade debtors will include '*Clients*' and '*Effets a recevoir*'.
4   While the various sub-headings under 'Stocks' have been shown, these are actually found on page 5 of the *Bilan*, on the Trading Account.
5   The *Bilan* only shows one year's accounts. To make comparisons, each year's accounts must be obtained separately.

GERMAN-ENGLISH

German	English
AKTIVA	*ASSETS*
ANLAGEVERMÖGEN	FIXED ASSETS, LONG-TERM LOANS AND INVESTMENTS
SACHANLAGEN UND IMMATERIELLE ANLA-GEWERTE	FIXED AND INTANGIBLE ASSETS
GRUNDSTÜCKE UND GRUNDSTÜCKGLEICHE RECHTE MIT GESCHÄFTS-, FABRIK- UND ANDEREN BAUTEN	LAND AND PROPERTY RIGHTS WITH OFFICE, FACTORY AND OTHER BUILDINGS ERECTED
GRUNDSTÜCKE UND GRUNDSTÜCKGLEICHE RECHTE OHNE BAUTEN	LAND, ETC., WITHOUT BUILDINGS
MASCHINEN UND MASCHINELLE ANLAGEN	MACHINERY AND INSTALLATIONS
BETRIEBS- UND GESCHÄFTAUS-STATTUNG	FACTORY AND OFFICE EQUIPMENT
WERKZEUGE	TOOLS
ANLAGEN IN BAU UND ANZAHLUNGEN AUF ANLAGEN	CONSTRUCTION IN PROGRESS AND ADVANCE PAYMENTS FOR SAME
KONZESSIONEN, GEWERBLICHE SCHUTZRECHTE UND ÄHNLICHE RECHTE	INTANGIBLE ASSETS
FINANZANLAGEN	FINANCIAL ASSETS
BETEILIGUNGEN	INVESTMENTS
WERTPAPIERE DES ANLAGEVERMÖGENS	SECURITIES
AUSLEIHUNGEN MIT EINER LAUFZEIT VON MINDE-STENS VIER JAHREN — DAVON DURCH GRUNDPFANDRECHTE GESICHERT	LOANS GRANTED FOR AT LEAST FOUR YEARS — AMOUNT OF SUCH LOANS SECURED BY MORTGAGES
UMLAUFVERMÖGEN	CURRENT ASSETS
VORRÄTE	STOCKS

ROH-, HILFS- UND BETRIEBSTOFFE	RAW MATERIAL AND SUPPLIES
UNFERTIGE ERZEUGNISSE	WORK-IN-PROGRESS
ERZEUGNISSE UND WAREN	FINISHED GOODS
ANDERE GEGENSTÄNDE DES UMLAUFVER-MÖGENS	OTHER CURRENT ASSETS
GELEISTETE ANZAHLUNGEN	PREPAYMENTS TO SUPPLIERS
FORDERUNGEN AUS LIEFERUNGEN UND LEISTUNGEN — DAVON MIT EINER RESTLAUFZEIT VON MEHR ALS EINEM JAHR . . .	TRADE DEBTORS, OF WHICH DUE IN MORE THAN ONE YEAR . . .
WECHSEL	BILLS RECEIVABLE
SCHECKS	CHEQUES
KASSENBESTAND, BUNDESBANK- UND POSTSCHECKGUTHABEN	CASH IN HAND AND BANK DEPOSITS
ANDERE BANKGUTHABEN or GUTHABEN BEI KREDITINSTITUTEN	OTHER SHORT-TERM DEPOSITS
SONSTIGE FORDERUNGEN	SUNDRY DEBTORS
FORDERUNGEN AN VERBUNDENE UNTERNEHMEN	AMOUNTS DUE FROM ASSOCIATE COMPANIES
SONSTIGE VERMÖGENSGEGEN-STÄNDE	OTHER CURRENT ASSETS
RECHNUNGSABGREN-ZUNGSPOSTEN	PRE-PAID EXPENSES
GESCHÄFTSWERT	GOODWILL
ABSCHREIBUNGEN	DEPRECIATION
PASSIVA	*LIABILITIES*
GRUNDKAPITAL	SHARE CAPITAL
OFFENE RÜCKLAGEN	CAPITAL RESERVES
GESETZLICHE RÜCKLAGE	LEGAL RESERVE
FREIE RÜCKLAGEN	OTHER RESERVES
WERTBERICHTIGUNGEN	ALLOWANCES OR PROVISIONS
RÜCKSTELLUNGEN	ACCRUED LIABILITIES

VERBINDLICHKEITEN MIT EINER LAUFZEIT VON MINDESTENS VIER JAHREN	LONG-TERM DEBTS (AT LEAST FOUR YEARS)
ANLEIHEN	LOANS
VERBINDLICHKEITEN GEGENÜBER KREDITIN-STITUTEN — DAVON DURCH GRUNDPFAN-DRECHTE GESICHERT	BANK LOANS — SECURED BY MORTGAGE
LASTENSAUSGLEICHS-VERMÖGENSABGABE	TAX EQUALISATION RESERVE
SONSTIGE BERBINDLICH-KEITEN	OTHER LIABILITIES
KURZFRISTIGE VERBIND-LICHKEITEN	CURRENT LIABILITIES
VERBINDLICHKEITEN AUS LIEFERUNGEN UND LEISTUNGEN	TRADE CREDITORS
WECHSELVERBINDLICH-KEITEN	BILLS PAYABLE
VERBINDLICHKEITEN GEGENÜBER KREDITINS-TITUTEN	BANK LOANS AND OVER-DRAFTS
VERBINDLICHKEITEN GEGENÜBER VER-BUNDENEN UNTERNEH-MEN	ACCOUNTS DUE FROM ASSOCIATE COMPANIES
STEUERN	TAXES
BILANZGEWINN	RETAINED EARNINGS
UMSATZERLÖSE	TURNOVER
AUFWENDUNG FÜR ROH-HILFS- UND BETRIEB-STOFFE	COST OF GOODS SOLD
GESAMTLEISTUNG	TOTAL REVENUE
ROHERTRAG (ROHAUF-WAND)	GROSS PROFIT (LOSS)
LÖHNE UND GEHÄLTER	WAGES AND SALARIES
ZINSEN UND ÄHNLICHE AUFWENDUNGEN	INTEREST AND FINANCIAL CHARGES
JAHRESÜBERSCHUSS (JAHRESFEHLBETRAG)	PROFIT FOR YEAR (LOSS)
SONSTIGE ERTRÄGE	OTHER INCOME
SONSTIGE AUFWEN-DUNGEN	OTHER EXPENSES

DUTCH-ENGLISH

Dutch	English
ACTIVA	*ASSETS*
DUURZAME PRODUKTIE-MIDDELEN or VASTE ACTIVA	FIXED ASSETS
TERREINEN	LAND
GEBOUWEN	BUILDINGS
MACHINES EN INSTALLATIES	MACHINERY AND EQUIPMENT
WERKTUIGEN	TOOLS
KANTOORINVENTARIS or KANTOORINRICHTINGEN	FURNITURE AND FITTINGS
WOONRECHTEN	LEASEHOLD PROPERTIES
AFSCHRIJVINGEN	DEPRECIATION
IMMATERIËLE ACTIVA	INTANGIBLES
DEELNEMINGEN	INVESTMENTS
NIET DIRECT REALISEERBARE WAARDEN	OTHER NON-CURRENT ASSETS
VLOTTENDE ACTIVA or VLOTTENDE MIDDELEN	CURRENT ASSETS
VOORADEN	STOCKS
GRONDSTOFFEN	RAW MATERIAL
GOEDEREN IN BEWERKING	WORK-IN-PROGRESS
GEREED PRODUKT	FINISHED GOODS
HANDELSDEBITEUREN	TRADE DEBTORS
VORDERINGEN OP GELEERDE ONDERNEMINGEN	INTERCOMPANY RECEIVABLES
WISSELS	BILLS RECEIVABLE
VOOR TUITBETALINGEN	PAYMENTS IN ADVANCE
OVERIGE VORDERINGEN or DIVERSE DEBITEUREN	SUNDRY DEBTORS
LIQUIDE MIDDELEN	CASH AND MARKETABLE SECURITIES
KASSE, BANKEN or BELEGDE MIDDELEN	CASH IN HAND AND AT BANKS
PASSIVA	*LIABILITIES*
KORTLOPENDE SCHULDEN or SCHULDEN OP KORTE TERMIJN	CURRENT LIABILITIES

CREDITEUREN *or* HANDELSVERPLICH-TINGEN	TRADE CREDITORS
BANKVERPLICHTINGEN	BANK OVERDRAFTS
BELASTING OP DE WINST	TAX
VERPLICHTINGEN TEGENOVER GELIEERDE ONDERNEMINGEN	DEBTS DUE TO SUB-SIDIARIES
VERPLICHTINGEN MOEDERMAATSCHAPPIJ	DEBTS DUE TO PARENT COMPANY
TE BETALEN KOSTEN	ACCRUED EXPENSES
WINSTUITKERING	DIVIDENDS PAYABLE
SCHULDEN OP LANGE TERMIJN	LONG-TERM DEBTS
AANDELENKAPITAAL	SHARE CAPITAL
INGEHOUDEN WINSTEN	RETAINED EARNINGS
EIGEN VERMOGEN	SHAREHOLDERS' FUNDS
VOORZIENINGEN	PROVISIONS
OBLIGATIELENINGEN	DEBENTURES
VERLIES – EN WINSTREKENING	*PROFIT AND LOSS ACCOUNT*
OMZET	TURNOVER
BEDRIJFSWINST or BEDRIJFSRESULTAAT	OPERATING PROFIT
BETAALDE INTEREST	INTEREST PAID
WINST VOOR AFTREK VAN BELASTING	PROFIT BEFORE TAX
WINST NA AFTREK VAN BELASTING	PROFIT AFTER TAX
NETTOWINST	NET PROFIT

FLEMISH-ENGLISH

Flemish	English
VASTLIGGEND *or* VASTE ACTIVA	FIXED ASSETS
ONSTOFFELIJK *or* IMMATERIELE VASTE ACTIVA	INTANGIBLES
EFFECTENBEZIT	INVESTMENTS
BESCHIKBAAR EN OMZETBAAR	CURRENT ASSETS
KLANTEN	TRADE DEBTORS
ONTWANGEN WISSELS	BILLS RECEIVABLE
INVENTARIES	STOCKS
HANDELSGEEDEREN	MERCHANDISE
WERK AAN DE GANG	WORK-IN-PROGRESS
FABRIKATEN	FINISHED GOODS
BESCHIKBAAR	CASH
VERWEZENLIJKBAAR	LIQUID ASSETS
NIET EISBAAR	SHAREHOLDERS' FUNDS
HYPOTHECAIRE LENING	MORTGAGE LOAN
LEVERANCIERS	TRADE CREDITORS
BETALEN DIVIDENDEN	DIVIDENDS PAYABLE
FISKALE PROVISIE	TAX PROVISION
VERSCHEIDENE SCHULDEISERS	SUNDRY CREDITORS
RESULTAAT	RETAINED EARNINGS
VERLIES – EN WINSTREKENING	*PROFIT AND LOSS ACCOUNT*
OVERGEDRAGEN SALDO	BALANCE BROUGHT FORWARD
OVERDRACHT OP NIEUW	CARRIED FORWARD
KAPITAAL IS VOLSTORT	CAPITAL IS FULLY PAID
TANTIÈMES	DIRECTORS' FEES
BEDRIJFSONKOSTEN	GENERAL AND ADMINIS-TRATIVE EXPENSES
BRUTOWINST	GROSS PROFIT

BELGIAN/FRENCH-ENGLISH

Belgian/French	English
IMMOBILISÉ BRUT	FIXED ASSETS
AMORTISSEMENTS	DEPRECIATION
ACTIFS CIRCULANTS	CURRENT ASSETS
RÉALISABLE	STOCKS, DEBTORS AND INVESTMENTS
INVENTAIRE *or* MAGASINS	STOCKS
TRAVAUX EN COURS	WORK-IN-PROGRESS
DISPONIBLE	CASH
NON EXIGIBLE *or* FONDS PROPRES	SHAREHOLDERS' FUNDS
EXIGIBLE À COURT TERME	CURRENT LIABILITIES
EMPRUNT HYPOTHÉCAIRE	MORTGAGE LOAN
PRÉVISION FISCALE	TAX PROVISION
DIVERS CRÉDITEURS	SUNDRY CREDITORS
BÉNÉFICE BRUT	GROSS PROFIT
RÉSULTAT	RETAINED EARNINGS
LE CAPITAL EST ENTIÈRE-MENT LIBÉRÉ	CAPITAL IS FULLY PAID
COMPTES D'ORDRES	CONTINGENT LIABILITY
PARTICIPATIONS	PERMANENT INVESTMENTS IN OTHER COMPANIES

ITALIAN-ENGLISH

Italian	English
ATTIVO or*ATTIVITA*	*ASSETS*
IMMOBILIZZI	FIXED ASSETS
TERRENO	LAND
MACHINARIO	MACHINERY
IMPIANTI	PLANT
FABRICATI	BUILDINGS
AUTOMEZZI	VEHICLES
ATTREZZI	EQUIPMENT
ARR. UFF & ATTR *or* MOBILI D'UFFICIO	FIXTURES AND FITTINGS
AMMORTAMENTI	DEPRECIATION
TITOLI A REDDITO FISSO	FIXED INTEREST SECURITIES
PARTICIPAZIONIE PORTA-FOGLIO TITOLI	INVESTMENTS AND MARKETABLE SECURITIES
ATTIVO CURRENTI	CURRENT ASSETS
MAGGAZINO *or* SCORTE	STOCKS
MATERIE PRIME & MERCI	RAW MATERIAL AND SUPPLIES
PRODOTTI IN CORSO DI FABRICAZIONE	WORK-IN-PROGRESS
PRODOTTI FINITI	FINISHED GOODS
CLIENTI	DEBTORS
ANTICIPI A FORNITORI	PAYMENTS IN ADVANCE
CAMBIALI ATTIVE *or* EFFETTI ATTIVI	BILLS RECEIVABLE
CASSA	CASH
DEPOSITI BANCARI	BANK DEPOSITS
CREDITI VERSI CON-SOCIATE	OWED BY SUBSIDIARIES
ATTIVI IMMATERIALE	INTANGIBLES
AVVIAMENTO	GOODWILL
PASSIVO	*LIABILITIES*
DEBITI CORRENTI *or* DEBITI A BREVE TERMINE	CURRENT LIABILITIES
FORNITORI	CREDITORS
EFFETI PASSIVI	BILLS PAYABLE
ANTICIPI DI CLIENTI	PREPAYMENTS
DEBITI VERSO SOCIETA COLLEGATA	DUE TO ASSOCIATE COMPANIES

169

DEBITI VERSO BANCHE *or* SCOPERTI BANCARI	BANK OVERDRAFTS
DEBITI VERSO IL FISCO	CURRENT TAXATION
DEBITI A LUNGO E MEDIO TERMINE	MEDIUM AND LONG-TERM DEBT
ACCANTONAMENTI	PROVISIONS
CAPITALE SOCIALE	SHARE CAPITAL
RISERVA	RESERVES
OBLIGAZIONI	DEBENTURES

PROFITTI E PERDITE – COSTI	*PROFIT AND LOSS – COSTS*
ACQUISISTI *or* COSTO DEI MATERIAL	PURCHASES
SPESE GENERALI	GENERAL EXPENSES
VENDITE	TURNOVER
IMPOSTE *or* ONERI TRIBUTARI	TAXATION
PROVENTI FINANZIARI	INTEREST RECEIVED
ONERI FINANZIARI	INTEREST CHARGES
UTILE DELL'ESERCIZIO *or* UTILE NETTO	NET PROFIT
AVANZO A NUOVO	BALANCE CARRIED FORWARD

DANISH-ENGLISH

Danish	English
AKTIVER	*ASSETS*
ANLAEGSAKTIVER	FIXED ASSETS
FAST EJENDOM	LAND
MASKINER OG INVENTAR	MACHINERY AND EQUIP-MENT
AKTIER	SHARES
VAERDIPAPIRER	SECURITIES
AFSKRIVNINGER	DEPRECIATION
OMSAETNINGSAKTIVER	CURRENT ASSETS
KASSEBEHOLDNING	CASH
VAREDEBITORER	DEBTORS
VEKSLER	BILLS RECEIVABLE
FORUDBETALING TIL LEVERANDORER	ADVANCE PAYMENTS TO SUPPLIERS
VARELAGER *or* VAREBEHOLDNINGER	STOCKS
IGANGVAERENDE ARBEJDER	WORK-IN-PROGRESS
ANDRE FORDRINGER	OTHER DEBTORS
PASSIVER or *GAELD*	*LIABILITIES*
KORTFRISTET GAELD	CURRENT LIABILITIES
KREDITORER	CREDITORS
VEKSELGAELD	BILLS PAYABLE
FORUDBETALING FRA KUNDER	ADVANCE PAYMENTS FROM CUSTOMERS
BANKGAELD	BANK OVERDRAFT
SKYLDIGT UDBYTTE	DIVIDENDS DUE
SKYLDIGE SKATTER	TAXES DUE
LANGFRISTET GAELD	LONG-TERM LIABILITIES
PRIORITETSGAELD	MORTGAGES
UDSKUDT SKAT	DEFERRED TAX
UDBYTTEGIVENDE GAELSBREVE	DEBENTURES
UDBYTTE TIL AKTIONAERERNE	DIVIDENDS DUE TO SHAREHOLDERS
INVESTERINGSFONDS	INVESTMENT FUNDS
EGENKAPITAL	NET CAPITAL
BUNDEN EGENKAPITAL	FIXED CAPITAL

AKTIEKAPITAL	SHARE CAPITAL
LOVPLIGTIG RESERVE-FOND	LEGAL RESERVES
FRI EGENKAPITAL	FREE CAPITAL
OVERFORSEL TIL NAESTE ÅR	RETAINED EARNINGS
GARANTIFORPLIGTELSER	CONTINGENT LIABILITIES
VARESALG	SALES
VAREFORBRUG	PURCHASES
BRUTTOFORTJENESTE *or* BRUTTOVERSKUD	GROSS PROFIT
FINANSIERINGSOM-KOSTNINGER	FINANCING COSTS
UDBYTTE	DIVIDEND
RENTEOMKOSTNINGER	INTEREST PAID
ORDINAERT DRIFTS-RESULTAT	OPERATING PROFIT
ÅRETS DRIFTSRESULTAT	PROFIT FOR YEAR
SELSKABSSKAT	COMPANY TAX
ÅRETS NETTORESULTAT *or* REGNSKABSMESSIGT OVERSKUD	NET PROFIT
SIDSTE ÅR	PRECEDING YEAR

172

Swedish	English
AKTIVA or TILLGÅNGAR	*ASSETS*
OMSÄTTNINGSTILL-GÅNGAR	CURRENT ASSETS
VÄXELFORDRINGAR *or* FRÄMMANDE VÄXLAR	BILLS RECEIVABLE
(KONTO) FORDRINGAR	DEBTORS
FORDRINGAR HOS KONCERNBOLAG	ASSOCIATE COMPANY DEBTORS
FÖRSKORT TILL LEVERANTÖRER	ADVANCE PAYMENTS TO SUPPLIERS
VARULAGER *or* VAROR	STOCKS
FÄRDIGA VAROR	FINISHED GOODS
HALVFABRIKAT	WORK-IN-PROGRESS
RAVATOR	RAW MATERIAL
MATERIALER	SUPPLIES
KASSA	CASH
BANKFORDRINGAR *or* BANKTILLGODOH *or* BANKKONTON	BANK BALANCES
ANLÄGGNINGSTILL-GÅNGAR	FIXED ASSETS
JORDOMRÅDEN *or* JORDFASTIGHETER	LAND
BYGGNADER	BUILDINGS
INDUSTRIFASTIGHETER	PLANT
MASKINERIER	MACHINERY
INVENTARIER	FIXTURES AND FITTINGS
AVSKRIVNING	DEPRECIATION
INVESTERINGSTILL-GÅNGAR	INVESTMENTS
VÄRDEPAPPER	SECURITIES
PASSIVA OR SKULDER OCH EGET KAPITAL	*LIABILITIES*
KORTFRISTIGA SKULDER	CURRENT LIABILITIES
VÄXELSKULDER	BILLS PAYABLE
BANKSKULDER	BANK DEBTS
LEVERANTÖRSSKULDER *or* KONTOSKULDER	CREDITORS

SKULDER TILL KONCERNBOLAG	ASSOCIATE COMPANY CREDITORS
SKATT	TAXATION
ERHÅLLNA FÖRSÅLJNING-SFÖRSKOTT	ADVANCE PAYMENTS FROM CUSTOMERS
LANGFRISTIGA SKULDER	LONG-TERM DEBTS
PENSIONFUND or PENSIONSKASSA	PENSION FUND
INTECKNINSLÅN	MORTGAGE LOAN
OBLIGATSONSLÅN	BOND LOAN
URVECKLINGSFOND	DEVELOPMENT FUNDS
DIVIDENDER	DIVIDENDS
RESERVING FÖR KREDITRISKER or KREDITFÖRLUSTRESERV	BAD DEBT RESERVE
SKATTERESERVFOND	TAX RESERVES
AKTIEKAPITAL	SHARE CAPITAL
RESERVFOND	CAPITAL RESERVES
FRÅN FÖREGÅENDE AR VINST	BROUGHT FORWARD BALANCE ON PROFIT AND LOSS
VINSTSALDO	PROFIT BALANCE
ÅRETS VINST	THIS YEAR'S PROFIT
ANSVARSFÖRBINDELSER	CONTINGENT LIABILITIES
FAKTURERAD FÖRSÄLJNING	TURNOVER
TILLVERKNINGS-, FÖRSÄLJNINGS OCH ADMINISTRATIONSKOSTNADER	COST OF SALES, SALES AND ADMINISTRATIVE EXPENSES
BRUTTORESULTAT	GROSS PROFIT
RÖRELSRESULTAT	OPERATING PROFIT
REDOVISAD NETTOVINST	NET PROFIT

SPANISH-ENGLISH

Spanish	English
ACTIVO	*ASSETS*
INMOVILIZADO	FIXED ASSETS
TERRENSO	LAND
INMUEBLES	PROPERTY
MAQUINARIA	MACHINERY
UTILES Y HERRAMIENTAS	TOOLS
INVERSIONES	INVESTMENTS
ACTIVO CIRCULANTE	CURRENT ASSETS
CUENTAS CORRIENTES or DEUDORES	DEBTORS
EFFECTOS A COBRAR	BILLS RECEIVABLE
ALMACANES or EXISTENCIAS	STOCKS
OBRA EN CURSO or TRABAJOS EN CURSO	WORK-IN-PROGRESS
FABRICACION EXISTENCIAS	FINISHED GOODS
MATERIA PRIMA	RAW MATERIAL
CAJA Y BANCOS	CASH AND BANK BALANCES
CARTERA DE VALORES	SECURITIES
ANTICIPOS EN COMPRAS	ADVANCE PAYMENTS TO SUPPLIERS
REALIZABLE A LARGO PLAZO	'LONG-TERM' CURRENT ASSETS
REALIZABLE A CORTO PLAZO	'SHORT-TERM' CURRENT ASSETS
PASIVO	*LIABILITIES*
EXIGIBLE A CORTO PLAZO	CURRENT LIABILITIES
SALDOS ACREEDORES	CREDITORS
PROVEEDORES	SUPPLIERS
CREDITOS BANCARIOS	BANK CREDIT
EFECTOS A PAGAR	BILLS PAYABLE
IMPTOS. YS. S. PTES DE PAGO	TAX PAYABLE
DIVIDENDO	DIVIDEND
EXIGIBLE A MEDI Y LARGO PLAZO	MEDIUM AND LONG-TERM LIABILITIES
FONDOS PROPIOS	SHAREHOLDERS' FUNDS
CAPITAL SOCIAL	SHARE CAPITAL

RESERVA	RESERVE
AMORTIZACIONES	DEPRECIATION
CUENTA PERDIDAS Y GANANCIAS	*PROFIT AND LOSS ACCOUNT*
BENEFICIO	PROFIT
REMANENTE EJERCICIO ANTERIOR	BALANCE FROM PREVIOUS FISCAL YEAR
IMPUESTOS	TAX
PREVISIONES	PROVISIONS
INGRESOS DE EXPLOTACION	GROSS REVENUE
RESULTADO BRUTO DE EXPLOTACION	GROSS PROFIT
GASTOS FINANCIEROS	FINANCIAL EXPENSES

NORWEGIAN-ENGLISH

Norwegian	English
EIENDELER OR AKTIVA	*ASSETS*
ANLEGGSMILDER *or* ANLEGGS AKTIVA	FIXED ASSETS
BYGNINGER	BUILDINGS
MASKINER OG INVENTAR	MACHINERY AND EQUIPMENT
OBLIGASJONER OG ANDRE VERDIPAPIRER	BONDS AND OTHER SECURITIES
INVESTERINGER	INVESTMENTS
OMLÖPSMILDER *or* OMLOPS AKTIVA	CURRENT ASSETS
LAGER	STOCKS
LAGER AV RÅVARER	RAW MATERIALS
HALVFABRIKATA UNDER TILVIRKNING *or* MATERIALE UNDER BEARBEIDUNG	WORK-IN-PROGRESS
VARER BEREGNET TIL VIDERESALG	FINISHED GOODS
DEBITORER	DEBTORS
VEKSELFORDRINGER	BILLS RECEIVABLE
KONTANTER, BANKINN-SKUDD OG INNESTÅENDE PÅ POSTGIRO	CASH IN HAND, BANK AND POST GIRO ACCOUNT
FORSKUDD TIL LEVERAN-DÖRER	PREPAYMENTS
GJELD OG EGENKAPITAL	*LIABILITIES AND EQUITY CAPITAL*
KORTSIKTIGE FORPLIK-TELSER *or* KORTSIKTIG GJELD	CURRENT LIABILITIES
KREDITORER	CREDITORS
VEKSELGJELD	BILLS PAYABLE
KASSA KREDITT	BANK OVERDRAFT
UTLIKNET SKATT	TAXATION
FORSKUDD FRA KUNDER	ADVANCES FROM CUSTOMERS
LANGSIKTIG GJELD	LONG-TERM DEBT

EGENKAPITAL *or*	SHARE CAPITAL
AKSJEKAPITAL	
RESERVE FOND	RESERVES
ÅRSOVERSKUDD *or*	YEAR'S PROFIT OR LOSS
ÅRSUNDERSKUDD	
PANTSTILLESLER	MORTGAGES
TAPS OG VINNINGS KONTO	*PROFIT AND LOSS ACCOUNT*
SALGS INTEKTER *or*	SALES
OMSETNING	
INNKJÖP	PURCHASES
AVSKRIVNINGER	DEPRECIATION
BRUTTO SALGSINNTEKT	TRADING PROFIT
RENTEUTGIFTER	INTEREST PAID
NETTO INNTEKT EFTER	NET PROFIT AFTER TAX
SKATTER	

PORTUGUESE-ENGLISH

Portuguese	English
ACTIVO	*ASSETS*
IMOBILIZADO	FIXED ASSETS
IMOVEIS	PROPERTY
MOVEIS E UTENSILIOS	FURNITURE AND FIXTURES
INCORPOREO	INTANGIBLE ASSETS
DISPONIVEL	LIQUID ASSETS
CAIXA	CASH
BANCOS	BANK BALANCES
REALIZAVEL	CURRENT ASSETS
CLIENTES	DEBTORS
PROV. P/COB. DUVID	BAD DEBT PROVISION
LETRAS A RECEBER	BILLS RECEIVABLE
FORNECEDORES	PAID IN ADVANCE TO SUPPLIERS
REMANESCENTES *or* ARMAZENA	STOCKS
ARMZ. MAT. PRIMAS	RAW MATERIAL
ARMZ. PROD. P/RECUP	WORK-IN-PROGRESS
PROV. P/DEPR. EXIST	PROVISION FOR STOCK DEPRECIATION
REINTEGRAÇOES	DEPRECIATION
CUSTOS ANTECIPADOS	PRE-PAID EXPENSES
DEVEDORES DIVERSOS	SUNDRY DEBTORS
PASSIVO	*LIABILITIES*
EXIGIVEL	CURRENT LIABILITIES
FORNECEDORES	CREDITORS
CLIENTES	CUSTOMERS
LETRAS A PAGAR	BILLS PAYABLE
EMPRESTIMO TERCEIROS	LOANS TO THIRD PARTIES
IMPOSTA	TAX
IMP. TRANSACÇOES	ADDED VALUE TAX
RENDAS	INCOME
CONTAS DE ORDEM	CONTINGENT LIABILITIES
LETRAS DESCONTADAS	DISCOUNTED BILLS
CANHOS E PERDAS *or* LUCROS E PERDAS	PROFIT AND LOSS
VENDAS	SALES
CUSTO DA MERCADORIA VENDIDA	COST OF SALES

DESPESAS C/O PESSOAL	LABOUR COSTS
ENCARGOS FINANCEIROS	FINANCIAL CHARGES
DESPESAS GER. DE FABRICO	PRODUCTION COSTS
DESPESAS GER. ADMINISTRATIVAS	ADMINISTRATION EXPENSES
DESPESAS DE VIAT. E DISTRIB	TRANSPORT AND DISTRIBUTION COSTS

FINNISH-ENGLISH

Finnish	English
OMAISUUS	*ASSETS*
KÄYTTÖOMAISUUS	FIXED ASSETS
INVESTOINNIT	INVESTMENTS
VARAT	CURRENT ASSETS
VARASTO	STOCKS
KESKENERÄISET TYOT	WORK-IN-PROGRESS
TILISAATAVAT *or* VELALLISET	DEBTORS
KÄTEINEN *or* KÄTEISTA	CASH
VELAT	*LIABILITIES*
TILIVELAT *or* VELKOJAT	CREDITORS
PANKKIVELAT	BANK OVERDRAFT
LYHYTAIKAISET VELAT *or* YHTEENSÄ	TOTAL CURRENT LIABILITIES
VEROJA	TAX
OSAKEPÄÄOMA	ISSUED CAPITAL
VARAUKSET	RESERVES
OMAPÄÄOMA	SHAREHOLDERS' FUNDS
LAINAT	LOANS
VIERAS PÄÄOMA	LOAN CAPITAL
VOITTO	PROFIT
MYYNTI	SALES
OSTOT	PURCHASES
LIIKEVOITTO	TRADING PROFIT
MAKSETUT KOROT	INTEREST PAID
VOITTO ENNEN VEROJA	PROFIT BEFORE TAX
VOITTO VEROT VÄHENNETTYINÄ	PROFIT AFTER TAX
PÄÄTTYNYT TILIKAUSI	YEAR ENDED
YHTEENSÄ	TOTAL

181

Chapter 12

Contract terms, documentation, payment terms and letters of credit

Compared to the domestic market, the export trade offers a bewildering choice of terms. The credit manager must not only understand how they work, but also how to make the most appropriate choice.

Export terminology

Before examining these terms, it is essential to understand the basic terminology and documents of the export trade. Full coverage of these leads into the study of contract, mercantile and international laws, which is beyond the scope of this book. The recognised authority on these and other related subjects is *The Export Trade* by Clive Schmithoff, (Stevens and Sons Ltd).

Shipping terms and their meaning are known as *Incoterms* — defined by the International Chamber of Commerce and accepted throughout the world. All quotations and invoices should state that Incoterms apply. The principle terms which the credit manager should be familiar with are as follows:

Ex-works

The price will include packing for export. The buyer must arrange for collection from the seller's premises and all carriage and insurance costs to his own premises. Property and risk pass from the seller when the buyer is notified that the goods are at his disposal. From a credit viewpoint, these are the best contract terms. So long as the buyer or his agent signs for the goods, there can be no problem about proof of delivery. No delivery period is involved so the credit period is clearcut.

FOB (free on board)

The principal obligations of the seller are:
a   To place on board ship the specified goods.
b   To pay all handling and transport charges.
c   To cover all expenses incurred to that point.
d   To notify the buyer to enable him to arrange marine insurance.
e   To bear any costs and charges in passing Customs.
   The principal obligations of the buyer are:
a   To advise the seller in good time which ship is to be used — in time to meet delivery requirements.
b   To ensure space is available in the vessel.
c   To bear any costs and charges in passing out of port.
d   To provide substitute vessels if necessary and to bear any costs arising therefrom.
   Other points to note are:
a   Buyer must arrange and pay for freight and marine insurance.
b   Property in goods passes when goods cross the ship's rail — unless otherwise stipulated.
c   Unless otherwise stated, it is seller's responsibility to obtain an export licence.

CIF

A CIF contract does not really relate to the sale of goods but a sale of the documents relating to the goods. *Delivery of shipping documents is equivalent to delivery of the goods.* The principal obligations of the seller are:
a   To ship at the port of shipment the specified goods.
b   To procure a contract of affreightment under which goods will be delivered to the specified destination.
c   **To arrange appropriate insurance.**

183

d   To make out a proper invoice.

e   To render these documents to the buyer so he may obtain delivery or recover for the loss of the goods.

   The principal obligations of the buyer are:

a   To bear all risks after goods have passed the ship's rail — provided seller has tendered proper documents.

b   Take up the documents — if in order — and pay according to the contract terms.

c   Pay even *before* arrival, receipt or examination of goods.

d   Take delivery at port of destination and bear costs of unloading and any freight not included in the seller's invoice.

e   Bear all cost incurred during voyage (except freight included in seller's invoice), including any demurrage.

f   Obtain any import licence or other necessary document.

g   Bear all costs of customs duties, taxes, etc.

C & F

As for CIF, except that the arrangement of insurance, paragraph *c* under CIF, is an obligation of the buyer rather than the seller.

Franco

Followed by the delivery address of the buyer, this gives the seller the responsibility for all costs 'door to door'.

Documentation (See also Appendix 3 — SITPRO)

Export documentation is many an exporter's nightmare. Payment delays are frequently the result of documentation errors, and while the credit manager will probably not be responsible for preparing documents, it is good practice for all export paperwork to be checked and despatched by the credit department. This should certainly apply to all documents going to a bank. The principal documents to consider are:

1   Commercial invoices.
2   Consular invoices.
3   Insurance certificates.
4   Bills of lading.
5   Airways bills.
6   Forwarding agent's receipt.

7   Certificates of origin.
8   Trust receipt.

Commercial invoices

Apart from the standard information which appears on all invoices, the following must also be included:

a   Type of contract, e.g. C & F Antwerp, after the invoice value.
b   Shipping marks and number.
c   Name of vessel.
d   Currency of invoice.
e   Declaration of origin of goods (commonly required by importing authorities).

Some countries require commercial invoices to be legalised by their embassy in the exporter's country or be certified by an authorised UK Chamber of Commerce.

Consular invoices

These are a common requirement in South America. A special form has to be obtained from the appropriate embassy in the UK and completed by the exporter. It then has to be stamped by the embassy, who will make a charge. There are specialist agencies providing a service in this field which can sometimes reduce or avoid bureaucratic delays through their use of regular contacts.

Insurance certificates

An insurance company's certificate is needed as evidence of insurance in any contract beyond C & F in terms of the exporter's responsibility. It is not sufficient to have a cover note or broker's certificate; these are not accepted by banks handling documents as evidence of insurance.

Bills of lading

The most important documents in overseas trade, since they are both a receipt for goods by the shipping company and also documents of title. Whoever possesses an original Bill of Lading is considered the owner of the goods. Bills are raised in sets, usually three or more originals plus copies. The presentation of one original is sufficient to obtain the goods. If goods are sold on open account terms, the Bill of Lading accompanies the goods with another original mailed direct to the buyer so that he can take possession on arrival in his country. If documentary terms are operating, the exporter must ensure that Bills of Lading are only given to the importer against payment or acceptance. In the 'Consignee' box, the word 'order' should be entered, and the exporter must endorse the reverse of the document. Alternatively, the words 'to order of the bank' (or another third party, if required under the terms of a Letter of Credit) may be entered — in this case ownership of the goods will not pass until the bank adds its endorsement. If the goods are to be sent direct to the buyer on open account terms, the name of the buyer is entered in the consignee box and the Bill of Lading is not a negotiable document.

A Bill of Lading is said to be 'clean' if it is signed by the shipping company without qualification. If goods or packing are received damaged or, in some respect, inconsistent with the Bill of Lading, the Bill will be 'claused' appropriately and it ceases to be a clean Bill. This is of great importance where payment is to be made under a Letter of Credit, as a clean Bill of Lading is normally a prerequisite. Clausing will also occur if dangerous goods are involved or goods are stowed on deck. To avoid this problem in trades such as chemicals, the buyer must try to have a Credit worded so as to allow shipment on deck.

Similarly a Letter of Credit may demand a 'shipped' Bill of Lading, which means that the word 'shipped' must be included. It can happen that instead of 'shipped' the Bill says 'received for shipment', which may mean that the goods are still at the docks awaiting loading. Any such endorsements must be dated by the shipping company and any alterations properly authenticated.

A problem frequently encountered is the difficulty in getting Bills of Lading to the bank within the time specified under a Letter of Credit. If no time limit is stipulated, banks will accept documents within 21 days of document date. This should be sufficient time but credits do sometimes demand presentation within a shorter period. Forwarding agents (who deal with the shipping company for the exporter) are not always able to meet such deadlines, unless prior arrangements are made. If sufficient attention is paid to this, the credit manager should be able to obtain Bills of Lading within three to four days.

Another common problem which can result in payment being withheld by the bank is the omission of the words 'freight prepaid' on the Bill of Lading on CIF and C & F contracts. Unless a credit account has been established, the seller is obliged to pay the shipping company or forwarding agent *before* Bills of Lading are handed over. Not being aware of this until too late is a frequent reason for late presentation of documents. Even where credit terms exist, payment is usually required within a very short period and special arrangements have to be made. The credit manager would do well to check on all the terms operating with the company's shipping lines or forwarding agents.

There are a number of special types of Bills of Lading, depending on the method of shipment and the route involved. Unless specifically prohibited in the terms of a Letter of Credit, the following types of Bill are accepted by the banks as being documents of title:

1   Short Form Bill of Lading.
2   Through Bill of Lading (also known as Combined Transport Document).
3   Container Bill of Lading.

Types of Bill *not* acceptable to a bank unless specifically authorised by a Credit are:

1   Bills of Lading issued by forwarding agents.
2   Charter-party Bills of Lading.
3   Bills of Lading covering shipment by sailing vessel.

Airway Bills

Also known as air consignment notes, these are *receipts only* and *not* documents of title. In order to retain control of goods, the exporter must consign the goods to a bank (through prior arrangement). This also applies to rail consignment notes.

Forwarding agent's receipt

As the name indicates, this does not give evidence of shipment but only of receipt for shipment.

Where goods are sent by 'groupage', i.e. several exporters' goods sharing one container, the forwarding agent's receipt (known in this instance as a 'House Bill of Lading') will be the only document available to the exporter, because the container bill will relate to the full container-load. The exporter sends the House Bill to his buyer, who presents it to the overseas forwarding agent who is responsible for distributing the container contents.

Certificate of origin

A declaration of the origin of the goods is frequently required from the exporter by the importing country. Sometimes a signed statement on the commercial invoice is sufficient. Some markets require a combined certificate of value and origin, others demand a separate document usually issued and stamped by a Chamber of Commerce.

Trust receipt

Where a bank is asked by the buyer to release title documents or goods before payment is made, on a 'documents against payment' transaction, it may choose to do so against a trust receipt. This binds the buyer to take the goods into safe keeping and to make the outstanding payment within an agreed period. Banks only accept trust receipts from customers of undoubted standing, since failure to pay leaves the bank fully responsible to the exporter.

Choosing payment terms

The first principle is to set the shortest possible terms that are compatible with winning or retaining business. The reasons for this are:

a   Time costs money and extended credit reduces profit margins.
b   The longer the period of credit, the greater the risk of non-payment.
c   A short credit period facilitates a greater volume of business within a credit limit.

The following payment terms will be considered in this chapter.
1   Cash with order.
2   Cash on delivery.
3   Letter of Credit.

Bills of Exchange and open account terms will be examined in Chapter 13.

Cash with order

This is obviously the safest method of trading, but its use is generally confined to 'one-off' orders from unknown buyers. Exchange control regulations in a number of markets do not permit advance payment, e.g. France (except by the approval of the Bank of France).

Cash on delivery

The success of COD terms depends largely on the efficiency of the postal service in the buyer's country, since there is no alternative to the Post Office if goods are to be sent on this basis. Other transporters and carriers will usually not handle goods if payment has to be obtained from the buyer at the time of delivery. It may be possible to have the parcel delivered to a bank in the buyer's locality, with instructions for it to be released only against payment. This method depends entirely upon a prior arrangement with the bank, and the exporter must not assume that an overseas bank will accept such an arrangement.

Putting the above two terms (CWO and COD) aside, conditions of payment are either documentary or open account. Documentary terms have been developed over many years as a means of enabling traders unknown to each other to buy and sell with varying degrees of security. This has been made possible by the international banking system acting as an intermediary. Banks operate under rules laid down by the International Chamber of Commerce, in particular the *Uniform Customs and Practice for Documentary Credits* and the *Uniform Rules for Collection* (Revised Edition 1979). These booklets are essential references for the export credit manager. They may be obtained from the British National Committee of the ICC, 6/14 Dean Farrar St, London SW1H 0DT or from one's own bank. The full text of both is given in the appendices to Chapters 12 and 13.

Letters of Credit

A documentary credit is an undertaking by the buyer's bank to pay an agreed sum of money to the seller under certain precisely defined conditions. This has clear benefits to both parties. The seller is now certain of payment from a bank — providing he complies with the Credit in every respect — as opposed to hoping for payment from an unknown buyer in an unknown market. The buyer knows that payment will only be made on his behalf against the evidence he is demanding.

For a buyer to agree Letter of Credit terms he must first arrange that his bank will issue a credit. This will only be possible if the buyer has adequate facilities with his bank. Refusal by a buyer to open a credit (in a market where it is normal practice) may therefore be interpreted by the exporter as an indication of strained resources, and requests for less secure terms should be examined cautiously. In some markets the issue of Letters of Credit is controlled by the central bank, and in time of economic stress, regulations may be imposed aimed at restricting the outflow of currency. Thus in the Nigerian Budget of April 1978 no credit could be opened without the importer first depositing 100 per cent of the value with the central bank. In 1976 the Government of

189

Brazil made a similar ruling, linking it with the issue of foreign exchange.

It should not be forgotten that the buyer also benefits from Letter of Credit terms. The precise documentation requirements which the buyer dictates will ensure that payment need only be made if the price, despatch dates, ports of loading and unloading, condition and description of the goods is exactly as ordered.

The confirming or advising bank acts strictly as an agent of the issuing bank, and it has no responsibility beyond checking the documents. It has been known for payment to be made under a credit, yet on arrival and inspection the goods are found to be totally incorrect, e.g. bananas instead of radios. The bank can only be held liable if it fails to detect a discrepancy or lack of conformity in the documents. The basic principle is that banks deal in documents, not in goods.

There are four types of Credit:

1 Revocable Credits Very rarely used, since they offer no protection to the seller. Once established they can be amended or cancelled either by the buyer or by the issuing bank.

2 Irrevocable Credits Once opened, an irrevocable credit cannot be modified or cancelled without the consent of both buyer and seller.

3 Unconfirmed Irrevocable Credits Payment remains the responsibility of the issuing or opening bank. The issuing bank in the buyer's country will normally contact the seller via an 'advising bank' in the seller's country. The advising bank has no obligation to pay the beneficiary, but it will generally do so providing, first, that the conditions of the credit are complied with and, secondly, that it has no serious doubts about being reimbursed by the issuing bank without delay. When advising unconfirmed credits, a bank usually adds the words 'this credit does not bear our confirmation' (or similar).

4 Confirmed Irrevocable Credits For the exporter these are the only safe type of credit. The advising bank is requested by the opening bank to 'add its confirmation'. By doing so it becomes the 'confirming bank' and assumes all the obligations of the issuing bank. Providing the beneficiary presents documents in complete conformity with the credit, the confirming bank has to pay — regardless of any doubts that may have arisen about reimbursement.

There are two advantages to the exporter in having a confirmed credit. Firstly, it eliminates any doubts about the standing of the opening bank. Commercial standards and regulations in some parts of the world fall far below those of the UK and not all establishments calling themselves banks are worthy of the name. Some markets are notorious for producing banks those existence goes no further than the name on their notepaper. A useful reference book is the *Bankers' Almanac*, an annual publication listing the principal banks of the world. A summary of the latest balance sheet is given, details of branches and the names of London and New York correspondents. Extreme caution should be exercised in dealing with any bank not listed in the *Bankers' Almanac*.

The second advantage is that the transfer risk is removed. The exporter, having contracted to receive payment in sterling or another currency of his choice and having obtained a Letter of Credit, must overcome the final problem of how to bring payment into his own bank. Confirmation by a UK bank solves their problem since payment is assured against correct presentation of documents. When this protection is most needed, however, it is often not available. There comes a point when shortage of foreign exchange in a market becomes so acute that UK banks will refuse to confirm credits because they can see a high risk of not being repaid by the issuing bank. This situation arose with credits opened by Turkish banks in 1977-9. Unless the opening bank actually had sterling funds in London which a UK bank could draw on, confirmation was not possible. It is not normally considered necessary to seek confirmation of credits raised by first-class banks, particularly when the advising bank is a branch or even the head office of the opening bank. This rule does not apply, however, if there is a severe foreign exchange problem in the buyer's country. Confirmation should always be sought in that situation.

It follows from the above that an exporter, on receiving an unconfirmed credit, is entitled to find a bank willing to confirm. The correct procedure is for the seller to try and arrange that the UK bank's confirmation is requested by the opening bank (on instructions from the buyer).

In this situation the seller should be prepared to pay confirmation costs. These will vary but will generally be as much again as the original opening cost.

Payment under Letter of Credit

Payment may be 'at sight', i.e. on presentation of specified documents or at a fixed future date up to 180 days from sight. Bank of England approval is required for a bank to advise or confirm a credit which is payable beyond 180 days. This is normally only allowed for capital

191

Exhibit 12.1

Term bill drawn on	Acceptance necessary?	Beneficiary obtains payment by
(a) *Advising bank*	*Yes*	*Discounting bill with advising bank (or his own bank) at a fine rate*
(b) *Issuing bank*	*Yes*	*Sight payment from advising bank*
(c) *Buyer*	*No*	*Negotiating bill with advising bank at ordinary market rate*

goods. In either case the credit will call for bills (sight or term) to be drawn, usually on the advising bank but sometimes on the buyer or on the issuing bank. The exporter enjoys the same security with a term bill as with a sight payment, since the documents are only passed to the customer after the bill is accepted. An accepted bill, drawn on the advising bank under a Letter of Credit, may be discounted by the exporter — at a fine rate because it bears the bank's name. A term bill drawn on the buyer may be negotiated by the exporter in the UK before it has been accepted but at a higher rate of interest, since it does not carry the bank's name although the issuing bank is ultimately responsible. Term bills drawn on and accepted by the issuing bank can be discounted, and the beneficiary is paid at sight by the advising bank. These different ways of obtaining payment before maturity are summarised as shown in Exhibit 12.1.

Assuming the credit is unconfirmed, there is a theoretical right of recourse from the advising bank to the beneficiary. In practice, if there are serious doubts about obtaining reimbursement on due date, the advising bank will not put its name to a bill [*(a)* above] or will only negotiate [*(b)* and *(c)* above] where the *beneficiary's* standing is beyond question.

When a Letter of Credit calls for term bills, it is sometimes referred to as a Documentary Acceptance Credit. This should not be confused with an Acceptance Credit (see Chapter 16).

Opening the credit

It is normal for a buyer to request a pro-forma invoice containing details to be included in the Letter of Credit. At this stage the exporter should do his utmost to ensure a favourable credit. Points to note are as follows:

a   Allow as big a safety margin as possible in the shipment date. If the credit expires too soon after the promised date, the exporter may have to seek an extension which can take a long while to arrive. If the validity of the credit is linked to the expiry of an import licence or the availability of foreign exchange, extension or renewal may be refused.

b   Specify that shipment may be made from any UK port. A dock strike could prevent shipment from the original chosen port. 'UK' is better than 'English' in this context.

c   If there is any possibility that part-shipment or transshipment may be necessary, request permission to be given in the credit.

d   Ask that the buyer instructs his bank to advise the credit through the exporter's bank, with a request that the latter be asked to add their confirmation. If the exporter's bank is not a correspondent of the opening bank this will not work, but it is worth trying.

e   The seller must check his pro-forma carefully for any spelling errors, incorrect part numbers, descriptions, etc. If there are any, they will be repeated on the credit which can easily lead to problems.

Checking the credit

The Letter of Credit is generally received by the sales office. Copies should immediately be given to the credit department and the shipping department. All these offices should have a checklist, and the credit must be examined line-by-line to ensure that its conditions can be fulfilled and payment obtained. A specimen checklist is given in Appendix 1 to this chapter.

If discrepancies or errors are found, the buyer must be asked to arrange an amendment, if time permits. Some errors, such as incorrect spelling, may be easier to accept than have amended, providing the same errors are repeated in the documents. Any amendment request must be made direct to the buyer, since he alone can instruct the opening bank.

Serious problems arise when a necessary amendment has not arrived before the expiry date for shipping. If the buyer has cabled that the amendment is 'on its way', the exporter must decide whether to ship or whether to await the amendment. When sailings to the buyer's country are infrequent or it is difficult to book shipping space at short notice it is tempting to take a chance, especially if failure to deliver on time could mean missing an opportunity. In this situation, however, the exporter would be well advised *not* to take a chance unless his relationship with and knowledge of the buyer gives sufficient confidence in the buyer's good faith. Even when this confidence exists, however, the exporter must check that any import licence or exchange control regulations are not being infringed.

Presenting the documents

Bankers never grow tired of telling exporters about the high percentage of documents containing errors. If thorough checks are made in providing information to the buyer to open the credit and against the credit when it arrives, the chances of error on presentation are greatly reduced.

While the task of obtaining, preparing and collating documents will usually fall to the shipping office or possibly the invoice department, the credit manager should have the final responsibility of getting the documents to the bank. This is because part of the credit manager's job is to ensure that payment of all sales arrives on time. In export business this demands close relationships with all banks who are involved in the payment process. Nonetheless, situations will occur where documents do not comply with the credit terms, such as where the Bill of Lading is claused or where documents are presented outside the validity of the credit. Some errors can be corrected by the exporter, providing there is sufficient time. These include for example the omission of the words 'freight prepaid' on a Bill of Lading (necessary on C & F and CIF contracts), or omitting to endorse the Bill of Lading. When discrepancies occur which cannot be put right, the exporter has a choice of one of three actions:

1   Ask the advising/confirming bank to cable the issuing bank for approval to pay or accept despite the errors.
2   Ask the advising/confirming bank to send the documents to the issuing bank on a collection basis.
3   Ask the advising/confirming bank to pay against an indemnity, either from the exporter or from his bank. (That is, the bank has recourse to the beneficiary or his bank if the opening bank refuses to accept the documents.)

The first of these is generally preferable to the others, although in some markets inefficient banks can take weeks to reply to a cable. Sending documents out on a collection basis means surrendering the protection of the credit. The issuing of indemnities, while sometimes unavoidable, is a bad practice because if it is done often, it inevitably encourages careless handling of documentation.

A bank has a duty to examine all documents presented under a credit. If the exporter includes documents which are not actually required but which are found to be inconsistent with those that are required, the bank can refuse to pay.

Documentary credits always have a time limit, beyond which documents will not be accepted. Sometimes two expiry dates are given, one for the latest shipment date and one for presentation of documents. If no deadline is indicated for presentation of documents, under the *Uniform Customs and Practices for Documentary Credits*, the exporter must submit documents within 21 days of the date of shipment. This 21-day period is nonetheless subordinate to the final expiry date of the credit.

The exporter can request his buyer to renew or extend the validity of a credit. It should be noted that the renewal of confirmation of a credit is not given automatically when the credit itself is renewed. An example of this occurred in 1977 with credits which had been opened by Turkish banks with UK confirmation before the foreign exchange crisis. Exporters who subsequently applied for renewal of these credits found that confirmation by the UK banks was no longer available, except in those cases where the opening bank still had funds in the UK which had approval from the Central Bank of Turkey to be used against the credits in question.

Credits opened in foreign currency operate in precisely the same way as those in sterling. Since the exporter receives payment in foreign currency, he will probably want to eliminate his exchange risk through a forward contract. This is explained in Chapter 18.

There are a number of special kinds of credit, details as follows:

Revolving credits These enable a series of payments to be made, usually within a fixed period, up to a maximum figure for each presentation. A payment of £10,000 against a revolving credit of £100,000 results in an automatic topping-up or renewal to the full £100,000. This is a useful facility where a series of regular shipments are to be made within a known period, whose total value is unknown. Another form of revolving credit is where regular payments of fixed amounts (of say £10,000) have to be made over a fixed period of time. The credit will be opened for £10,000, available on each presentation according to the agreed timetable.

Transferable credits The beneficiary of a transferable credit is en-titled to instruct the advising bank to transfer all or part of the value of the credit to a second beneficiary. The second beneficiary obtains payment by presenting documents to the bank, in accordance with the terms of the credit. By this is meant that an export agent in the UK can ensure that his UK suppliers obtain payment out of the credit, leaving a balance (representing the agent's profit) to be drawn directly by the agent.

Appendix 1   Checklist for Letters of Credit

A   Preparing information on which customer opens Letter of Credit

1   Allow sufficient time for possible production delays, e.g. request Letter of Credit to be valid one month beyond scheduled delivery date.
2   Ensure all particulars are complete and accurate.
3   State whether part-shipment and transshipment must be permitted.
4   For FOB contracts ask that the payment be made against presentation of freight forwarder's receipt.
5   If your goods are specially made to customer specification, ask for the Letter of Credit to be opened and in your possession *before* you start manufacturing.

B   On receipt

1   Is the Letter of Credit *irrevocable*? It must be.
2   Is the Letter of Credit *confirmed by a UK or US bank*? It is infinitely preferable but not mandatory. Please contact credit department if it is not.
3   Is our name and address correct — spelling particularly?
4   Is the name of our customer correct and spelled correctly?
5   Do validity, expiration and shipping dates give sufficient time to get documents together in time to assure payments, special attention to the juxtaposition of these dates and shipping and airline schedules?
6   Is the Letter of Credit amount enough to cover our quotation? Check:
   a   Cost of goods plus profit.
   b   Inland transport to dock or airport, including wharfage and handling charges.
   c   Ocean/airline transportation charges.
   d   Forwarding fees.
   e   Consular charges.
   f   Insurance costs.
   g   Miscellaneous charges.

7   Is description of goods correct? If you decide not to ask for amendment then the customer's description of the goods must appear on *all* documents as well as your description.
8   Is quantity of goods correct?
9   If required, is partial shipment permitted?
10   Is shipment required at a given rate or amount? If so, can you conform?
11   Is shipment permitted from any place in the UK or only from one named place?
12   Does named destination (port of discharge) you quoted, or you and buyer agreed on, agree with Letter of Credit?
13   Do you require export licences?
14   Is the import licence shown? (it is usually required to be shown on the invoice).
15   Is Letter of Credit in a foreign currency? If so, please contact credit department.
16   Are guarantees of any sort required by buyer?
17   Can properly executed documents be obtained to conform with Letter of Credit in the language of the buyer if required?
        Bill of Lading
        Air waybill
        Parcel post receipt
        Invoices — commercial, preferential, consular, legalised
        Packing list
        Certificate of origin
        Insurance policy certificate
        Certificate of inspection
        Certificate of Quality
     Is any specified agency required to issue or authenticate any of these documents?
18   Can you comply with cover of insurance risks required by the Letter of Credit? Does credit require policy or certificate?
19   Compare the conditions of the contract of sale with the Letter of Credit.
20   Where is payment to be made? If not in UK, does the expiry date allow sufficient time for documents to be presented at the overseas bank?

If, after having made examination of the Letter of Credit against this checklist and having compared the sales contract with the Credit, you find need for amendment or clarification of the Credit, cable your customer requesting necessary clarification or amendment, bearing in mind shipping and validity dates and the chance of amendments being received in time to honour shipping and validity dates.

Appendix 2 The Uniform Customs and Practice

General provisions and definitions

a These provisions and definitions and the following articles apply to all documentary credits and are binding upon all parties thereto unless otherwise expressly agreed.

b For the purposes of such provisions, definitions and articles the expressions 'documentary credit(s)' and 'credit(s)' used therein mean any arrangement, however named or described, whereby a bank (the issuing bank), acting at the request and in accordance with the instructions of a customer (the applicant for the credit),

> **i** is to make payment to or to the order of a third party (the beneficiary), or is to pay, accept or negotiate bills of exchange (drafts) drawn by the beneficiary, or

> **ii** authorises such payments to be made or such drafts to be paid, accepted or negotiated by another bank, against stipulated documents, provided that the terms and conditions of the credit are complied with.

c Credits, by their nature, are separate transactions from the sales or other contracts on which they may be based and banks are in no way concerned with or bound by such contracts.

d Credit instructions and the credits themselves must be complete and precise. In order to guard against confusion and misunderstanding, issuing banks should discourage any attempt by the applicant for the credit to include excessive detail.

e The bank first entitled to exercise the option available under Article 32 (b) shall be the bank authorised to pay, accept or negotiate under a credit. The decision of such bank shall bind all parties concerned.
  A bank is authorised to pay or accept under a credit by being specifically nominated in the credit.
  A bank is authorised to negotiate under a credit either
    i by being specifically nominated in the credit, or
    ii by the credit being freely negotiable by any bank.

f A beneficiary can in no case avail himself of the contractual relationships existing between banks or between the applicant for the credit and the issuing bank.

A   Form and notification of credits

Article 1
a   Credits may be either
  i   revocable, or
  ii   irrevocable.

b   All credits therefore should clearly indicate whether they are revocable or irrevocable.

c   In the absence of such indication the credit shall be deemed to be revocable.

Article 2
A revocable credit may be amended or cancelled at any moment without prior notice to the beneficiary. However, the issuing bank is bound to reimburse a branch or other bank to which such a credit has been transmitted and made available for payment, acceptance or negotiation, for any payment, acceptance or negotiation complying with the terms and conditions of the credit and any amendments received up to the time of payment, acceptance or negotiation made by such branch or other bank prior to receipt by it of notice of amendment or of cancellation.

Article 3
a   An irrevocable credit constitutes a definite undertaking of the issuing bank, provided that the terms and conditions of the credit are complied with:

  i   to pay, or that payment will be made, if the credit provides for payment, whether against a draft or not;

  ii   to accept drafts if the credit provides for acceptance by the issuing bank or to be responsible for their acceptance and payment at maturity if the credit provides for the acceptance of drafts drawn on the applicant for the credit of any other drawee specified in the credit;

  iii   to purchase/negotiate, without recourse to drawers and/or bona fide holders, drafts drawn by the beneficiary, at sight or at a tenor, on the applicant for the credit or on any other drawee specified in the credit, or to provide for purchase/negotiation by another bank, if the credit provides for purchase/negotiation.

b An irrevocable credit may be advised to a beneficiary through another bank (the advising bank) without engagement on the part of that bank, but when an issuing bank authorises or requests another bank to confirm its irrevocable credit and the latter does so, such confirmation constitutes a definite undertaking of the confirming bank in addition to the undertaking of the issuing bank, provided that the terms and conditions of the credit are complied with:

i to pay, if the credit is payable at its own counters, whether against a draft or not, or that payment will be made if the credit provides for payment elsewhere:

ii to accept drafts if the credit provides for acceptance by the confirming bank, at its own counters, or to be responsible for their acceptance and payment at maturity if the credit provides for the acceptance of drafts drawn on the applicant for the credit or any other drawee specified in the credit;

iii to purchase/negotiate, without recourse to drawers and/or bona fide holders, drafts drawn by the beneficiary, at sight or at a tenor, on the issuing bank, or on the applicant for the credit or on any other drawee specified in the credit, if the credit provides for purchase/negotiation.

c Such undertakings can neither be amended nor cancelled without the agreement of all parties thereto. Partial acceptance of amendments is not effective without the agreement of all parties thereto.

Article 4
a When an issuing bank instructs a bank by cable, telegram or telex to advise a credit, and intends the mail confirmation to be the operative credit instrument, the cable, telegram or telex must state that the credit will only be effective on receipt of such mail confirmation. In this event, the issuing bank must send the operative credit instrument (mail confirmation) and any subsequent amendments to the credit to the beneficiary through the advising bank.

b The issuing bank will be responsible for any consequences arising from its failure to follow the procedure set out in the preceding paragraph.

200

c Unless a cable, telegram or telex states 'details to follow' (or words of similar effect), or states that the mail confirmation is to be the operative credit instrument, the cable, telegram or telex will be deemed to be the operative credit instrument and the issuing bank need not send the main confirmation to the advising bank.

Article 5
When a bank is instructed by cable, telegram or telex to issue, confirm or advise a credit similar in terms to one previously established and which has been the subject of amendments, it shall be understood that the details of the credit being issued, confirmed or advised will be transmitted to the beneficiary excluding the amendments, unless the instructions specify clearly any amendments which are to apply.

Article 6
If incomplete or unclear instructions are received to issue, confirm or advise a credit, the bank requested to act on such instructions may give preliminary notification of the credit to the beneficiary for information only and without responsibility; in this event the credit will be issued, confirmed or advised only when the necessary information has been received.

B *Liabilities and responsibilities*

Article 7
Banks must examine all documents with reasonable care to ascertain that they appear on their face to be in accordance with the terms and conditions of the credit. Documents which appear on their face to be inconsistent with one another will be considered as not appearing on their face to be in accordance with the terms and conditions of the credit.

Article 8
a In documentary credit operations all parties concerned deal in documents and not in goods.

b Payment, acceptance or negotiation against documents which appear on their face to be in accordance with the terms and conditions of a credit by a bank authorised to do so, binds the party giving the authorisation to take up the documents and reimburse the bank which has effected the payment, acceptance or negotiation.

c If, upon receipt of the documents, the issuing bank considers that they appear on their face not to be in accordance with the terms and conditions of the credit, that bank must determine, on the basis of the documents alone, whether to claim that payment, acceptance or negotiation was not effected in accordance with the terms and conditions of the credit.

d   The issuing bank shall have a reasonable time to examine the documents and to determine as above whether to make such a claim.

e   If such claim is to be made, notice to that effect, stating the reasons therefor, must, without delay, be given by cable or other expeditious means to the bank from which the documents have been received (the remitting bank) and such notice must state that the documents are being held at the disposal of such bank or are being returned thereto.

f   If the issuing bank fails to hold the documents at the disposal of the remitting bank, or fails to return the documents to such bank, the issuing bank shall be precluded from claiming that the relative payment, acceptance or negotiation was not effected in accordance with the terms and conditions of the credit.

g   If the remitting bank draws the attention of the issuing bank to any irregularities in the documents or advises such bank that it has paid, accepted or negotiated under reserve or against a guarantee in respect of such irregularities, the issuing bank shall not thereby be relieved from any of its obligations under this article. Such guarantee or reserve concerns only the relations between the remitting bank and the beneficiary.

Article 9
Banks assume no liability or responsibility for the form, sufficiency, accuracy, genuineness, falsification or legal effect of any documents, or for the general and/or particular conditions stipulated in the documents or superimposed thereon; nor do they assume any liability or responsibility for the description, quantity, weight, quality, condition, packing, delivery, value or existence of the goods represented thereby, or for the good faith or acts and/or omissions, solvency, performance or standing of the consignor, the carriers or the insurers of the goods or any other person whomseovever.

Article 10
Banks assume no liability or responsibility for the consequences arising out of delay and/or loss in transit of any messages, letters or documents, or for delay, mutilation or other errors arising in the

transmission of cables, telegrams or telex. Banks assume no liability or responsibility for errors in translation or interpretation of technical terms, and reserve the right to transmit credit terms without translating them.

Article 11
Banks assume no liability or responsibility for consequences arising out of the interruption of their business by Acts of God, riots, civil commotions, insurrections, wars of any other causes beyond their control or by any strikes or lockouts. Unless specifically authorised, banks will not effect payment, acceptance or negotiation after expiration under credits expiring during such interruption of business.

Article 12
a Banks utilising the services of another bank for the purpose of giving effect to the instructions of the applicant for the credit do so for the account and at the risk of the latter.

b Banks assume no liability or responsibility should the instructions they transmit not be carried out, even if they have themselves taken the initiative in the choice of such other bank.

c The applicant for the credit shall be bound by and liable to indemnify the banks against all obligations and responsibilities imposed by foreign laws and usages.

Article 13
A paying or negotiating bank which has been authorised to claim reimbursement from a third bank nominated by the issuing bank and which has effected such payment or negotiation shall not be required to confirm to the third bank that it has done so in accordance with the terms and conditions of the credit.

C Documents

Article 14
a All instructions to issue, confirm or advise a credit must state precisely the documents against which payment, acceptance or negotiation is to be made.

b Terms such as 'first class', 'well known', 'qualified' and the like shall not be used to describe the issuers of any documents called for under credits and if they are incorporated in the credit term banks will accept documents as tendered.

C1   Documents evidencing shipment or dispatch or taking in charge (shipping documents)

Article 15
Except as stated in Article 20, the date of the Bill of Lading, or the date of any other document evidencing shipment or dispatch or taking in charge, or the date indicated in the reception stamp or by notation on any such document, will be taken in each case to be the date of shipment or dispatch or taking in charge of the goods.

Article 16
a   If words clearly indicating payment or prepayment of freight, however named or described, appear by stamp or otherwise on documents evidencing shipment or dispatch or taking in charge they will be accepted as constituting evidence of payment of freight.

b   If the words 'freight payable' or 'freight to be prepaid' or words of similar effect appear by stamp or otherwise on such documents they will not be accepted as constituting evidence of the payment of freight.

c   Unless otherwise specified in the credit or inconsistent with any of the documents presented under the credit, banks will accept documents stating that freight or transportation charges are payable on delivery.

d   Banks will accept shipping documents bearing reference by stamp or otherwise to costs additional to the freight charges, such as costs of, or disbursements incurred in connection with, loading, unloading or similar operations, unless the conditions of the credit specifically prohibit such reference.

Article 17
Shipping documents which bear a clause on the face thereof such as 'shipper's load and count' or 'said by shipper to contain' or words of similar effect, will be accepted unless otherwise specified in the credit.

Article 18
a   A clean shipping document is one which bears no superimposed

clause or notation which expressly declares a defective condition of the goods and/or the packaging.

b Banks will refuse shipping documents bearing such clauses or notations unless the credit expressly states the clauses or notations which may be accepted.

C1.1 Marine Bills of Lading

Article 19
a Unless specifically authorised in the credit, Bills of Lading of the following nature will be rejected:

    i Bills of Lading issued by forwarding agents.

    ii Bills of Lading which are issued under and are subject to the conditions of a Charter-party.

    iii Bills of Lading covering shipment by sailing vessels.

b However, subject to the above and unless otherwise specified in the credit, Bills of Lading of the following nature will be accepted:

    i 'Through' Bills of Lading issued by shipping companies or their agents even though they cover several models of transport.

    ii Short Form Bills of Lading (i.e. Bills of Lading issued by shipping companies or their agents which indicate some or all of the conditions of carriage by reference to a source or document other than the Bill of Lading).

iii Bills of Lading issued by shipping companies or their agents covering unitized cargoes, such as those on pallets or in Containers.

Article 20
a Unless otherwise specified in the credit, Bills of Lading must show that the goods are loaded on board a named vessel or shipped on a named vessel.

b Loading on board a named vessel or shipment on a named vessel may be evidenced either by a Bill of Lading bearing wording indicating loading on board a named vessel or shipment on a named vessel, or by means of a notation to that effect on the Bill of Lading signed or initialled and dated by the carrier or his agent, and the date of this notation shall be regarded as the date of loading on board the named vessel or shipment on the named vessel.

Article 21
a   Unless transshipment is prohibited by the terms of the credit, Bills of Lading will be accepted which indicate that the goods will be transshipped en route, provided the entire voyage is covered by one and the same Bill of Lading.

b   Bills of Lading incorporating printed clauses stating that the carriers have the right to tranship will be accepted notwithstanding the fact that the credit prohibits transshipment.

Article 22
a   Banks will refuse a Bill of Lading stating that the goods are loaded on deck, unless specifically authorised in the credit.

b   Banks will not refuse a Bill of Lading which contains a provision that the goods may be carried on deck, provided it does not specifically state that they are loaded on deck.

C1.2   Combined transport documents

Article 23
a   If the credit calls for a combined transport document, i.e. one which provides for a combined transport by at least two different modes of transport, from a place at which the goods are taken in charge to a place designated for delivery, or if the credit provides for a combined transport, but in either case does not specify the form of document required and/or the issuer of such documents, banks will accept such documents as tendered.

b   If the combined transport includes transport by sea the document will be accepted although it does not indicate that the goods are on board a named vessel, and although it contains a provision that the goods, if packed in a Container, may be carried on deck, provided it does not specifically state that they are loaded on deck.

C1.3   Other shipping documents, etc.

Article 24
Banks will consider a Railway or Inland Waterway Bill of Lading or Consignment Note, Counterfoil Waybill, Postal Receipt, Certificate of Mailing, Air Mail Receipt, Air Waybill, Air Consignment Note or Air Receipt. Trucking Company Bill of Lading or any other similar document as regular when such document bears the reception stamp of the carrier or his agent, or when it bears a signature purporting to be that of the carrier or his agent.

Article 25
Where a credit calls for an attestation or certification of weight in the case of transport other than by sea, banks will accept a weight stamp or declaration of weight superimposed by the carrier on the shipping document unless the credit calls for a separate or independent certificate of weight.

C2   Insurance documents

Article 26
a   Insurance documents must be as specified in the credit, and must be issued and/or signed by insurance companies or their agents or by underwriters.

b   Cover notes issued by brokers will not be accepted unless specifically authorised in the credit.

Article 27
Unless otherwise specified in the credit, or unless the insurance documents presented establish that the cover is effective at the latest from the date of shipment or despatch or, in the case of combined transport, the date of taking the goods in charge, banks will refuse insurance documents presented which bear a date later than the date of shipment or dispatch or, in the case of combined transport, the date of taking the goods in charge, as evidenced by the shipping documents.

Article 28
a   Unless otherwise specified in the credit, the insurance document must be expressed in the same currency as the credit.

b   The minimum amount for which insurance must be effected is the CIF value of the goods concerned. However, when the CIF value of

207

the goods cannot be determined from the documents on their face, banks will accept as such minimum amount the amount of the drawing under the credit or the amount of the relative commercial invoice, whichever is the greater.

Article 29
a Credits should expressly state the type of insurance required and, if any, the additional risks which are to be covered. Imprecise terms such as 'usual risks' or 'customary risks' should not be used; however, if such imprecise terms are used, banks will accept insurance documents as tendered.

b Failing specific instructions, banks will accept insurance cover as tendered.

Article 30
Where a credit stipulates 'insurance against all risks', banks will accept an insurance document which contains any 'all risks' notation or clause, and will assume no responsibility if any particular risk is not covered.

Article 31
Banks will accept an insurance document which indicates that the cover is subject to a franchise or an excess (deductible), unless it is specifically stated in the credit that the insurance must be issued irrespective of percentage.

C3 Commercial invoices

Article 32
a Unless otherwise specified in the credit, commercial invoices must be made out in the name of the applicant for the credit.

b Unless otherwise specified in the credit, banks may refuse commercial invoices issued for amounts in excess of the amount permitted by the credit.

c The description of the goods in the commercial invoice must correspond with the description in the credit. In all other documents the goods may be described in general terms not inconsistent with the description of the goods in the credit.

C4 Other documents

Article 33
When other documents are required, such as Warehouse Receipts, Delivery Orders, Consular Invoices, Certificates of Origin, of Weight, of Quality or of Analysis etc. and when no further definition is given, banks will accept such documents as tendered.

D Miscellaneous provisions
Quantity and amount

Article 34
a The words 'about', 'circa' or similar expressions used in connection with the amount of the credit or the quantity or the unit price of the goods are to be construed as allowing a difference not to exceed 10% more or 10% less.

b Unless a credit stipulates that the quantity of the goods specified must not be exceeded or reduced a tolerance of 3% more or 3% less will be permissible, always provided that the total amount of the drawings does not exceed the amount of the credit. This tolerance does not apply when the credit specifies quantity in terms of a stated number of packing units or individual items.

Partial shipments

Article 35
a Partial shipments are allowed, unless the credit specifically states otherwise.

b Shipments made on the same ship and for the same voyage, even if the Bills of Lading evidencing shipment 'on board' bear different dates and/or indicate different ports of shipment, will not be regarded as partial shipments.

Article 36
If shipment by instalments within given periods is stipulated and any instalment is not shipped within the period allowed for that instalment, the credit ceases to be available for that or any subsequent instalments, unless otherwise specified in the credit.

Expiry date

Article 37
All credits, whether revocable or irrevocable, must stipulate an expiry date for presentation of documents for payment, acceptance or negotiation, notwithstanding the stipulation of a latest date for shipment.

Article 38
The words 'to', 'until', 'till', and words of similar import applying to the stipulated expiry date for presentation of documents for payment, acceptance or negotiation, or to the stipulated latest date for shipment, will be understood to include the date mentioned.

Article 39
a When the stipulated expiry date falls on a day on which banks are closed for reasons other than those mentioned in Article 11, the expiry date will be extended until the first following business day.

b The latest date for shipment shall not be extended by reason of the extension of the expiry date in accordance with this Article. Where the credit stipulates a latest date for shipment, shipping documents dated later than such stipulated date will not be accepted. If no latest date for shipment is stipulated in the credit, shipping documents dated later than the expiry date stipulated in the credit or amendments thereto will not be accepted. Documents other than the shipping documents may, however, be dated up to and including the extended expiry date.

c Banks paying, accepting or negotiating on such extended expiry date must add to the documents their certification in the following wording: 'Presented for payment (or acceptance or negotiation as the case may be) within the expiry date extended in accordance with Article 39 of the Uniform Customs'.

Shipment, loading or dispatch

Article 40
a Unless the terms of the credit indicate otherwise, the words 'departure', 'dispatch', 'loading' or 'sailing' used in stipulating the latest date for shipment of the goods will be understood to be synonymous with 'shipment'.

b Expressions such as 'prompt', 'immediately', 'as soon as possible' and the like should not be used. If they are used, banks will interpret them as a request for shipment within thirty days from the date on the advice of the credit to the beneficiary by the issuing bank or by an advising bank, as the case may be.

c The expression 'on or about' and similar expressions will be interpreted as a request for shipment during the period from five days before to five days after the specified date, both end days included.

Presentation

Article 41
Notwithstanding the requirement of Article 37 that every credit must stipulate an expiry date for presentation of documents, credits must also stipulate a specified period of time after the date of issuance of the Bills of Lading or other shipping documents during which presentation of documents for payment, acceptance or negotiation must be made. If no such period of time is stipulated in the credit, banks will refuse documents presented to them later than 21 days after the date of issuance of the Bills of Lading or other shipping documents.

Article 42
Banks are under no obligation to accept presentation of documents outside their banking hours.

Date terms

Article 43
The terms 'first half', 'second half' of a month shall be construed respectively as from the 1st to the 15th and the 16th to the last day of each month, inclusive.

Article 44
The terms 'beginning', 'middle', or 'end' of a month shall be construed respectively as from the 1st to the 10th, the 11th to the 20th, and the 21st to the last day of each month, inclusive.

Article 45
When a bank issuing a credit instructs that the credit be confirmed or advised as available 'for one month', 'for six months' or the like, but

does not specify the date from which the time is to run, the confirming or advising bank will confirm or advise the credit as expiring at the end of such indicated period from the date of its confirmation or advice.

E   Transfer

Article 46
a   A transferable credit is a credit under which the beneficiary has the right to give instructions to the bank called upon to effect payment or acceptance or to any bank entitled to effect negotiation to make the credit available in whole or in part to one or more third parties (second beneficiaries).

b   The bank requested to effect the transfer, whether it has confirmed the credit or not, shall be under no obligation to effect such transfer except to the extent and in the manner expressly consented to by such bank, and until such bank's charges in respect of transfer are paid.

c   Bank charges in respect of transfers are payable by the first beneficiary unless otherwise specified.

d   A credit can be transferred only if it is expressly designated as 'transferable' by the issuing bank. Terms such as 'divisible', 'fractionable', 'assignable', and 'transmissible' add nothing to the meaning of the term 'transferable' and shall not be used.

e   A transferable credit can be transferred once only. Fractions of a transferable credit (not exceeding in the aggregate the amount of the credit) can be transferred separately, provided partial shipments are not prohibited, and the aggregate of such transfers will be considered as constituting only one transfer of the credit. The credit can be transferred only on the terms and conditions specified in the original credit, with the exception of the amount of the credit, of any unit prices stated therein, and of the period of validity or period for shipment, any or all of which may be reduced or curtailed.
Additionally, the name of the first beneficiary can be substituted for that of the applicant for the credit, but if the name of the applicant for the credit is specifically required by the original credit to appear in any document other than the invoice, such requirement must be fulfilled.

f   The first beneficary has the right to substitute his own invoices for those of the second beneficiary, for amounts not in excess of the original amount stipulated in the credit and for the original unit prices if stipulated in the credit, and upon such substitution of invoices the first beneficiary can draw under the credit for the difference, if any, between his invoices and the second beneficiary's invoices. When a credit has been transferred and the first beneficiary is to supply his own invoices in exchange for the second beneficiary's invoices but fails to do so on first demand, the paying, accepting or negotiating bank has the right to deliver to the issuing bank the documents received under the credit, including the second beneficiary's invoices, without further responsibility to the first beneficiary.

g   The first beneficiary of a transferable credit can transfer the credit to a second beneficiary in the same country or in another country unless the credit specifically states otherwise. The first beneficiary shall have the right to request that payment or negotiation be effected to the second beneficiary at the place to which the credit has been transferred, up to and including the expiry date of the original credit, and without prejudice to the first beneficary's right subsequently to substitute his own invoices for those of the second beneficiary and to claim any difference due to him.

Article 47
The fact that a credit is not stated to be transferable shall not affect the beneficiary's rights to assign the proceeds of such credit in accordance with the provisions of the applicable law.

Appendix 3   SITPRO

A considerable amount of work on export documentation has been done by SITPRO (Simplification of International Trade Procedures Board), 11-12 Waterloo Place, London SW1Y 4AU. It has published *Systematic Export Documentation*, which shows how exporters can both improve efficiency and save money by streamlining their documentation systems. Further information is obtainable from the above address (telephone 01-839 3393).

Chapter 13

Payment terms (continued) — Bills of Exchange and open account

Bills of Exchange

The legal definition (*The Bills of Exchange Act, 1882*) cannot be improved: 'An unconditional order in writing, addressed by one person to another, signed by the person giving it, requiring the person to whom it is addressed to pay on demand or at a fixed or determinable future time a sum certain in money to, or to the order of a specified person, or to a bearer'.

The exporter raises a Bill as the 'Drawer' and the buyer is the 'Drawee'. The 'Payee' is usually the exporter but can be a third party. If payment is to be made 'on demand' the bill is known as a *sight draft*. Payment at a future date makes it a *tenor, time* or *usance bill*.

Sight drafts

Payment by documentary sight draft gives the exporter a good measure of security, without the full protection afforded by a Letter of Credit. The only real disadvantage is that there is no safeguard against the possibility of the buyer refusing to take up the goods on arrival.

The procedure to be adopted in a sight draft transaction is as follows: When the goods have been despatched, the exporter must gather together all the required documents and raise a sight draft on the customer. Drafts are usually raised in sets of three, each one being identified as 'this first of exchange (second and third of same date being unpaid)', etc. All documents are then sent to the exporter's bank (the remitting bank) under cover of an instruction schedule (or bank lodgement form). The exporter's bank is thereby instructed to release documents to the buyer against payment. To perform this duty the remitting bank sends the documents to a bank in the buyer's country (the collecting bank). The name of the collecting bank may already have been provided by the exporter — normally when the buyer has requested the use of a particular bank. If no instructions have been given, the remitting bank will select a correspondent bank. However the collecting bank is chosen, it acts as the agent of the remitting bank and is fully responsible for handling and disposing of documents in accordance with the instruction schedule.

An alternative method, offered especially by American banks in the UK, is known as *direct collections*. The exporter's bank gives the exporter a supply of lodgement forms which the exporter completes and sends with all the documents direct to the collecting bank. A copy of the lodgement form goes to the remitting bank, who then assumes the usual responsibilities for following up. Time is clearly saved by this method, but the exporter loses the benefit of his own bank checking documents prior to sending them overseas. This checking procedure is *not* part of the remitting bank's responsibilities, but it is often undertaken as part of the bank's service to its customers.

Careful completion of the instruction schedule by the exporter is important. The following points should be noted:

a   Is the bill to be presented on receipt or should presentation await the arrival of the vessel? In some markets it is normal practice for payment (or acceptance) of bills to be deferred until the goods arrive.

b   Is payment or non-payment to be advised by cable or by airmail? To minimise costs, it may be considered sufficient for non-payment only to be advised by cable.

c   How is payment to be remitted? By airmail or by cable? The interest-saving on a cable transfer will outweigh the cost on payments over a certain level (see Chapter 14 for further consideration of this point).

d   Who should the collecting bank contact in 'case of need', i.e. if payment is refused or some other problem occurs? This will normally be the exporter's local agent. What powers does he have in determining the action to be taken?

e   Is the bill to be protested? This is examined late in this chapter.

215

f   What action is the bank to take with regard to the care and disposal of the goods if payment is not made?

g   Are the charges of both collecting and remitting banks to be paid by the buyer or by the exporter, or are they to be shared? The intention of the exporter can also be expressed through the use of a clause on the bill (see 'clauses' below).

The term 'cash against documents (CAD)', is sometimes used as an alternative to payment by sight draft. The difference is that CAD terms do not involve the raising of a Bill of Exchange. The exporter sends all the documents to his bank for release against payment. There may be a cost saving for the buyer in respect of local stamp duties on bills, but the exporter gains nothing. The absence of a properly numbered and dated Bill of Exchange from the exporter's records can also be inconvenient.

The term 'cash against goods' is occasionally encountered. The exporter is required to send documents with the goods, having first arranged that the buyer will either pay or accept a Bill of Exchange on receipt of documents. The bill is thus a clean bill, and the whole transaction is really a form of open account, since the exporter has no control over goods and relies entirely on the good faith of the customer. It occurs generally in situations which would normally call for documentary terms. Because goods arrive ahead of documents, the customer cannot clear them through customs. To avoid this problem, 'cash against goods' may be suggested. Unless the buyer is entirely trustworthy, the procedure is not recommended. A variation on this idea is to address the Bill of Lading to the collecting bank, sending it as before 'in the ship's bag'. For this method to be successful, it is essential to make prior arrangements with the bank, which will need to be located in the port of disembarkation (or near to the frontier in the case of an overland shipment).

Term bills

Term, tenor or usance bills are drawn by the exporter to be paid, either at a fixed future date or at a calculable future date, e.g. '90 days from Bills of Lading' or '60 days after sight', there is clear advantage in commencing the credit period from Bill of Lading date, and in the absence of any specific arrangements to the contrary the exporter should always do this. Expressing a bill as payable '90 days after sight' means that the period of shipment and dock clearance is effectively added on to the credit period. Also the exporter does not know the due date until advised by the collecting bank.

Under a term bill arrangement the buyer is permitted to receive documents (and therefore goods) only after 'accepting' the bill for payment on the due date. Regardless of the credit period, accepted bills are usually held by the collecting bank until maturity unless the exporter is arranging to discount them. If a collecting bank releases documents to a customer before the bill is paid or accepted and the bill is not honoured on presentation, the collecting bank is held responsible.

Term bills sometimes require documents to be released against payment. For example, on a 90-day D/P bill, after the bill is accepted the goods are placed in a bonded warehouse and the buyer has 90 days in which to pay. During this period he has an opportunity of finding customers ready to take delivery and pay him as soon as he pays the bank and takes possession of the goods.

Payment before maturity of a term bill may be obtained by the seller by negotiation through his bank. The exporter sells his bill to his bank — normally before acceptance has been obtained from the customer. If payment is not made on due date, the bank has recourse to the drawer. A sight bill may also be negotiated if the exporter prefers not to suffer the one or two months' delay normal with sight payments. The existence of an ECGD Comprehensive Short-term Guarantee, assigned to the bank, covers 90-95 per cent of the risks of non-payment, providing of course that the sale is within the agreed credit limit. If less than 100 per cent of the face value of a bill is paid by the bank, this becomes an advance rather than a negotiation.

The act of 'discounting' a bill is different. A bill must be accepted first and be payable in the locality of the discounting bank. Discounting is usually restricted to bills drawn on banks under Letters of Credit.

Bill clauses

The addition of a clause to a bill enables the drawer to give precise instructions about payment. Clauses in common use include:

'Payable with interest at . . . per cent per annum from the date hereof until arrival of funds in London.' This was known as the Eastern Clause, because it was frequently used in trade with the Far East which involved long delays in the transmission of funds.

'Payable at the current rate of exchange for sight drafts on London.' This ensures that the buyer must provide sufficient local currency to meet the sterling value of the bill on due date.

'Payable with all bank collection charges.' This assumes that the buyer has agreed to meet these costs.

'Payment may be made in local currency pending exchange control approval for the transfer of sterling.' In practice, collecting banks, unless instructed to the contrary, release documents against local currency payments without such a clause.

While the exporter can include any of the above instruction clauses on the bank lodgement form, there is clearly an advantage in entering them on the bill itself. They remain in full view to any person handling the bill, whereas a lodgement form can become separated from the bill.

Bill of Exchange problems

Demurrage

A frequent problem is demurrage, by which is meant costs imposed by port authorities when goods arrive ahead of documents and cannot be cleared from the docks. When the shipment period is only a few days, i.e. for all European and Near Eastern destinations, the exporter must either ensure that documents are obtained from the forwarding agent within 24 hours or make an arrangement with the collecting bank. By no means are all banks equipped or prepared to take delivery of goods and store them.

Article 6 of the *Uniform Rules for Collections* (see Appendix to this chapter) states: 'In the event of goods being despatched direct to the address of a bank or consigned to a bank for delivery to a drawee against payment or acceptance or upon other terms without prior agreement on the part of that bank, the bank has no obligation to take delivery of the goods, which remain at the risk and responsibility of the party despatching the goods.'

Shipments by air, road or rail

Complete security in documentary transactions is only possible where documents of title are passed to the collecting bank. (The phrase 'complete security' is not strictly accurate, since it takes no account of the possibility of fraud.)

Where shipment is by rail or road there is no document of title unless a Combined Transport Bill of Lading is used or, in the case of container deliveries, a Container Bill of Lading. Since a container bill relates to the total contents of a container, it is not usually available to an exporter as a document of title. When shipment is by air, the Airway Bill is not a document of title.

The usual answer to the question of security in these situations is that the goods should be consigned to a bank. Very often this is either not possible or not acceptable to the buyer. As far as air-freight is concerned, the prime object is speed — to deliver goods as fast as possible to the buyer. If a bank has to take possession (assuming a prior arrangement has been made), this adds considerably to the time. Some countries permit airlines to operate on a 'cash-on-delivery' basis, but many do not. Not all airlines are willing to undertake this responsibility.

Release against local currency

It is normal practice for the collecting bank to release documents (on a 'D/P' collection) against payment in local currency, although Article 12 of the *Uniform Rules* only permits this if the amount paid can be remitted immediately. Since the buyer has parted with his money, from his point of view it is entirely reasonable that he be allowed to take possession of the merchandise. For the exporter, however, the picture is quite different. In markets that are short of foreign exchange, there can be long delays before payment is permitted. To guard against the possibility of the exporter losing as a result of a devaluation of the local currency between the lodging of local currency and its transfer to the seller, the collecting bank should be asked to release documents only against a 'shortfall undertaking', i.e. the buyer guarantees to provide enough additional local currency as is needed to produce the right value for the exporter.

For example, a UK exporter supplies goods to a Ghana importer on documentary sight draft, value £1,000. The importer pays enough cedis (Ghanian currency) to buy £1,000 and obtains the documents also giving a shortfall undertaking to the collecting bank. No sterling is available for six months, and during that time the cedi is devalued by 20 per cent. In accordance with the shortfall undertaking, the buyer must give the bank additional cedis so that the total held will still buy £1,000.

Often, however, these undertakings are not effective. Local controls may prevent extra payments being made or long delays can occur, depending on the degree of priority given by the central bank to the merchandise.

219

The solutions to this problem are either to sell under a Letter of Credit, confirmed by a UK bank, or to continue on a bill basis under the protection of ECGD. Neither of these solutions is satisfactory, since in extreme cases — those that cause the most problems — UK confirmation is not available, and it is not possible to take out ECGD cover on occasional business at short notice.

Dishonour of bills

When sending a bill to the bank, the exporter must at that time decide whether to have it protested in the event of non-payment. Protesting is done by having a notary public complete a deed of protest to the effect that payment has been refused on due date. This evidence of non-payment can be produced in court, and in many countries it is a necessary first step towards court action for the recovery of payment.

The regulations for protesting bills vary from country to country, some requiring protest to be made within 24 hours of presentation and others allowing several years before the right to protest disappears. The best reference book on this subject is *British Exports and Exchange Restrictions Abroad*, published by the Swiss Bank Corporation, 99 Gresham St, London EC2.

The effect of protest also differs according to the market. In some countries the protesting of a bill is tantamount to an act of bankruptcy on the part of the buyer, and in others his reputation will be severely damaged.

It is, therefore, important that the exporter should check both on the protest regulations and on the effect of protesting in all markets where bill terms are used and to mark his records accordingly. If an ECGD policy is held, the exporter is normally expected to protest bills, since failure to do so may mean that the legal right to sue for an unpaid account is lost.

Open account

When the buyer is an established company with a good reputation on a market free from serious political or transfer risks, goods may be supplied on open account. The shipper or transporter is instructed to deliver direct to the buyers, documents of title (where existing) accompanying the goods. The payment terms may be on arrival of goods, or at an agreed number of days after invoice date or after arrival.

The decision on the period of credit to be offered will be influenced by the local practice and by competition. Terms of 60 or 90 days are common in France, sometimes being stretched even further by the use of complicated arrangements, such as 'payment on the 10th or the 20th of the third month following the month of invoice'. Such requests should be resisted by the credit manager because credit costs money, which reduces profit margins, and because control over unpaid accounts becomes more difficult the older they are. If a market is to be entered where it is known that long terms will be expected, prices must be adjusted to cover this. A further problem is caused by the period of shipment, since many buyers will start counting the credit period from the date of receipt of goods. Shipments by sea to the USA, for instance, will take up to 14 days to arrive, and then there is a further delay before the goods arrive at the customer's premises. There are two alternative ways of tackling this situation. Terms can be set at 30 days from receipt of goods. This may suit the customer, but the exporter can never precisely fix the due date, unless a special arrangement is made with the carrier. It may be better to agree on, say, 60 days from invoice date providing that the total delivery period is somewhere near but not exceeding four weeks.

It is the practice in some European countries to agree discount terms, often with an alternative. Thus in Germany one often finds buyers offering to pay '2 per cent 10 days, 30 days net'. In other words the buyer has the option of a 2 per cent discount for paying in 10 days from invoice date or paying net after 30 days. Generally these arrangements are not recommended because, with a short period such as ten days, most or all of that time will elapse before the customer receives the invoice. Any benefit to cash flow will therefore be lost.

The credit decision, as to payment terms and credit limit, is examined in Chapter 14 together with the question of export cashflow.

Appendix   Uniform Rules for Collection

General provisions and definitions

A   These provisions and definitions and the following articles apply to all collections as defined in (B) below and are binding upon all parties thereto unless otherwise expressly agreed or unless contrary to the provisions of a national, state or local law and/or regulation which cannot be departed from.

B   For the purpose of such provisions, definitions and articles:
1   **i**   'Collection' means the handling by banks, on instructions

221

received, of documents as defined in (**ii**) below, in order to:

a   obtain acceptance and/or, as the case may be, payment, or

b   deliver commercial documents against acceptance and/or, as the case may be, against payment, or

c   deliver documents on other terms and conditions.

ii 'Documents' means financial documents and/or commercial documents:

a   'financial documents' means Bills of Exchange, promissory notes, cheques, payment receipts or other similar instruments used for obtaining the payment of money;

b   'commercial documents' means invoices, shipping documents, documents of title or other similar documents, or any other documents whatsoever, not being financial documents;

iii 'Clean collection' means collection of financial documents not accompanied by commercial documents.

iv 'Documentary collection' means collection of:

a   financial documents accompanied by commercial documents;

b   commercial documents not accompanied by financial documents.

2   The 'parties thereto' are:

i the 'principal' who is the customer entrusting the operation of collection to his bank;

ii the 'remitting bank' which is the bank to which the principal has entrusted the operation of collection;

iii the 'collecting bank' which is any bank, other than the remitting bank, involved in processing the collection order;

iv the 'presenting bank' which is the collecting bank making presentation to the drawee.

3   The 'drawee' is the one to whom presentation is to be made according to the collection order.

C   All documents sent for collection must be accompanied by a collection order giving complete and precise instructions. Banks are only permitted to act upon the instructions given in such collection order, and in accordance with these Rules.

If any bank cannot, for any reason, comply with the instructions given in the collection order received by it, it must immediately advise the party from whom it received the collection order.

Liabilities and responsibilities

Article 1   Banks will act in good faith and exercise reasonable care.

Article 2   Banks must verify that the documents received appear to be as listed in the collection order and must immediately advise the party from whom the collection order was received of any documents missing.
Banks have no further obligation to examine the documents.

Article 3   For the purpose of giving effect to the instructions of the principal, the remitting bank will utilise as the collecting bank:
i   The collecting bank nominated by the principal, or, in the absence of such nomination,
ii   Any bank, of its own or another bank's choice, in the country of payment or acceptance, as the case may be.
The documents and the collection order may be sent to the collecting bank directly or through another bank as intermediary.
Banks utilising the services of other banks for the purpose of giving effect to the instructions of the principal do so for the account of and at the risk of the latter.
The principal shall be bound by and liable to indemnify the banks against all obligations and responsibilities imposed by foreign laws or usages.

Article 4   Banks concerned with a collection assume no liability or responsibility for the consequences arising out of delay and/or loss in transit of any messages, letters or documents, or for delay, mutilation or other errors arising in the transmission of cables, telegrams, telex, or communication by electronic systems, or for errors in translation or interpretation of technical terms.

Article 5   Banks concerned with a collection assume no liability or responsibility for consequences arising out of the interruption of their business by Acts of God, riots, civil commotions, insurrections, wars, or any other causes beyond their control or by strikes or lockouts.

Article 6   Goods should not be dispatched direct to the address of a bank or consigned to a bank without prior agreement on the part of that bank.
In the event of goods being dispatched direct to the address of a bank or consigned to a bank for delivery to a drawee against payment or acceptance or upon other terms without prior agreement on the part of that bank, the bank has no obligation to take delivery of the goods,

which remain at the risk and responsibility of the party dispatching the goods.

Presentation

Article 7 Documents are to be presented to the drawee in the form in which they are received, except that remitting and collecting banks are authorised to affix necessary stamps, at the expense of the principal unless otherwise instructed, and to make any necessary endorsements or place any rubber stamps or other identifying marks or symbols customary to or required for the collection operation.

Article 8 Collection orders should bear the complete address of the drawee or of the domicile at which presentation is to be made. If the address is incomplete or incorrect, the collecting bank may, without obligation and responsibility on its part, endeavour to ascertain the proper address.

Article 9 In the case of documents payable at sight the presenting bank must make presentation for payment without delay.

In the case of documents payable at a tenor other than sight the presenting bank must, where acceptance is called for, make presentation for acceptance without delay, and where payment is called for, make presentation for payment not later than the appropriate maturity date.

Article 10 In respect of a documentary collection including a bill of exchange payable at a future date, the collection order should state whether the commercial documents are to be released to the drawee against acceptance (D/A) or against payment (D/P).

In the absence of such statement, the commercial documents will be released only against payment.

Payment

Article 11 In the case of documents payable in the currency of the country of payment (local currency), the presenting bank must, unless otherwise instructed in the collection order, only release the documents to the drawee against payment in local currency which is immediately available for disposal in the manner specified in the collection order.

Article 12   In the case of documents payable in a currency other than that of the country of payment (foreign currency), the presenting bank must, unless otherwise instructed in the collection order, only release the documents to the drawee against payment in the relative foreign currency which can immediately be remitted in accordance with the instructions given in the collection order.

Article 13   In respect of clean collections partial payments may be accepted if and to the extent to which and on the conditions on which partial payments are authorised by the law in force in the place of payment. The documents will only be released to the drawee when full payment thereof has been received.

In respect of documentary collections partial payments will only be accepted if specifically authorised in the collection order. However, unless otherwise instructed, the presenting bank will only release the documents to the drawee after full payment has been received.

In all cases partial payments will only be accepted subject to compliance with the provisions of either Article 11 or Article 12 as appropriate.

Partial payment, if accepted, will be dealt with in accordance with the provisions of Article 14.

Article 14   Amounts collected (less charges and/or disbursements and/or expenses where applicable) must be made available without delay to the bank from which the collection order was received in accordance with the instructions contained in the collection order.

Acceptance

Article 15   The presenting bank is responsible for seeing that the form of the acceptance of a bill of exchange appears to be complete and correct, but is not responsible for the genuineness of any signature or for the authority of any signatory to sign the acceptance.

Promissory notes, receipts and other similar instruments

Article 16   The presenting bank is not responsible for the genuineness of any signature or for the authority of any signatory to sign a promissory note, receipt, or other similar instrument.

Protest

Article 17   The collection order should give specific instructions regarding protest (or other legal process in lieu thereof), in the event of non-acceptance or non-payment.

In the absence of such specific instructions the banks concerned with the collection have no obligation to have the documents protested (or subjected to other legal process in lieu thereof) for non-payment or non-acceptance.

Any charges and/or expenses incurred by banks in connection with such protest or other legal process will be for the account of the principal.

Case-of-need (principal's representative) and protection of goods

Article 18   If the principal nominates a representative to act as case-of-need in the event of non-acceptance and/or non-payment the collection order should clearly and fully indicate the powers of such case-of-need.

In the absence of such indication banks will not accept any instructions from the case-of-need.

Article 19   Banks have no obligation to take any action in respect of the goods to which a documentary collection relates.

Nevertheless in the case that banks take action for the protection of the goods, whether instructed or not, they assume no liability or responsibility with regard to the fate and/or condition of the goods and/or for any acts and/or omissions on the part of any third parties entrusted with the custody and/or protection of the goods. However, the collecting bank must immediately advise the bank from which the collection order was received of any such action taken.

Any charges and/or expenses incurred by banks in connection with any action for the protection of the goods will be for the account of the principal.

Advice of fate, etc.

Article 20   Collecting banks are to advise fate in accordance with the following rules:
i   *Form of advice*   All advices or information from the collecting bank to the bank from which the collection order was received, must bear appropriate detail including, in all cases, the latter

226

bank's reference number of the collection order.

ii   *Method of advice* In the absence of specific instructions, the collecting bank must send all advices to the bank from which the collection order was received by quickest mail but, if the collecting bank considers the matter to be urgent, quicker methods such as cable, telegram, telex, or communication by electronic systems, etc. may be used at the expense of the principal.

iii   *(a) Advice of payment* The collecting bank must send without delay advice of payment to the bank from which the collection order was received, detailing the amount or amounts collected, charges and/or disbursements and/or expenses deducted, where appropriate, and method of disposal of the funds.

(b) Advice of acceptance The collecting bank must send without delay advice of acceptance to the bank from which the collection order was received.

(c) Advice of non-payment or non-acceptance The collecting bank must send without delay advice of non-payment or advice of non-acceptance to the bank from which the collection order was received.

The presenting bank should endeavour to ascertain the reasons for such non-payment or non-acceptance and advise accordingly the bank from which the collection order was received.

On receipt of such advice the remitting bank must, within a reasonable time, give appropriate instructions as to the further handling of the documents. If such instructions are not received by the presenting bank within 90 days from its advice of non-payment or non-acceptance, the documents may be returned to the bank from which the collection order was received.

Interest, charges and expenses

Article 21 If the collection order includes an instruction to collect interest which is not embodied in the accompanying financial document(s), if any, and the drawee refuses to pay such interest, the presenting bank may deliver the document(s) against payment or acceptance as the case may be without collecting such interest, unless the collection order expressly states that such interest may not be waived. Where such interest is to be collected the collection order must bear an indication of the rate of interest and the period covered. When payment of interest has been refused the presenting bank must inform the bank from which the collection order was received accordingly.

If the documents include a financial document containing an

unconditional and definitive interest clause the interest amount is deemed to form part of the amount of the documents to be collected. Accordingly, the interest amount is payable in addition to the principal amount shown in the financial document and may not be waived unless the collection order so authorises.

Article 22 If the collection order includes an instruction that collection charges and/or expenses are to be for account of the drawee and the drawee refuses to pay them, the presenting bank may deliver the document(s) against payment or acceptance as the case may be without collecting charges and/or expenses unless the collection order expressly states that such charges and/or expenses may not be waived. When payment of collection charges and/or expenses has been refused the presenting bank must inform the bank from which the collection order was received accordingly. Whenever collection charges and/or expenses are so waived they will be for the account of the principal, and may be deducted from the proceeds.

Should a collection order specifically prohibit the waiving of collection charges and/or expenses then neither the remitting nor collecting nor presenting bank shall be responsible for any costs or delays resulting from this prohibition.

Article 23 In all cases where in the express terms of a collection order, or under these Rules, disbursements and/or expenses and/or collection charges are to be borne by the principal, the collecting bank(s) shall be entitled promptly to recover outlays in respect of disbursements and expenses and charges from the bank from which the collection order was received and the remitting bank shall have the right promptly to recover from the principal any amount so paid out by it, together with its own disbursements, expenses and charges, regardless of the fate of the collection.

Chapter 14

Credit decisions and export cash-flow

The last three chapters have been devoted to risk evaluation and payment terms. When the credit manager has satisfied himself on these issues, the moment of credit decision has arrived.

There are a number of guidelines which can help in deciding on the right payment terms and controls, and these should be followed in a logical sequence. Assuming that a new enquiry is received, the following questions should be asked:

Is there a serious political or transfer risk in the importing country?

If yes, terms should be Confirmed Irrevocable Letter of Credit. If a credit period is demanded, this can be given by term bills under the Letter of Credit. If the market risk appears acceptable:

Is the buyer of high standing and good reputation?

If yes, then credit can be given, either on open account terms or by the use of term bills. Open account is generally reserved for well established buyers in Europe or the USA, where reliable commercial information is obtainable.

If the answer to the second question is no, the choice is generally between documentary sight draft or Letter of Credit (lack of confirmation may be acceptable assuming the absence of serious market risk). Where the product is made-to-measure against customer specification, a Letter of Credit is preferable. Providing work is not started until the credit arrives, the pre-shipment risk can be avoided. If the contract is ex-works or FOB, however, there is still the danger that the buyer will decide not to arrange for collection or for shipment. Where non-standard goods are involved and the buyer is unknown, it is always advisable to quote CIF or delivered terms, payment to be made by Letter of Credit.

Some markets, especially amongst the developing countries, present difficulties even though there are no serious political or transfer risks. Incompetent banking systems or a corrupt and inefficient bureaucracy (or both) frequently result in payment delays which can drag on for months. To recognise these problems and be prepared for them is part of the credit manager's job. Through regular liaison with other exporters (already discussed in Chapter 11) and expert advice from his bank, the credit manager must be able to meet these difficulties and to find answers.

Complete freedom of choice of terms is often not possible. Regulations may be imposed on importers by their governments, attempting to limit the outflow of foreign exchange. The exporter will then be expected to offer more liberal terms in order to do business. The terms offered by competitors can also have an effect. In a market where similar products are sold on 90-day terms or 30 days less 3 per cent discount (often found in Germany), the exporter who insists on 30 days net will find it hard to win orders.

While a detailed consideration of ECGD services is reserved for Chapter 15, it is important to note that the holding of an ECGD policy can play an important role in the choice of terms. Markets which would otherwise demand Letter of Credit terms may sometimes be sold to on documentary bills under the protection of ECGD. To insist on a Letter of Credit will certainly mean extra costs for the buyer. Also the conditions specified in the Letter of Credit may be so strict that compliance by the exporter is almost impossible. The alternative of term bills with ECGD cover may be very attractive.

Credit decisions often have to be made quickly with no time available for comprehensive information gathering and detailed risk evaluation. At such times, just as in the home market, the credit manager has to live on the telephone, and his ability to make good decisions will depend very much on the contacts and information sources he has developed. The following example illustrates this.

In the late afternoon of Day 1, a UK manufacturer of automotive parts (G) received a telephone order from a company in West

Germany asking for despatch on Day 3 of goods to the value of £11,000. The buyer was totally unknown. Within 24 hours credit clearance had been given, and the goods were despatched on Day 3. This was the result of several telexes and telephone calls to credit agencies and insurance companies. While G did not hold an ECGD policy, discreet enquiries established that ECGD had no file on the buyer. A UK credit agency also had no information. Direct approaches to two German reporting agencies produced a few basic facts which together indicated that the company was small (3-4 persons), long established (30 years) and of good reputation. No details of net worth, turnover or profitability were available, since it was registered as a sole trader.

Telephone calls direct to the buyer (who spoke no English) revealed he was willing to pay on a 45-days documentary sight draft basis, but there was no time to contact his bank to make the necessary arrangements. Without insurance cover, this was clearly a very marginal case, and the credit manager would have preferred that documentary terms were used.

The decision was made to ship, payment to be by 45-day clean draft. Payment was received on due date.

Credit limits

When credit terms are given, either open account or on term bills, credit limits should be set. The same principles should be observed as in the home market, questions being asked in the following sequence:

> *On the payment terms agreed or requested, what credit limit is needed to cater for the expected volume of business?*

A problem not generally encountered in the domestic market is the period of shipment, which can vary from a few days to several weeks. This may be built into the terms, as when documentary bills are dated from Bill of Lading date, or when 60 days from invoice are agreed in place of 30 days from date of arrival.

A further complication can be the slow movement of funds back to the UK, which will distort the credit period. If a delay of four weeks is commonly experienced in receiving the proceeds of a 60-day term bill from a particular market, should the credit limit be increased to allow for this? While a 60-day bill may run from Bill of Lading date, the goods may have left the factory three weeks earlier and been at the docks waiting for a vessel.

Fortunately, as far as documentary terms are concerned, where the credit manager would aim to build in an extra month for slow payment with a domestic buyer, that extra month can be used to cover delays in shipping, since he will have a bill accepted for payment on the due date. Thus, for a buyer on 60 days sight averaging £5,000 monthly, a credit limited of £15,000 should be sufficient. While the payment itself may not arrive until several weeks after due date of the bill, the collecting bank will send a telex advice if payment is not made, and an immediate hold can be placed on further deliveries.

Should a bill not be accepted within a reasonable period, this in itself will alert the credit manager to a potential problem.

Open account customers present a slightly different set of problems. On the one hand, being on open terms should mean that the delivery period is relatively short. The risk of shipping delays is normally less with container traffic across Europe than with ocean transport. Against this, the absence of a bank advice about payment plus transfer delays can prolong the period of uncertainty before payment actually arrives.

Experience with different markets will give the credit manager a guide as to where payment delays can be expected. Market conditions change, and the prudent credit manager will look as much at the financial strength of his customers as at the liquidity problems of their territories.

As a general rule, a credit limit for a buyer on open account needs to be high enough to cover the credit period plus an extra month.

Can this credit limit be justified on the information available?

As we saw in Chapter 11, hard financial information is difficult to obtain. Judgements often have to be made on business reputation rather than balance sheet figures. Selling into Germany, for example, very frequently means dealing with firms who have no legal obligation to publish accounts. To insist on documentary terms may result in lost business since they expect to be granted open terms. Unless he is protected by an ECGD or Trade Indemnity Policy, the credit manager has a very difficult task in these situations. There is no formula for the right answer. All he can do is to develop to the maximum the sources of information that are available and hope that his past experience does not lead him to false judgements. In many cases he will open an account on a small limit and aim to increase it gradually as the customer proves his ability and intention to pay.

Is the credit limit to be a restriction or a guideline? What risk category is the customer to be allocated?

As in the domestic market, these decisions determine the nature of order-referral controls.

Category A is reserved for government buyers (Western industrial markets only!) and national/international companies of the highest standing. The principles followed in the UK are not always applicable, even to the Western industrial markets. Italian hospitals, for example, should on no account be given 'blue-chip' status.

Category C will include any buyers whose credit limit is restrictive. Because of information problems, this category will probably include a bigger proportion of overseas customers than the domestic sales ledger.

Category B will include all those not coming under 'A' or 'C', and order referral limits will be set to ensure that credit limits are not breached.

Market risk limits

In selling to markets with a transfer risk, on sight draft or unconfirmed Letter of Credit, it is prudent to set a credit limit which is, firstly, related to the buyer and, secondly, to the market.

An example from real life concerns a UK supplier (W) of a standard product to a Portuguese buyer (F) in 1977-8. The credit standing of F was rather low. When this was put against the background of Portugal's financial problems, terms of documentary sight draft were clearly well justified. In late 1977 the Portuguese government increased its already strict controls over foreign exchange, import licences and Letters of Credit. F applied for credit terms because of the internal liquidity squeeze. A term Letter of Credit was considered, but UK confirmation was doubtful, and, more importantly, Portuguese restrictions on the use of credits would have made it almost impossible for W to arrange the required delivery programme. Eventually the following steps were taken:

1   F provided a bank guarantee, initially from a West German bank but later from a Portuguese bank, which could be called in the event of W not receiving sterling funds in the UK. [This was far better than merely guaranteeing payment by F, since local currency might have been paid, thus releasing the bank from its obligation. It can be regarded as similar in effect to a confirmed Letter of Credit, but without the restrictions and conditions of a Letter of Credit.]
2   Payment terms were set at 90-day documentary bills.
3   A credit limit of £100,000 was set. Not only did this match the

value of the bank guarantee, but it also represented the maximum value W was prepared to ship and risk having returned to the UK should bills not be accepted.

Operating the controls

It is clear that even more flexibility is needed than with home customers, because of the additional problems of shipping, documentation and payment delays.

The credit manager needs to have some knowledge of shipment methods and also of documentation. This is often complicated and can easily lead to delays which will make nonsense of a credit limit system. With regard to delays in the transfer of funds, this is a subject on its own covered later in this chapter.

Special care is needed where non-standard products are involved, since the amount at risk must be calculated to include work-in-progress and finalised stock.

The following examples (from practical experience) illustrate this:

1 An American company (B) wished to order specially made engineering products from S, a UK firm. S was eager to have this business which could well develop into a substantial volume within a few years. On the other hand, the status information on B was not good, showing losses over recent years and a very poor liquid position. Normal terms for the product were 30 days from arrival of goods. A Letter of Credit was suggested but turned down by B (because of lack of bank support). Shipments would be required monthly, at an average value of £17,500.

One big advantage was that B, being a US company, was fully aware of the need to prove its credit standing. Accounts up to the last half-year were produced, plus evidence of US government contracts which needed the UK product. The other advantage was that S had credit insurance, not with ECGD but with Trade Indemnity, which included work-in-progress cover.

It was eventually agreed that the account would be opened on a limit of £35,000 on terms of 45 days from date of invoice. This was both the minimum amount that would permit the required sales to be made and also the maximum figure that could be insured. Careful controls were set up to ensure the amount at risk did not exceed £35,000, which had to cover both unpaid deliveries, any finished goods, plus work-in-progress.

2 A French buyer (L), purchasing non-standard products on 60 days'

open account from a UK supplier (B), ran into financial difficulties. The existing debt was frozen under a form of moratorium, but L wished to continue buying. The proprietor of L had given B his personal guarantee on part of the outstanding debt. He offered to buy on cash terms for a price artificially increased by 20 per cent, this extra amount being set against the frozen debt. B agreed, since not only would the debt be reduced, but more product would be sold at no risk.

Over a period of 12 months the debt was reduced by nearly 50 per cent, but the system was not trouble free. Imports into France cannot be paid for on 'pro-forma' terms without Bank of France approval. To avoid this, on receipt of a cable advice of the next shipment value, L would give his bank an irrevocable instruction to remit the required amount to B, when his bank received the necessary customs entry document. Because the product was 'made-to-measure', B would not start manufacture until L's bank advised that they had the money available against receipt of documents. B then had to arrange for the transporter to deliver the customs document to the bank immediately after customs clearance, so that payment could be sent to the UK. A lengthy and cumbersome procedure but it did work. The alternative for B (apart from accepting the terms of the moratorium and not supplying any further goods) was to take L's proprietor to court for his personal guarantee. Doubts about the costs involved and whether he had sufficient personal assets persuaded B to choose the method described.

This is also an interesting reflection on the value of personal guarantees. They should never be taken if it seems likely they will be called, unless a very careful check has been made of the legal procedures and costs involved in the country concerned. In the example above, it was fortunate for B that the existence of a guarantee (and the threat of calling it) was sufficient in itself.

Distributor credit

A common feature of export marketing is the appointment of a distributor to be responsible for selling in a particular market.

The credit manager should be contributing to this decision by the provision of information. A major problem is often the amount of credit to be given and on what terms, since distributors usually expect better terms than direct buyers to enable them to build up stocks and give a good service to the market. The nature of the end-market will have a big effect on the amount of distributor credit granted. If a distributor has to give 2-3 months' credit to his customers, he will expect at least the same from his UK supplier; otherwise he will be forced to borrow locally to maintain his cash-flow. Borrowing costs, which may be high, reduce his profit margin. By the nature of their business, distributors have usually little in the way of fixed assets, so the exporter is often confronted with the choice of limiting credit to what the balance sheet will stand, thereby restricting sales and preventing expansion in the export market and giving more credit with some form of security. It may sometimes be possible to take a first charge on the distributor's receivables.

If an ECGD policy is held, this can be particularly valuable in financing distributors. Providing a full disclosure is made and ECGD can be persuaded that the customer is fundamentally sound and healthy, a credit limit can often be obtained which would be completely unjustifiable to a supplier without insurance cover.

Payment methods

Regrettably, many companies believe that fixing the payment terms is all that needs to be done. As a result of this, control of export cash-flow is very neglected and misunderstood.

We have already seen how the international banking system enables exporters and importers to trade with varying degrees of security. It is vital that the credit manager understands how to use this system so that the transfer of funds from the customer to the seller's bank is achieved with the minimum delay. Payment methods can be matched to different payment terms as shown in Exhibit 14.1.

Exhibit 14.1

Payment methods	Documentary terms	Open account
Customer's cheque	No	Yes
Bank cheque	Yes	Yes
Bank transfer	Yes	Yes
SWIFT	Yes	Yes
Clean bill	No	Yes

Sterling payments

1 Customer's cheque Cheques drawn by overseas buyers on their local bank are expressed in the currency of that country, with one exception. This exception is when the buyer's bank is operating a sterling hold account, having obtained permission from the

236

appropriate monetary authorities on the grounds that there is sufficient volume of sterling transactions (both imports and exports). Such a sterling account is classed as an external account.

If possible, buyers should be dissuaded from making this type of payment because 'cleared funds' cannot be provided by the exporter's bank until the cheque has been returned to the bank it is drawn on, presented and cleared. While the exporter's bank may often be prepared to give immediate face value, this will be with recourse and is equivalent to the negotiation of a bill of exchange drawn and payable abroad. A delay of at least one week is unavoidable between receipt of the cheque in the UK bank and receipt of cleared funds, and this period can easily stretch to two or even three weeks depending on the location of the buyer's bank and the efficiency of the local clearing system. If, at the end of this period, the exporter is told that the cheque has bounced, he has lost all that intervening time and may even have shipped further goods. His bank will also charge interest on the money advanced pending cheque clearance, plus commission and postage.

2 Bank cheque The only type of cheque payment which is satisfactory is a cheque drawn on a UK bank, usually a branch of the customer's own local bank. Cleared funds can be obtained within two to three days, since the UK bank is merely honouring a cheque raised by its overseas branch or by a correspondent. This method of payment is commonly known as a banker's draft. Problems can still arise with this system, since the UK paying bank may refuse to give value without a covering advice from the issuing bank abroad.

3 Bank transfer This is achieved by the buyer instructing his bank to transfer funds to the bank of the seller. This method is generally used for the payment of documentary bills as well as for open account transactions. While apparently simple, bank transfers give rise to a high volume of frustration and bitterness amongst UK exporters, who invariably blame the banking system when payments take longer than expected. Many complaints can be avoided if some trouble is taken at the outset to determine the timing and routing of transfers. Some points to note are as follows:

a Type of transfer A high proportion of bank transfers are sent by mail (abbreviated as MT), because without other instructions this is the normal method. The time taken for an MT to be credited to the exporter's bank will vary greatly, depending on the number of banks involved in the transfer and on the efficiency of those banks. A minimum period of one week should be expected. While most MTs should arrive within two to three weeks, longer delays are not unknown.

237

The alternative is to request cable or telegraphic transfer (TT). This should reduce the transfer period to a minimum of two days. Quite apart from the greater speed, a TT has the further advantage over MT that it cannot be lost in the post. Banks charge more for TT payments, and the credit manager should be ready to offer to pay these costs, providing it is economic to do so. A figure between £1,500 and £5,000 is generally accepted as the 'break-point', above which the interest saving outweighs the cable costs.

It is worth remembering that the customer's bank account is debited at precisely the same time regardless of whether MT or TT is used.

b *Precise instructions* The customer should be asked to give his bank full particulars of where and how the payment is to go. An example of inadequate instructions is:

'Please pay £5491.65 to General Manufacturers Ltd, 99 Oxford Street, London, England.'

This should be worded:

'Please pay by cable transfer £5491.65 to National Westminster Bank Ltd, 100 Oxford St, London, England, for the credit of A/C No. 1234567 General Manufacturers Ltd. Cable charges for the payee.'

This identifies the account number and the name and the branch of the supplier's bank. If the exporter also wants to receive a separate advice of payment, the following should be added:

'Under advice to General Manufacturers Ltd, 99 Oxford St, London, England.'

c *The banking chain* The more banks a payment has to pass through, the longer it will take and the more chances there are of error and mishandling. The first step in establishing payment arrangements with a new buyer is to check whether his bank (or one of his banks) has a direct relationship with, i.e. is a correspondent of, the exporter's bank. A common problem arises when the customer is using an out-of-town branch and payment has to come to the local branch of the exporter's bank. The sequence of events can be as follows:

i Buyer instructs local branch to pay.
ii Local branch passes instruction to main office.
iii Main office transfers to UK correspondent.

238

iv   UK correspondent transfers to main office of supplier's bank.

v   Main office transfers to supplier's local branch.

Even when the original instruction is to pay by TT, delays will occur in this type of situation because a cable transfer instruction only covers the movement of funds between two international centres, e.g. Paris to London. A payment which starts in Société Général in Evreux and has to move via Paris and London to Banbury is only on cable between Paris and London. Where the use of a local branch at both the start and the finish of a bank transfer is unavoidable, several extra days will be added to the two days' cable transfer period.

If there is a choice of banks for the importer to use, it will help the supplier to request that payment be remitted from a bank which is a correspondent of his bank. Failing this, it can sometimes be quicker to request the buyer to arrange payment by a bank draft drawn on a London bank with instructions for the funds to be telephoned to the exporter's bank on arrival in the UK.

The same principles apply with the transfer of funds from the payment of bills. Delays tend to be longer because documentary transactions are more common in distant markets where communications are poor and standards of banking competence are low compared to the industrial nations.

A final point to remember is that customers have to buy sterling in order to pay it. Very few markets can offer the facilities taken for granted in the City of London for the purchase of currency.

d   *Swift*   A new system of inter-bank transfer by computer began in 1977, known as SWIFT (Society for World-wide Interbank Financial Telecommunications). Banks connected to a computer network are able to communicate with each other and to transfer payments with complete security and privacy. At the time of writing (early 1979) only certain large branches of the major banks in Western Europe and North America are connected, but rapid growth is expected. Ultimately it is hoped that all transfers will be made via SWIFT.

When a remitting bank has to make a payment through another bank and both banks are on SWIFT, payment will be made by SWIFT automatically. A SWIFT payment instruction must include a value date, currency of payment, the amount, the name of the remitter and the beneficiary, and the name and branch of the reimbursing bank. Unless a forward value date is given, the transfer is made the same day.

Since many banks and branches of banks are not yet connected (especially provincial branches), exporters should still ask their customers to remit by TT. If there is a SWIFT link, payment will probably follow this route anyway and it will arrive faster than by cable — except that just as TT only operates between international centres, so SWIFT can only operate between connected banks and there may be additional transfer time to the beneficiary's bank.

The real benefit of SWIFT lies with the banks themselves, who hope to reduce paperwork considerably and to eliminate the danger of losing documents in the post. No extra charge is made when payments are sent by SWIFT, and as yet the existing MT and TT charges are not being reduced. SWIFT payments in currency other than that of the country of the remitting bank, e.g. sterling paid from outside the UK, will normally have a value date two days ahead of the date of despatch.

4   Clean bill   In a number of European markets it is normal practice for domestic payments to be made by clean bill. By this is meant a Bill of Exchange drawn by the seller on the buyer, dated to mature at an agreed future date, which is accepted by the buyer and 'domiciled', i.e. the buyer enters the name and address of the bank where payment will be made. No documents are attached to the bill, which is merely a means of payment as opposed to a method of controlling the delivery of goods. Its use is common in France, Belgium, Portugal and Norway and less frequent in Spain, Italy and Germany.

Payment by clean bill for goods exported on open account terms offers a number of advantages over payment by cheque or bank transfer:

a   Acceptance of a bill gives a limited amount of security. The customer knows it will be presented to his bank on the due date, and he will probably ensure that funds are available. To have a bill dishonoured is regarded as an extremely serious offence in all overseas markets.

b   The exporter does not have to remind the buyer to send a cheque or transfer. It is easier to omit to send a bank transfer on due date than to ignore the fact that a bill is falling due.

c   An accepted bill fixes the amount which has to be paid.

d   It can be used as a form of security where documentary terms are not practicable. For example, an order is received from a customer in Norway who has a history of slow payment on open account. The supplier accepts the order *subject* to acceptance of a clean bill dated to mature 30 days (the normal credit period) from the agreed despatch date. Only when the bill is returned accepted will shipment be made. This avoids the usual problem with clean

240

bills of releasing the goods and then having no leverage on the customer to accept the bill.

An accepted bill should be presented for payment through the exporter's bank, with clear instructions about the disposal of funds, advice of non-payment by telex, etc., and whether the bill is to be protested. Since the customer will be choosing the paying bank, there is no way of minimising transfer delays, which can easily be lengthy when the exporter's bank has no account with the buyer's bank.

A country with its own payment peculiarities is France. While payment by clean bill is normal practice, French buyers have a habit of amending, i.e. retarding, the due date on a bill so that 60-day terms turn into 90. This is especially likely to happen on a bill dated to mature in August. The whole of French industry and commerce appears to close for the month and bills are pushed into September. It is also quite common for a French customer, who has agreed open account terms, to raise his own *billet à ordre*. This is a promisory note, which is payable by the customer's bank on the date indicated. It cannot be discounted but may be negotiated with recourse by a bank.

German buyers occasionally request their suppliers to draw a Bill of Exchange on them for the same value as the payment which has just been made for goods supplied. If payment terms are 90 days, the draft would be payable at that maturity and the cheque or bank transfer payment would have a discount deduction. The buyer then has a bill which can be sold to his bank at 2-3 per cent below the rate of interest for overdraft borrowing. It is a method of financing which has developed because of the difference in interest charges. The drawer of the bill has, of course, been paid for his goods, but he has a contingent liability until the bill is paid on maturity.

Foreign currency payments

Many exporters invoice in the currency of the buyer or in a third currency. The reasons for doing so and the problems and benefits arising are examined in Chapter 18. In this chapter we are concerned with the handling of currency payments. Two basic principles must be observed.

The first is to remember that every currency payment into the UK has to be cleared through its country of origin. Thus all US dollar payments have to be routed through and cleared by a bank in the USA (generally in New York), regardless of where the buyer is located. Similarly payments in German Marks or French Francs have to come from a bank in Germany or France.

The second principle is that there must be a market for the foreign currency when it arrives in the UK. A buyer in Ghana will be delighted to pay in cedis, but the UK exporter will not be able to convert them into the required amount of sterling.

1   Customer's cheque   This is to be avoided for the same reasons that applied to receipt of a sterling cheque from an external account. All cheques must be cleared in the country in which they are domiciled.

If sales are being made to a number of buyers in a particular market, it may be worth applying for Bank of England permission to hold a foreign currency account in that market. Thus an exporter with many customers in France could arrange to open a franc account in Paris. Customers would be asked to send their cheques (or arrange bank transfers) in francs to that account. At agreed intervals — daily, weekly or monthly — the balance can be transferred back to the UK. There is a saving on bank charges because of the reduction in transfers. If required, the exporter can arrange to have a daily telex listing payments received so that control over credit limits and overdue accounts is maintained. This arrangement also overcomes a problem which can arise in markets operating strict exchange control regulations. For example, payments from France are not valid unless the paying bank has checked the evidence of import before authorising the despatch of funds. An exporter who goes to Paris and brings back a cheque direct from his customer may find the cheque is dishonoured because it lacks the bank's approval.

2   Other methods   Payments by bank draft, bank transfer and clean bill have the same characteristics whether they are made in sterling or in the currency of the buyer, except that the exporter has to arrange for all currency payments to be converted into sterling (see Chapter 18).

Additional problems occur when payment is made in a third currency. A big proportion of world trade is conducted in US dollars. All dollar payments have to be cleared through a bank in the United States. The result is that the clearing system in New York has an enormous volume of business to handle which often results in delays.

The most common cause of delays in bank transfers, however, is that the customer's bank at the end of the chain is not in direct correspondence with the same US bank which is finally crediting funds to the exporter's bank. For example, a UK supplier sells to a customer in Greece on documentary sight draft terms in US dollars. In order to take up the documents, the customer instructs his bank to pay $1 million to the UK supplier. The Greek bank has a dollar account with a New York bank and an instruction is given to transfer $1 million from that account to the Midland Bank, London, for the account of the exporter.

Providing there are sufficient funds in the Greek bank's New York account, the New York bank makes the transfer. But if the New York bank's account with the Midland, London, is temporarily overdrawn, the transfer will be routed via another New York bank which makes the final transfer to London. This chain of events can easily be lengthened if the Greek buyer has to deal through his local branch and if the UK supplier banks with an out-of-town branch of the Midland.

Payment methods – conclusions

1 Payment by TT is usually the fastest method — providing there are not going to be too many banks in the chain.
2 Payment in local currency into a currency hold account may be worthwhile if there is sufficient volume.
3 Delays are frequently the result of too many banks handling a transfer.

Exporters often find that it pays to use several different banks. The City of London has the biggest and most diverse banking community in the world. Many banks have developed from specialising in particular markets or areas — West Africa, South America, the Middle East, the Far East, etc. As a result, their knowledge of these markets is first-class and they often have a strong branch network. An exporter with a concentration of business in a particular area should find out which bank has the expertise and then take advantage of it. It is generally not necessary to open an account in order to have collection work done. A number of banks, including the UK clearers, some UK merchant banks and some US banks in London, offer a cash management service which may include advice and help on a wide range of topics, such as documentation, currency invoicing and market risk in addition to the basic function of accelerating cash flow.

Overdue accounts

Everthing said so far about payment methods assumes that customers are paying in accordance with the agreed terms. It is now necessary to look at how the exporter should tackle overdue accounts. This will be covered under the following headings, relating primarily to open account customers:
1 Invoices.
2 Statements.
3 Interest.
4 Letters.

5   Telephone.
6   Telex.
7   Visiting.
8   Agents.
9   Collection agents.
10 Legal action.
11 Political and transfer problems.

Invoices

Should export invoices be designed or presented differently from home trade? The UK supplier traditionally expects his overseas buyers to understand English, but it is worth considering whether a little trouble taken to present an invoice in the buyer's language might not have a beneficial effect on the timing of payment. This is particularly true where sales are made to small buyers. The problem of language occurs throughout the collection cycle. While English may be readily understood by multinational companies, this knowledge begins to fade the lower down the scale the contact exists. Some countries are renowned for their understanding of English, e.g. Holland, Denmark and Germany, but even so, it is wrong for the UK exporter to presume that he can correspond with and talk to these customers as if they were in Birmingham or Leeds.

It is not difficult to produce invoices with headings and pre-printed information in the main European languages — French, German, Dutch, Spanish and Italian. The invoice should carry a clear instruction about the method of payment, including full details of the bank account where funds are to be sent.

Statements

The UK practice of monthly statements is not followed on the Continent, with the exceptions of Belgium and Norway. In Austria and Germany, however, it is normal for customers to be sent a statement on or shortly after the due date.

This non-usage of statements derives from the fact that payment terms are invariably X days from invoice date, in contrast to the UK custom of monthly account. If statements are to be sent, to be of any value they must include the due date of every invoice.

244

Interest

In the UK the charging of interest for late payment is not generally accepted, although proposals for a statutory interest charge were put forward by the Law Commission in June 1978.

These ideas are hardly likely to be of any assistance to credit managers, however, since the suggested rate of interest is only 1 per cent over base lending rate. To be effective, interest must be charged at a penal rate; otherwise buyers may regard it as an alternative payment term.

In Europe interest charges are accepted as normal in France, Italy and all of Scandinavia. They are found less commonly in Germany, the Benelux countries, Austria, Switzerland, Spain and Portugal.

Suppliers suffering from bank transfer delays should not hesitate to charge interest to the banks responsible, providing that definite proof can be given that the bank was at fault.

Letters

Collection letters are not an effective way to chase overdue accounts, whether the customer is in Manchester, Munich or Milwaukee. But sometimes they have to be used, perhaps because there is no practicable alternative or because of the volume of accounts. The first rule must be to write in the buyer's language — unless that language is not one of the major European languages, in which case English must be used. A useful reference book is *Debt Collection Letters in Ten Languages*, published in 1978 by the Gower Press. This includes a good selection of pro-forma letters and telexes covering many situations, in French, German, Dutch, Italian, Spanish, Portuguese, Flemish, Danish, Swedish and Norwegian. The obvious drawback is how to understand the answers, but in the majority of cases the meaning is not too difficult to grasp with the aid of a dictionary.

Many buyers do understand English, but the chances of receiving a reply are much higher if they are addressed in their own language.

Telephone

Unless the credit manager is fluent in the appropriate language, there is no point in chasing by telephone without first knowing *(a)* the name of the person who can help and *(b)* that he can speak English. As mentioned previously, there is a good chance of finding English speakers in Holland, Germany, Denmark, Sweden, Norway and in any multinational company, but this is of little use unless the language is spoken by the individuals controlling payment. When the language problem hardly exists, as with the USA, one five-minute call establishing a personal contact is worth more than a dozen letters.

Telex

The preferred method of follow-up by many exporters is by telex, but here again it pays dividends to use the buyer's language and to address it for the attention of the particular person known to be in a position to help.

Visits

Not many credit managers have the opportunity to visit overseas buyers, but the economics of an occasional trip should be examined. A one- or two-day visit to a major centre in any of the nearer European countries will cost (in 1978) between £150 and £300. If the result is the clearance of many thousands of pounds several months earlier than expected, such a trip is easily justified. An alternative is to ask the export sales manager to include the problem on the agenda for his next visit.

The agent

Just as an agent should regard the gathering of information as part of his job, so should he be ready to assist in the follow-up of overdue invoices.

An agent covering a market or group of markets should be sent details of all overdue accounts in those areas every month. Those he cannot visit, he can telephone, with the advantage of speaking their language. Where an agent's commission on sales is not payable until the sales have been paid, this provides an excellent incentive!

Collection agencies

Many collection agencies in the UK (and others overseas) offer to collect export debts. The credit manager should be very wary of these offers. While the debt will probably be handled on a 'no collection — no charge' basis, a great deal can be lost if, after six months, the agency passes the debt back, having failed to collect.

The credit manager must find out exactly what arrangements the collector has in the market in question. Preferably he should obtain the names of 'satisfied clients' and check on their experience. Collection rates are inevitably higher for overseas debts — between 10 and 25 per cent are not uncommon.

Legal action

The last resort is to take the customer to court. This will be very expensive and will probably drag on for many months. Choosing a solicitor is the first problem. It is clearly preferable to use an English-speaking lawyer and the best way is by recommendation. Holders of ECGD policies are given a choice of names in nearly every market and are expected to pursue their debtors through the courts. This is only reasonable if ECGD are paying a claim, and the Department may be satisfied if the client can provide evidence that to take court action would be fruitless. Legal costs are recoverable from ECGD pro-rata to the proportion of the total debt which is paid.

Assistance in obtaining legal aid is also often provided by the commercial section of British Consulates and Embassies. Full details of the help available should be requested from the British Overseas Trade Board.

Political or transfer problems

Non-payment due to political reasons or lack of foreign exchange is a hazard of exporting which few companies succeed in avoiding at one time or another. The reasons for these problems were examined in Chapter 11.

There is very little the credit manager can do when told by his bank that his customer in Turkey has paid in local currency but no sterling will be available for an indefinite period. Nonetheless he should take the following steps:

a   Ensure that sales and marketing departments are fully aware of the problem, and that no further business is sought or accepted unless on a Confirmed Irrevocable Letter of Credit. If an ECGD policy is held, any restrictions imposed on policy holders must, of course, be adhered to.

b   Keep checking (through the bank and the press) on the status of blocked debts. A recommendation may well be required at year-end on the amount of bad debt provision to be made.

247

c   Keep his ear to the ground for news of possible ways of getting round the problem. Even in 1977-8 some UK exporters managed to keep on supplying goods to Turkey, whether through a UK buyer willing to take a risk or through payment from an account outside Turkey but controlled by a Turkish importer, through a barter deal or by finding a bank outside the UK willing to confirm a Turkish credit.

Chapter 15

ECGD — comprehensive short-term guarantees

All the industrial nations of the West offer some form of government insurance and subsidised finance to their exporters. The services provided by the British Government through the Export Credits Guarantee Department (ECGD) are the most highly developed and sophisticated.

The purpose of this chapter is to survey the facilities offered in broad outline and to concentrate on three questions:

1   How should an exporter decide whether to use ECGD?
2   What problems are likely to be encountered?
3   How should a policy be used to best effect?

ECGD services

Exhibit 15.1 (reproduced with the approval of the ECGD), illustrates the range of services available. For ease of reference these may be classified under three main headings:

1   Comprehensive short-term guarantee — also embracing the 'extended terms guarantee'.
2   Specific guarantees for supplier or buyer credit.
3   Specialised facilities.

This chapter is concerned only with the first of these. The others are covered in Chapter 16.

Exhibit 15.1 EGCD facilities

ECGD

EXPORT CREDITS GUARANTEE DEPARTMENT

THE EXPORT CREDITS GUARANTEE DEPARTMENT (ECGD) IS A GOVERNMENT DEPARTMENT WHICH ASSISTS EXPORTERS OF UK GOODS AND SERVICES BY INSURING THEM AGAINST THE RISKS OF NOT BEING PAID – WHETHER THROUGH THE DEFAULT OF THE BUYER OR THROUGH OTHER CAUSES SUCH AS RESTRICTIONS ON THE TRANSFER OF CURRENCY. AS AN ADDITION TO THIS BASIC INSURANCE ECGD ALSO GIVES UNCONDITIONAL GUARANTEES OF 100 PER CENT REPAYMENT TO BANKS PROVIDING FINANCE TO INSURED EXPORTERS, WHICH ENABLE THE BANKS TO PROVIDE THE FINANCE AT FAVOURABLE INTEREST RATES.

CREDIT INSURANCE

With an ECGD credit insurance policy, the exporter is assured that if the customer does not pay him for goods and services, then ECGD will do so. The exporter is insured for 90 per cent of his loss if it has occurred because of the insolvency or default of his buyer or for 95 per cent if it is due to 'country' risks such as exchange difficulties, and import or export licence impositions.

ECGD's Comprehensive Short Term Guarantee usually covers the whole of an exporter's turnover, but it can cover an agreed proportion which will give ECGD a reasonable spread of risk. This guarantee is basically designed for goods or services provided on payment terms of 6 months or less, but it can be extended to cover production line engineering goods sold on longer terms. An exporter of capital goods can insure a 'one—off' contract at a higher premium under ECGD's Specific Guarantee – one contract, one policy.

GUARANTEES FOR EXPORT FINANCE

ECGD does not directly provide finance for export credit, but over the years it has become increasingly important in facilitating lending by the banks. With an ECGD 100 per cent unconditional guarantee, the banks will make finance available to exporters at special export interest rates.

For contracts worth £1 million or more with credit of 2 years or longer, UK banks with ECGD backing are able to offer low interest loans ('buyer credit') direct to overseas buyers or their banks at a special export interest rate to finance up to 85 per cent of the contract value of capital goods and services supplied by UK firms. Buyer credits for large project cases (in some markets all buyer credits) are usually financed in foreign currencies – US dollars or deutschmarks – for which ECGD guarantees the availability of funds for the loan as well as the repayment of credit.

250

SPECIAL FACILITIES FOR EXPORTERS OF CAPITAL GOODS

ECGD can give a measure of cover against UK cost escalation for major capital goods contracts worth at least £2 million with a manufacturing period of 2 years or more.

For contracts on cash or very short payment terms with a UK content of £½ million or over, ECGD may support the issue of performance bonds.

ECGD cover is available selectively for pre—shipment bank finance for overseas contracts worth £1 million or more; such bank finance is not at the special interest rate.

ECGD is able to help consortium members contracting overseas for major projects, worth £50 million or more, by covering some of the risks arising from their joint and several responsibilities.

INSURANCE FOR OVERSEAS INVESTMENT

ECGD insures both capital and interest of new overseas investment against the risks of war, expropriation and restriction on remittances, for a period of 3 to 15 years. Enquiries to Overseas Investment Branch at ECGD's headquarters.

HOW TO GET IN TOUCH

ECGD HAS OFFICES COVERING EVERY PART OF THE UK CENTRED IN BELFAST, BIRMINGHAM, BRISTOL, CAMBRIDGE, GLASGOW, LEEDS, MANCHESTER, AND LONDON. THE DIRECTOR OF EVERY ECGD OFFICE IS THERE TO EXPLAIN TO EXPORTERS HOW THE DEPARTMENT CAN HELP SOLVE THEIR CREDIT INSURANCE PROBLEMS.

JANUARY 1978

PUBLICITY AND PUBLIC RELATIONS BRANCH
EXPORT CREDITS GUARANTEE DEPARTMENT
ALDERMANBURY HOUSE
ALDERMANBURY
LONDON
EC2P 2EL   Tel: 01—606 6899

(Continued)

Exhibit 15.1 *(continued)*

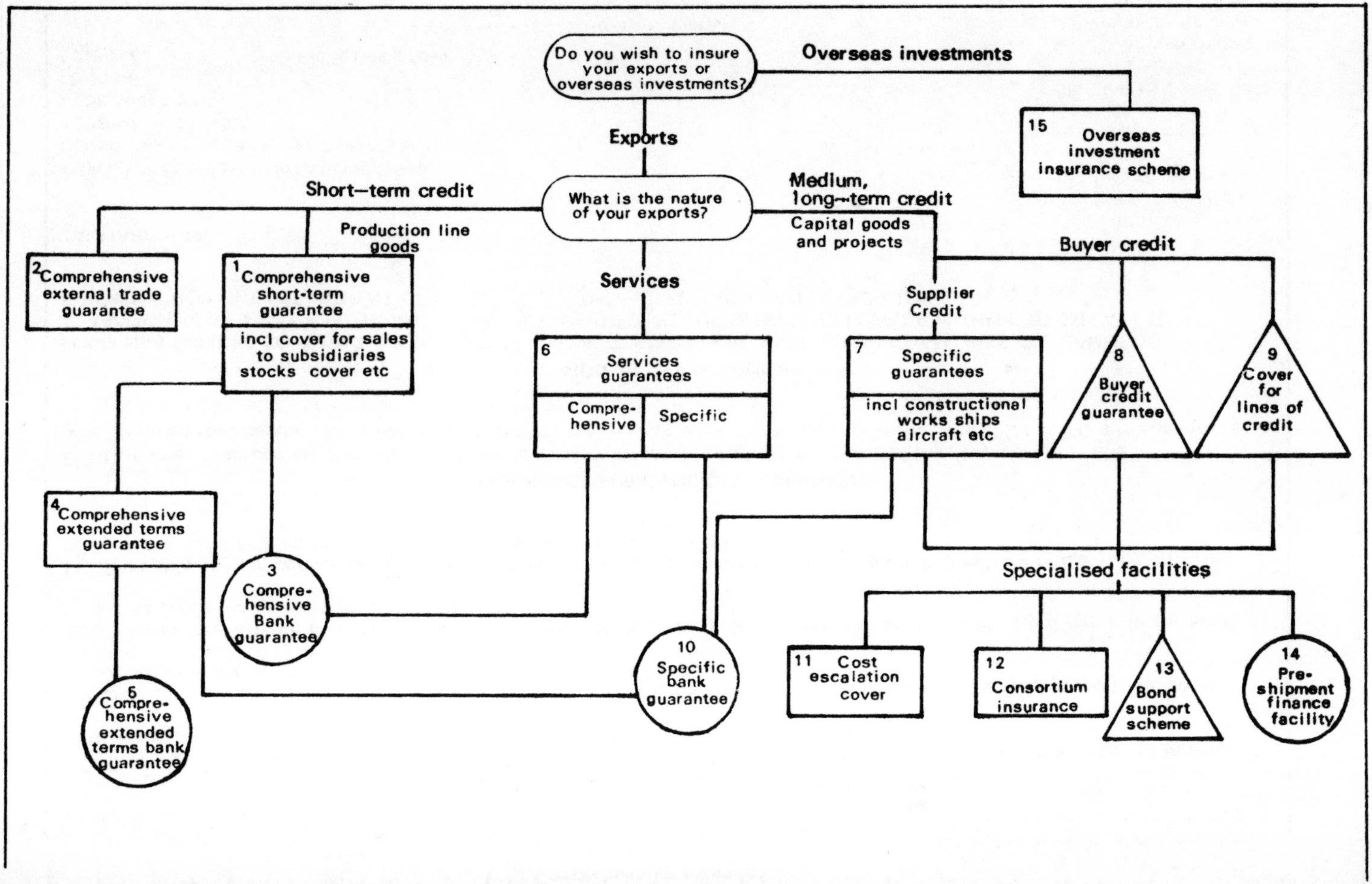

Insurance guarantees

Bank guarantees

Facilities combining insurance and finance

1 Comprehensive short-term guarantee

Intended for exporters of consumer or consumer durable goods sold on terms of payment not exceeding 180 days.

2 Comprehensive external trade guarantee

Protects UK merchants or confirmers trading in goods dispatched from one overseas country to another against risk of non-payment. Goods must be sold on credit not exceeding 180 days.

3 Comprehensive bank guarantee

Holders of 1, trading on credit terms of less than two years, can supplement their policy by a 100 per cent ECGD guarantee direct to financing banks. Finance is provided from date of shipment at 5/8 per cent above base rate.

4 Comprehensive extended terms guarantee

Holders of 1 trading in goods sold on longer than six months credit but less than five years can obtain cover through this guarantee.

5 Comprehensive extended terms bank guarantee

For holders of 4 this guarantee helps provide finance in the same way as 3.

6 Services guarantees

For firms who carry out services for principals overseas, the comprehensive option is suitable for a recurrent pattern of business whereas the specific, option is for where only one service is to be carried out.

7 Specific guarantees

Provide insurance for exporters whose goods are unsuitable for ECGD's comprehensive policies — this could be major capital goods projects, or business which involves substantial work on site or a long manufacturing period.

8 Buyer credit guarantee

ECGD guarantees UK bank loan direct to an overseas buyer — this enables the UK exporter to be paid on cash terms and can also facilitate progress payments during manufacture. Minimum eligible contract value is £1 million.

9 Cover for lines of credit

Credit made available to an overseas bank by a UK bank, guaranteed by ECGD. Amount of credit, period for which it is available, terms and interest rates, minimum size of contract, specified for each line.

10 Specific bank guarantee

For exporters (holding 7 or 4) with contract on credit or longer than two years ECGD gives a guarantee to financing bank, which provides finance at preferential export interest rate which varies according to buyer's country and length of credit.

11 Cost escalation cover

This provides partial protection against certain UK cost increases for firms with capital goods contracts worth over £2 million with a manufacturing period of at least two years.

12 Consortium insurance

This covers UK consortium members contracting overseas for major projects of £50 million or more against some of the risks arising from their 'joint and several' responsibilities.

13 Bond support scheme

ECGD can support the issue of performance and other bonds for contracts worth £½ million of more.

14 Pre-shipment finance

This provides pre-shipment finance for overseas contracts insured with ECGD with a contract value of £1 million or more, this finance is not at a preferential interest rate.

15 Overseas investment insurance scheme

Provides UK investors with insurance for up to 15 years against political risks in respect of new investment overseas. Investor must be a company carrying on business in the UK or a subsidiary of such a company.

Comprehensive short-term guarantee (CSTG)

This offers protection against both commercial and political risk. Exporters are required to offer the whole of their export business. ECGD will generally permit the exclusion of markets which include associate or subsidiary company buyers. The inclusion of UK export buyers is optional. Premium rates are lowest for companies insuring 100 per cent of turnover, rising fairly steeply as more markets are excluded. The premium rate may also be affected by the 'mix' of business, i.e. the proportion of strong buyers in low risk markets. An additional premium of 0.11 per cent is payable if cover is required against pre-shipment risk (not available for exports routed through a UK buyer).

Credit up to £250 can be given, providing no adverse information is known to the exporter. A discretionary limit of £5,000 is normally available, providing the exporter obtains at least one agency or bank report which justifies the amount of credit given. This discretionary limit may be subsequently increased up to a maximum of £20,000 providing the policy holder has a good claims record. Exhibit 15.2 illustrates how credit limits should be obtained. At times, however, ECGD withdraws all discretionary limits on markets where serious political or transfer problems arise. Similarly underwriters have the right to impose a ceiling on the total limit agreed for an individual overseas buyer or on a particular market. In such situations it is a case of 'first come, first served'.

Terms of payment must be within 180 days, unless the policy holder obtains an Extended Terms Guarantee (ETG) which covers business on terms of up to five years. This facility is limited to engineering products, vehicles, equipment, etc., which are normally sold on long terms. It is intended for continuous business of this nature and individual contracts not suitable for specific guarantees. A discretionary limit does not normally apply to an ETC.

ECGD has the right to make cover on any market conditional upon certain payment terms being used. A list (Schedule 2 of a CSTG policy) is published, summarising all the special conditions operative for those markets considered problem areas.

Where the policy holder is covering his exports routed through a UK buyer, payment terms to that buyer are limited to 30 days.

Business covered may be in sterling or any approved currency. Exporters losing money as a result of forward selling of foreign currency borrowing can obtain up to an extra 10 per cent on a valid claim, providing they hold a Foreign Currency Contracts Endorsement.

Claims under the policy may be submitted in the event of one of the

254

following causes of loss (with percentage cover shown in parentheses):
1 Insolvency of the buyer (90 per cent).
2 Buyer's failure to pay within six months of due date for goods accepted (90 per cent).
3 Buyer's failure or refusal to accept goods despatched providing the policy holder is not at fault and ECGD has confirmed that legal proceedings need not be taken (90 per cent after the policy holder takes a first loss of 20 per cent).
4 A general moratorium on external debt by the government of the buyer's country or of a third country through which payment must be made (95 per cent).
5 Any other action by the government of the buyer's country which prevents wholly or, partly, performance of the contract (95 per cent).
6 Political, economic, legislative or administrative difficulties outside the UK which prevent or delay the transfer of payments (95 per cent).
7 A shortfall in payment caused by exchange rate changes, when payment has been made in foreign currency in the buyer's country (95 per cent).
8 War, civil war, etc., preventing contract performance (95 per cent).
9 Cancellation or non-renewal of a UK export licence or other legal restriction on the export of goods (95 per cent).
10 Failure or refusal of a 'public buyer' to fulfill any of the terms of the contract. ECGD must have confirmed 'public buyer' status (95 per cent).

On causes of loss (4) to (10) inclusive, if a claim is made before goods have been despatched, the cover is reduced from 95 to 90 per cent. Claims become payable four months after the event causing loss or immediately after loss is sustained (whichever is the later), on numbers (4) to (10). On number (3) payment can be made one month after resale of goods.

Comprehensive guarantees to banks

The holder of a CSTG may use his policy to obtain bank finance at preferential rates. In 1978 this meant 0.625 per cent over base lending rate.

The procedure to be followed depends on whether terms of payment are open account (including 'cash against documents') or Bills of Exchange (including promissory notes). This is illustrated in Exhibit 15.3.

START HERE - NEW ORDER

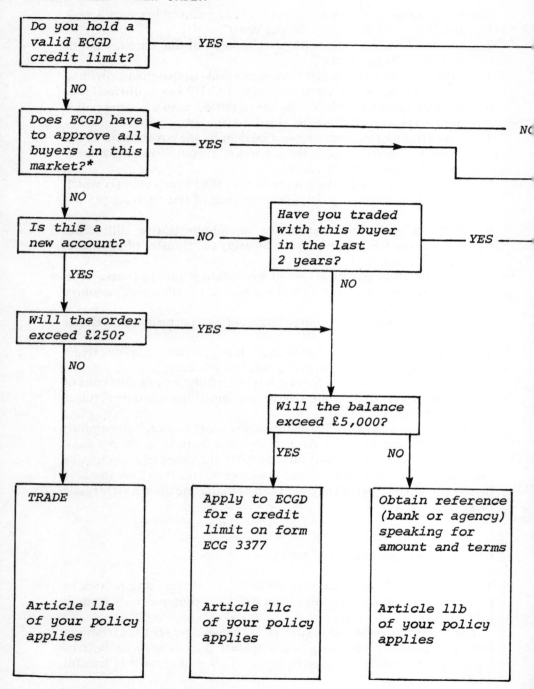

*See Schedule 2 issued by ECGD giving details of such markets

Exhibit 15.2

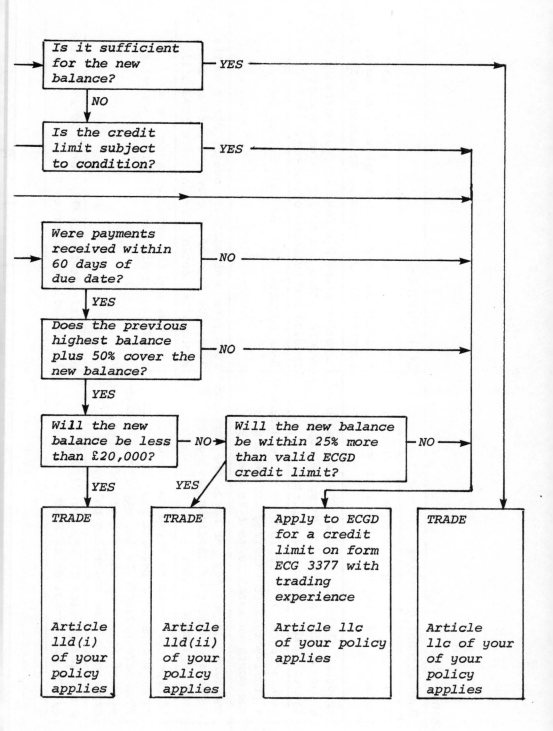

Exhibit 15.3

	Open account guarantee	Bill guarantee
1	ECGD gives exporter's bank a guarantee that exporter will repay amounts borrowed	ECGD gives exporter's bank guarantee that bills or notes plus interest will be paid. Exporter signs a recourse agreement with ECGD.
2	Exporter gives his bank an ECGD warranty of export within his policy terms, a copy invoice and evidence of export.	Exporter gives his bank an ECGD warranty of export within his policy terms, a copy invoice and evidence of export.
3	Bank advances 100% of invoice value against a promissory note maturing at the end of the month in which payment is due.	Bank advances 100% of the bill or note.
4	The bank charges 50p per note. One note can cover any number of invoices having the same repayment month.	ECGD pays bank unconditionally three months after due date of an accepted bill or one month after demand for an unaccepted bill.
5	If exporter fails to repay on due date, bank obtains 100% payment from ECGD. ECGD then have recourse to the exporter. If non-payment is due to the failure of buyer, the exporter claims under his policy.	The bank and the exporter agree on a revolving credit limit, reviewed annually.
6	A special premium of 15p per £100 is by the policy-holder to ECGD.	A special premium of 15p per £100 is payable by the policy-holder to ECGD

Other facilities available to CSTG policy holders include:

a *Subsidiaries guarantee* Cover may be given for sales made by the overseas subsidiary of goods sold to it by its parent or associate company in the UK. ECGD generally insist on insuring the original sale to the overseas subsidiary before offering such protection.

b *Supplementary stocks guarantee* ECGD will cover losses to stocks held overseas arising from political causes, i.e. expropriation, war damage. It is available for goods held at an overseas trade fair or for goods kept abroad on trial and demonstration.

An external trade guarantee can be obtained which offers similar protection to the CSTG in respect of foreign goods shipped direct from the supplying country to the export market without entering the UK. Causes of loss not covered are the failure of the buyer to take up goods, the imposition of export or import licensing and the cancellation or non-renewal of licences. The maximum cover is 90 per cent and the maximum credit period 180 days. Premiums are higher than for the CSTG.

By far the greater part of ECGD's business is conducted under CSTGs, as described above. The value of a CSTG should be considered under three questions:

1 How should an exporter decide if a policy is right for his business?
2 What are the main problems encountered by policy holders?
3 What steps should a policy holder take to ensure he gets the best use from it?

How to decide about ECGD

The first step towards a decision should be a market analysis of the next year's forecast export sales, dividing markets into two broad groups, comprising:

1 Europe, USA, Australia, New Zealand, Canada and Japan.
2 All other markets.

If this analysis shows that a very high proportion of sales (say 90 per cent) is directed to Group A — the areas of negligible political and transfer risk — the argument for ECGD cover is very slender. On the other hand, if a substantial proportion is going to Group B — say 30 per cent — there is a *prima facie* case that ECGD protection will be worth having.

The second step — necessary if under, say, 30 per cent of exports is being made to high-risk markets — is to examine the buyers. If a very high proportion of buyers in the low-risk markets are known to be sound and reputable concerns on whom up-to-date information can be obtained, the case for ECGD loses further weight. If the business is well spread over a large number of companies, there is less reason for protection than if sales are concentrated in a small number of buyers.

Having done these analyses the exporter should then step back and consider whether there still appears to be a case for insurance. The following example illustrates this:

Total exports   – £1 million
Exports to Group A – £750,000
Exports to Group B – £250,000
Business in Group A is well-spread.

The exporter has several associate companies, but in only one Group A market is he willing to exclude all the sales from cover — value £100,000.

The likely cost of a new policy (1979) would be around 0.37 per cent. Around half of the premium will be spent on insuring what are believed to be good buyers in strong markets. It is not possible to take this example further because so much depends on the quality of the buyers, the bad debt record of the exporter and the size of the limits that will be needed. Credit insurance is not a licence to trade with any willing buyer, and if restrictions are indicated on certain buyers, this should be taken as a warning and not used as an excuse for turning down a policy quotation.

The question of access to subsidised finance brings another dimension to the problem. If the exporter would not take advantage of a Comprehensive Bank Guarantee, his decision should rest entirely on the market and buyer analyses — and on the alternative quotations offered to him. The option which is always available is to do without insurance cover. Self-insurance on the 'Group B' markets will probably mean insisting on more secure terms, e.g. Letter of Credit instead of usance Bills, than might be necessary under a policy. A fairly high budget must be allowed for the cost of obtaining and up-dating credit information on all buyers. An exporter with a special product may be fortunate in that he can demand secure terms, but against that he has to carry a pre-shipment risk of making to order and then finding he has no buyer. Another alternative for exporters selling mainly to Europe and the USA is a Trade Indemnity policy. This protects against insolvency and protracted default only and is normally limited to those markets. On the other hand, terms are more flexible and there is more possibility of an individually tailored package than with ECGD.

How can a policy holder ensure he gets good value for his policy?

Once the decision is taken to have a policy, the first principle to be observed is that it is not a substitute for credit management. There are many exporters who fail to understand this and consequently they do not make the best use of their policies.

ECGD themselves indicate a number of points which cause problems:

1 Discretionary limits are not used. Only too often exporters apply for limits which are within their own discretion, whether this is £5,000 or higher. It is a simple matter to obtain a bank or agency report, but if this is left to ECGD, the result is that time which ought to be spent on the difficult underwriting decisions has to be devoted to routine enquiries. The whole system slows down, and both ECGD staff and exporters become more and more frustrated.

2 The handling of the policy — enquiries, declarations, claims, etc. — is relegated to a junior person who frequently does not understand it.

3 Not enough attention is paid to the need for correct names and addresses, both of buyers and of their bankers and to the need to give advance notice of new names rather than expecting a limit to be agreed within one or two days.

A controversial question is whether to use an insurance broker in dealing with ECGD. There are very good brokers who give excellent service through their skill in presenting a case to ECGD, either on renewal terms or on a marginal limit decision. Constant liaison with ECGD should mean knowledge of which underwriter to approach, which precedents to draw on and which aspects of a case to emphasise. ECGD personnel are moved around between departments quite often, making it difficult for an exporter to build up close relationships with underwriters, whereas a broker should be more able to keep in touch.

The most important factor in making a policy successful is the approach of the exporter. A professional credit manager will make a policy work for his company, with or without a broker. If it is left to an inexperienced and probably uninterested clerk, the result will be frustrations and 'misunderstandings on both sides.

What are the main problems and difficulties likely to be encountered by policy holders?

Complaints about ECGD are heard frequently, but many of them are the inevitable result of the exporter's belief that he has no need of any form of credit management. Included in this is the accusation of long delays in obtaining limit decisions. ECGD maintains status files on over 200,000 overseas buyers, and claims that over 60 per cent of all enquiries are dealt with within seven days. Reliable information is nonetheless very hard to obtain in most developing countries. Even when full details of buyers and their bankers are given, delays of a few weeks are sometimes unavoidable. More legitimate problems include the following:

1 *UK buyers* The exporter has to decide on the total inclusion or exclusion of UK buyers. Payment terms to these buyers have to be a maximum of 30 days. If the exporter wishes to obtain finance under the Comprehensive Bank Guarantee, a copy Bill of Lading must be provided. This is a far stricter requirement than is imposed on business direct with overseas buyers, where proof of export is accepted in a wide variety of forms. Since goods can sometimes wait at the docks for several days or even weeks, the exporter selling through a UK buyer is at a disadvantage compared to the direct exporter.

2 *Evidence of shipment* An exporter making a large number of low-value shipments has a problem in that his bank will not provide finance on a whole month's despatches unless immediate evidence of shipment can be given on 100 per cent of those transactions.

3 *Pre-shipment finance* While pre-credit risk protection can be obtained under a CSTG, pre-shipment finance is only available for capital goods contracts, and even then it is limited to contracts with a value of at least £1 million.

Chapter 16

Specific guarantees and export finance

Specific guarantees — supplier credit

Exporters selling capital equipment on terms exceeding two years may seek ECGD cover on specific contracts. These are negotiated individually, according to the degree of commercial and market risk. In addition to the causes of loss described under the CSTG, cover is available against the default of a public buyer (either before or after shipment). The maximum protection is 90 per cent regardless of the cause of loss. Specific guarantees normally take effect from date of contract, thus protecting the exporter against losses due to the insolvency of the buyer or frustration of the contract from causes beyond his control and that of his buyer.

Specific Bank Guarantees (SBG) are available to help the exporter finance his contracts. The main conditions of SBGs are as follows:

1   At least 15 per cent of contract value must be paid on or before delivery of goods.

2   Fixed rates of interest are charged, based on minimum rates agreed by the Berne Union, comprising ECGD and other credit insurance organisations operated by foreign governments. These are based on their view of overseas markets as either 'poor', 'intermediate' or 'rich'. For contracts up to five years, minimum

interest rates are between 7.25 and 7.75 per cent, moving slightly higher on contracts exceeding five years.

3   These preferential rates are *not* available for contracts made with buyers in the EEC except for the sale of ships and (on a case-by-case basis) aircraft and aero-engine projects.

4   For sterling contracts, the bank provides non-recourse finance against accepted bills or promissory notes. Evidence of export and a warranty confirming that the ECGD cover is in order is also required. In many cases 'with recourse' finance is available against presentation of shipping documents, the bank arranging to have bills accepted by the buyer. Once acceptance is obtained, the finance moves onto a non-recourse basis.

5   Contracts may be expressed in either sterling, US dollars or Deutschemarks. The normal minimum for foreign currency contracts is £1 million. (This facility first became available in July 1978.)

6   While five years is the normal maximum credit period, ECGD will consider longer periods for very large projects or where there is evidence that such terms are being offered by foreign competition.

7   Pre-shipment finance can be provided — at *non-preferential* rates —on contracts exceeding £1 million.

8   Before an SBG is issued, ECGD require the exporter to sign a Recourse Agreement, for which there is a charge of 32p per £100. This covers ECGD for money paid to the bank not covered by the policy.

The provision of SBGs used to be limited to the UK clearing banks, but in 1978 this restriction was removed. UK merchant banks and foreign banks are entitled to loan money under ECGD guarantees, and consequently there is far more competition for exporters' business. The result is a reduction of bank charges. Whereas under the old system the clearing banks had fairly standard charges of 1 per cent flat commitment fee plus a negotiation fee of around 2 per mill. flat plus a 1 per mill. annual management fee, the exporter should be able to find cheaper rates by shopping around.

Exhibit 16.1 illustrates the supplier credit procedure.

Buyer credit

Under a buyer credit, finance is provided direct to the buyer by a bank covered by an ECGD guarantee. This involves a fundamentally different series of arrangements compared to supplier credits. The main elements are as follows:

264

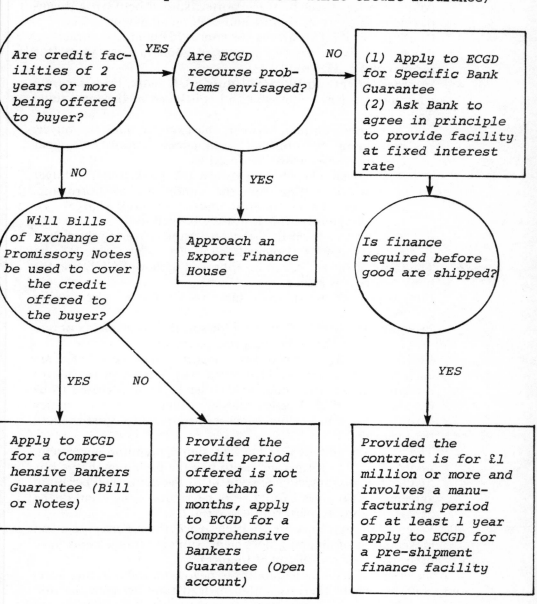

1   A minimum contract value of £1 million is normally required.
2   The overseas buyer is usually required to pay 15 or 20 per cent of contract price direct to the exporter, spread between a down-payment on contract signing and cash on shipment.
3   Credit terms of 5-15 years may be approved but most contracts do not exceed five years (for supply of goods) or ten years (for turnkey projects).
4   In order for cash to be provided by a UK bank, three separate contracts must be negotiated and concluded at the same time. These are:
    a A supply contract between the exporter and the buyer, containing the normal commercial details. Payment conditions are cross-referenced to:
    b A financial agreement between the bank and the buyer (borrower), setting out the conditions of borrowing, repayment details, interest and other bank charges. To become operative this has to be backed by:
    c A guarantee from ECGD to the bank, covering the risk of non-payment of prinicipal or interest.
5   The supply contract has to be approved by both ECGD and the bank before it is signed.
6   Interest rates are fixed, on the same basis as those under supplier credits.
7   Providing the supply contract allows it, the exporter can obtain pre-shipment finance, i.e. progress payments.
8   ECGD encourages exporters to transact buyer credits in foreign currency (US dollars or Deutschemarks), although the use of foreign currencies for contracts under £5 million ceased to be mandatory in 1978. Interest rates are usually lower on currency loans compared to sterling, which is of course a positive benefit to the exporter.
9   The exporter and ECGD have to sign a premium agreement, under which the former agrees to pay the premium charged by ECGD for guaranteeing repayment to the bank. The premium agreement also gives ECGD recourse rights in the event of the exporter failing to perform the contract.
10 When all the agreements have been signed, the exporter is paid on presentation of shipping documents (unless arrangements have been made for pre-shipment finance).

A buyer credit takes many months to negotiate, and it is, therefore, only suitable where there is sufficient lead time between the first approach and the commencement of manufacture. This, in turn, will be dictated by the buyer's required completion date.

The advantages of buyer over supplier credit are as follows:

a   Pre-shipment finance is more readily available and can be drawn out of the loan itself, whereas on a supplier credit a separate arrangement must be made with the bank and any pre-shipment finance is not available at preferential interest rates.

b   Payments received under a supplier credit are a contingent liability on the exporter until the bills are paid — even though the exporter is covered by an ECGD specific guarantee. Payments received under a buyer credit do not affect the exporter's borrowing facilities because the repayment contract is between the buyer and the banks.

c   All bank commissions and charges are payable by the buyer, so the exporter can exclude all such items from his costings (except for the ECGD premium).

d   Overseas buyers may prefer to borrow direct from a UK bank, rather than accept a series of bills raised by the supplier.

Exhibit 16.2 illustrates the buyer credit procedure.

The following example illustrates how a manufacturer can use a buyer credit to obtain pre-shipment finance:

Contract value — £1 million

Credit period — 5 years

Amount of loan — 80 per cent = £800,000

Buyer credit arranged with ECGD at an interest rate of 7 per cent p.a.

Period between contract signing and shipment — 12 months.

Manufacturer's costs before shipment — £750,000.

The two options open, A and B, are shown in Exhibits 16.3 and 16.4. The costs of Option B have to be compared with the costs of Option A — £112,500. There is a net saving of £79,333 because the contract price will reduce to £887,500 with additional loan costs of £32,667 payable by the buyer. Not only is the contract price more competitive, but the exporter does not have to tie up finance during the manufacturing period.

(Acknowledgement and thanks to Barclays Bank International Ltd for permission to base this example on a paper issued by them in October 1976.)

Lines of credit

Another form of buyer credit occurs when finance is made available to overseas borrowers (usually governments) on a line of credit. This facility is often provided by a consortium of banks and can either be used for a 'shopping basket' of capital goods and services (a general purpose line of credit) or a single project. In both cases a number of

Exhibit 16.2 Guide to establishing a single project buyer credit facility

EXPORTER	BUYER ALSO BORROWER*	UK BANK	ECGD
Prepares to tender and approaches		To investigate finance availability	For indication of their support
		Agree in principle to provide finance based on extent of ECGD support	
			Letter of indication given
Tender submitted			
	Tender accepted. Contractual negotiations begin		
		Contract terms examined and loan agreement drafted	
Supply contract drafted and sent to			Contract terms examined to see that ECGD requirements are met

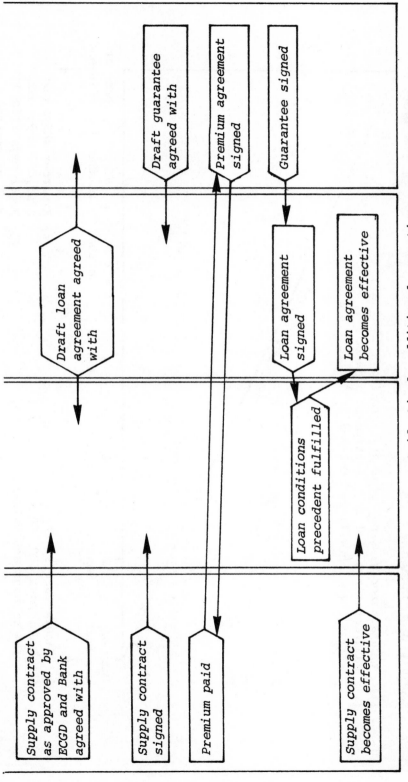

*where the buyer and the borrower are not identical, additional operations are necessary

Exhibit 16.3 Option A

(i) *Manufacturer's normal cost of borrowing – 15% p.a.*
(ii) *Manufacturer's cost of pre-shipment finance –*
£112,500 (which will be included in contract price)

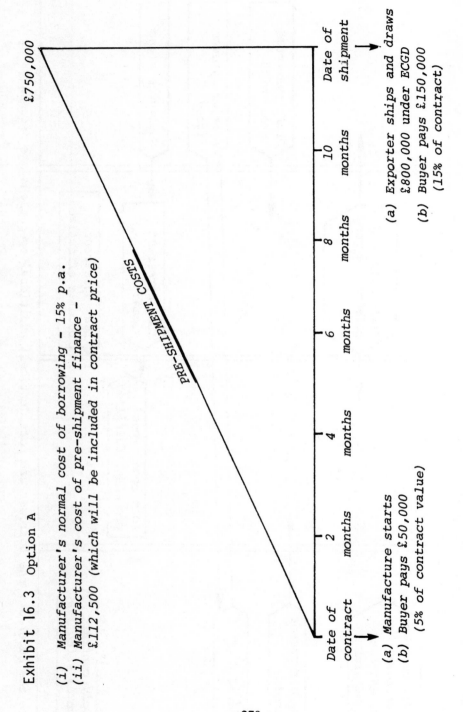

Exhibit 16.4 Option B

Providing the buyer credit can be negotiated appropriately, the manufacturer can be authorised to receive stage payments during manufacture. The diagram shows how four payments of £200,000 each out of the loan can have a dramatic effect on the manufacturer's cash-flow

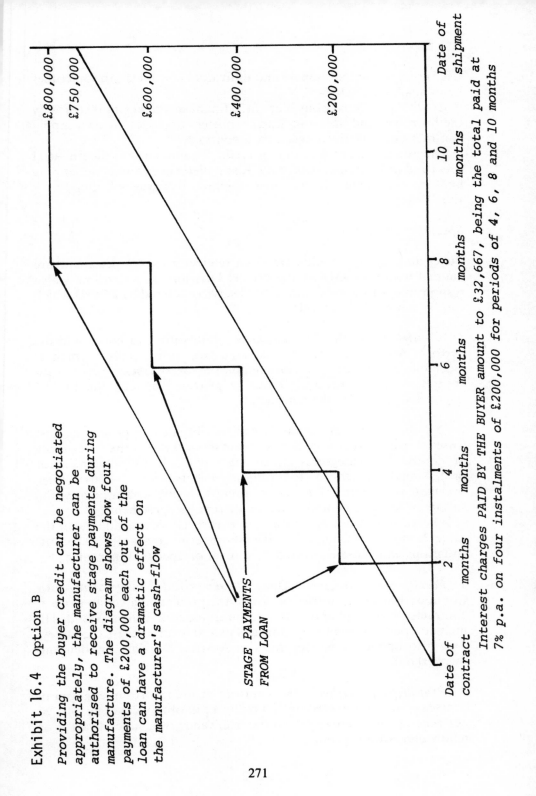

Date of contract

Date of shipment

2 months

4 months

6 months

8 months

10 months

£200,000

£400,000

£600,000

£750,000

£800,000

STAGE PAYMENTS FROM LOAN

Interest charges *PAID BY THE BUYER* amount to £32,667, being the total paid at 7% p.a. on four instalments of £200,000 for periods of 4, 6, 8 and 10 months

271

UK suppliers can participate and individual contracts can sometimes be as small as £10,000.

As with an ordinary buyer credit, a financial agreement is signed by the borrower and the bank. Each exporter concludes his own supply contract and effectively has a cash contract.

The establishment of a line of credit is announced in the financial press and in *Trade and Industry*. UK suppliers then contact the lending bank to determine whether their potential business will qualify for EGCD support.

Specialised facilities

Buyer and supplier credits are often referred to as 'projects' and are handed within ECGD by the Project Division. This division is also responsible for the other specialised services offered by ECGD which can be summarised as follows:

1 Constructional Works Guarantee Both supply of goods and the performance of services are covered uner this facility, which is available either for a private employer or overseas government contracts. Ninety per cent cover is provided against the loss of payments due under the contract.

2 Services guarantee Policies can be obtained to protect against losses of overseas earnings derived from services rather than the supply of goods. The categories which are eligible include technical or professional assistance to overseas clients; refits, conversions, overhaul or repairs of ships or aircraft; hiring arrangements; the supply of know-how under licence or royalty agreements.

Where services are of a recurring nature, cover is available on the same basis as a Comprehensive Short-term Guarantee. 'One-off' situations can also be covered by a form of Specific Guarantee.

3 Foreign subcontractors There are reciprocal arrangements with Common Market countries by which the protection given to a main contractor in a supplier or buyer credit transaction can be extended to include a percentage of sub-contracts placed in another EEC country. This also applies to subcontracts in Austria, Norway, Sweden and Switzerland.

4 Project participation UK members of a consortium engaged in overseas contracts exceeding £20 million can obtain cover against 90 per cent of losses arising from the insolvency of a subcontractor or fellow consortium member.

5   *Cost escalation cover*   This gives protection against losses caused by rapidly rising costs in capital goods contracts worth at least £2 million with a minimum manufacturing period of two years. This is a complex facility, and early communication with ECGD is essential before any commitments are made.

6   *Performance bonds and unfair calling of bonds*   These topics are examined in Chapter 17.

7   *Tender to contract cover*   This policy offers the exporter protection against fluctuations in exchange rates and is dealt with in Chapter 18.

8   *Overseas investment insurance*   New overseas investments in the form of equity capital (cash, plant or know-how) or loans can be protected against political risk, e.g. expropriation, war damage and transfer delay, for periods up to 15 years. Cover can also be given for certain guarantees of loans raised outside the UK.

Contact with ECGD

It is desirable for the exporter to keep in touch with ECGD from an early stage in negotiations which may result in the need for supplier or buyer credit facilities. Contact may be either direct or through a broker. A good broker can give valuable advice on the timing and manner of an approach to ECGD underwriters. Basically, contact should be made at two crucial stage:

1   At the quotation stage, to check whether cover is likely to be available for the approximate size and type of contract in view, to obtain an indication of the likely premium rate and to be advised of any limitations which ECGD may impose. These will be dictated by the view taken of the market in question and by the amount of money already at risk. Limitations could be made on the value of the loan portion of the contract or on the credit period, or both. At the same time as this approach is made to ECGD, the exporter should be sounding out a number of banks as to their services and costs in that market.

2   Immediately prior to contract signature, a firm written proposal form must be submitted to ECGD. Strictly speaking, an exporter should not seek ECGD support after a contract is signed, but it is not always possible to predict the progress of negotiations or to have all the contract details available to ECGD in sufficient time before signature. Providing the exporter does not 'spring' a

proposition on the Department without any prior warning, ECGD are generally sympathetic to such cases.

A recommended clause to be included in contracts is as follows: 'This contract will not become operative without the approval of the UK monetary authorities.' This is a polite fiction, intended to preserve the rule that an exporter should not disclose ECGD's interest to his buyer.

Where contract values are large and the markets are considered high-risk, the decisions on the amount of ECGD support to be made available are taken in Whitehall by the Treasury. These are usually referred to as Section 2 business, since they fall outside the scope of ECGD's normal business where decisions are based on commercial criteria. To obtain a favourable decision under Section 2, the exporter has to demonstrate that ECGD support for the proposed contract is in 'the national interest'. Where particularly long credit terms are being requested, it is necessary to give evidence that similar credit terms are being offered by overseas competitors. ECGD's attitude in such situations is that they will try and match competition terms, but they will not take the lead and risk starting a 'credit race'.

In the final analysis the decision has to turn on whether the political or economic importance of supporting trade in a particular market outweighs the risks of non-payment. In 1978-9, for example, there were a small number of markets whose risks were so great as to prevent virtually any form of support for long- or medium-term finance. These included Turkey, Peru, Zambia and Uganda.

Export finance

Sources of export finance can be grouped under the following headings:
1   Overdraft.
2   Bill advances and negotiations.
3   Discounting of term bills under Letter of Credit.
4   ECGD comprehensive guarantees (open account or bill).
5   ECGD's specific bank guarantees (supplier credit).
6   ECGD buyer credit.
7   Acceptance credits.
8   Confirming houses/export finance houses.
9   Export merchants.
10   Leasing.
11   Instalment finance.
12   Forfaiting.
13   Factoring.

Apart from the straightforward overdraft facility, (1)-(6) above have already been covered. Exporters selling wholely on very short-term credit (up to 90 days) to markets and buyers which they feel do not justify an ECGD policy may be able to turn over their overseas debtors fast enough to live inside their normal overdraft arrangements. A request for an increase in the overdraft caused by slow payments or lengthening terms will, however, be more favourably received if the bank can see that the export receivables are protected by ECGD or Trade Indemnity. The last entry, Factoring, has also been covered in Chapter 9.

Acceptance credits

Finance through acceptance credits may be regarded as a more flexible alternative to overdraft finance.

An exporter can arrange with an acceptance house (now usually referred to as a merchant bank, of which there are 17 in the City being members of the Accepting Houses Committee) to draw on a line of credit. Acceptance credits (which are clean bills) are drawn by the exporter on the merchant bank for an agreed per iod — normally 30, 60 or 90 days. The bills are accepted by the bank and immediately discounted at a very fine rate to give the exporter the funds he needs. The security behind acceptance credits is normally specific documentary bills (preferably covered by ECGD) covering the exporter's overseas sales, but they may be used to provide working capital in a more general way. In the latter case the bank will look directly at the exporter's balance sheet for its security.

The precise terms of the line of credit are contained in a 'Facility Letter' which will require the exporter to repay the sums advanced on the due date of each acceptance. In practice the exporter will often choose to draw fresh bills, thus 'rolling over' the facility. Bills can be drawn in sterling or other currencies, which allows them to be used with great flexibility. The bank charges a fee (acceptance commission) which is deducted from the face value of each bill together with the discount charges when bills are discounted.

The total cost of an acceptance credit will vary according to the cost of money in the City. Because the bank's name is on it, the finest possible rate is obtained, which will be highly competitive with other short-term facilities such as overdrafts.

Confirming houses/export finance houses

The original function of a confirming house was to confirm orders placed through it by overseas buyers, thereby eliminating the export credit risk of the UK exporter. This role is still carried out, but confirming houses today offer a wide range of services and are of particular value to exporters who wish to avoid the administrative effort demanded by an ECGD policy or who lack the expertise required to handle all the problems of exporting.

Typical of the facilities offered is the following, quoted by Grindlay Brandts Export Finance Ltd, one of the leading export finance houses.

1 Short-term facilities   Our short-term financing operation is geared mainly to the purchase of raw materials, consumer durables, low cost machinery, etc. where credit up to 180 days is required.

A facility could either be of a specific or revolving nature; the former would relate to specific purchases and the latter would provide a means of finance for unknown quantities of known goods up to a maximum credit limit with a repayment period of up to 180 days. No deposit is needed for credit of up to 180 days from shipment and we are able to offer a high degree of flexibility designing a facility to suit a particular buyer's specific requirement. Facilities can be arranged in either sterling or a major foreign currency. The cost of a sterling facility is related to the UK clearing bank base rate and where foreign currency financing is involved costs will be related to the London Inter Bank Offer Rate (LIBOR).

Depending on the type of transactions and the values involved it may be possible where foreign currency financing is required to offer a fixed rate of interest for the six-month period.

2 Medium-term facilities   We are able to provide up to five year's credit for purchases from the UK of capital and semi-capital goods such as tractors, cranes, plant, machinery, aircraft, etc. Where the credit period is two years or more, we take advantage of the preferential interest rates available through ECGD. The actual terms negotiated with ECGD depend on the type and value of the equipment, but contracts in excess of £120,000 would normally qualify for up to five years' credit. In certain circumstances it is possible to negotiate longer terms, but in any event a down-payment of between 15 and 20 per cent of the contract value is required, with the balance payable over the credit period by equal six-monthly instalments commencing six months from shipment or commissioning. Financing can be arranged in either sterling or US dollars at fixed rates of interest.

3   Distributor financing   The short- and medium-term finance facilities described above can also apply to distributors operating overseas; the terms, however, are usually shorter than those for actual users of the equipment and depend to a large extent upon the on-sale terms. For credit periods of two years and over the distributor will be charged the preferential ECGD fixed-interest rate and can thus extend low-cost financing to his customer which is, of course, a very important consideration in a competitive market.

The procedure for opening short- and medium-term facilities is relatively uncomplicated:

a   Upon receipt of a request to provide finance we telex by return an indication-in-principle of the terms and charges applicable to the transaction.

b   We make application under our own ECGD policy for approval and an indication of the terms available.

c   When ECGD approval is received, a separate financing agreement is prepared and sent to the customer who is requested to signify acceptance by signing and returning the duplicate copy of the agreement.

d   Immediately the acceptance is returned together with a copy of the order on the supplier and any necessary down-payment, we despatch a written undertaking to the supplier guaranteeing 100 per cent cash payment on shipment of the goods.

e   When the goods are despatched the supplier is paid and the shipping documents, together with a draft or drafts, are sent to the nominated collection bank with instructions to release the shipping documents against payment of any sight draft and acceptance of the other drafts covering the credit period.

f   The collection bank returns the accepted drafts which are then presented by us as and when they become due for payment.

There are several advantages to using our services and in addition to receiving cash immediately shipment takes place, by utilising our facilities you would be relieved of the following problems:

i   The problem of having to vet your buyer's creditworthiness.

ii   The problem of having to negotiate with ECGD for the necessary credit insurance policy and related bank guarantees.

iii   The problem of having to administer the financial package over a period of five or, in some cases, more years.

iv   The problem of having to 'chase' overdue accounts.

v   The problem of having to negotiate with ECGD should any of the credit instalments be unpaid. Such claims can be lengthy and will normally involve ECGD calling up recourse for at least 10 per cent of the loss.

vi   The problem of having to instigate prolonged and often expensive recovery action.

vii The problem of having to enter into any recourse agreement with ECGD.

It is our view that the above problems should be the responsibility of a specialist merchant bank and we, therefore, undertake such responsibilities, thus leaving you free to do the job of negotiating other sales, of manufacturing and delivering goods, a job which is of greater importance to you.

In addition to the above, a confirming house may also take over responsibility for shipping and documentation. The commission charged by confirming houses is either paid by the buyer separately or is included in the selling price. Either way it represents a price increase. In deciding whether to use a confirming house on a particular contract, the exporter must be satisfied that his buyer will accept this package which will be more expensive than a direct sale handled by the exporter himself. It should be possible for the exporter, however, through regular usage of a confirming house, not only to obtain a fine rate but also to reduce his own overhead costs.

Export merchants

Export merchants buy and sell goods as principals, in contrast to the confirming house which is not responsible for performance of the contract between exporter and buyer.

Other services offered by an export merchant may include the holding of stocks at home or overseas and the promotion of overseas sales.

Leasing

It is possible for an overseas buyer to lease UK capital goods. The lease may be arranged locally with the aid of a UK leasing company, or it may be established direct with a UK company. In either situation, the manufacturer sells to the leasing company and receives 100 per cent payment on installation. The lessee is enabled to obtain equipment it could not afford to buy (or which it chooses not to buy because of a high obsolescence risk).

Instalment finance

There are a number of London finance houses with branches or associates abroad, through whom deferred payment by instalments may be arranged for an overseas buyer. The exporter receives immediate payment.

This is a difficult field to enter because of different credit-sale and hire-purchase laws in different markets.

Forfaiting

In recent years a new source of export finance has developed. Forfaiting involves the discounting of documentary bills and notes, without recourse to the borrower, over a medium-term period (generally five years) at a fixed rate of interest. Transactions usually fall in the range of £250,000-£750,000, but can be considerably larger. Forfaiting is limited to Swiss francs, US dollars or Deutschemarks. Interest rates are calculated from a number of factors, principally the political/transfer risk of the market of the obligor, i.e. the overseas buyer, the need for a safety margin to cover unexpected cost increases, payment experience from the market in question and the level of supply and demand for financing in that market.

For the UK exporter, forfaiting may be attractive when the amount of ECGD-backed finance is limited on a particular market or is only available against very restrictive payment conditions. Interest rates are high by comparison with other borrowing rates but the benefits are worth considering:
1   Fixed interest for the total period.
2   No recourse to the borrower.
3   Ease of operation.

Forfaiting originated in Switzerland and this remains its centre, although some banks in London, West Germany and Austria have also entered the field. The specialist forfaiting company in London is Finanz AG London Ltd, owned by Credit Suisse. Further details may be found in a booklet, *The Forfaiting Manual*, published by Finanz AG London Ltd in February 1977.

It is becoming increasingly common for overseas buyers of capital goods to require 100 per cent finance from UK suppliers. The maximum proportion which ECGD will support on a buyer or supplier credit is 85 per cent, sometimes reducing to 80 or 75 per cent depending on the market and the product. 'Front-end financing' is the term used to describe a finance arrangement covering the remaining 15-25 per cent. It may also be used to describe the financing of local or other non-UK costs incurred by the buyer which are outside the scope of the ECGD guarantee.

It is clearly an advantage to the overseas buyer if a total finance package including the ECGD credit, the deposit and any local costs can be arranged by one bank, or by one bank leading a number of banks (a 'consortium'). This is known as 'Project financing' and the arranging bank is normally a merchant bank.

While supplier and buyer credits may be expressed in either sterling, US dollars or Deutschemarks, the front-end portion has to be denominated in non-UK funds. This arises from *The Exchange Control Act, 1947,* which requires that payment for goods exported from the UK must be received from outside the sterling area, and also that credit beyond 180 days cannot be given without Bank of England approval unless under a ECGD guarantee.

The source of additional financing is the Eurocurrency market, which requires some explanation.

A Eurocurrency is any freely convertible currency held outside the control of the monetary authorities of its country of origin. All dollars for example, owned by non-US banks, investors and depositors are held on the accounts of American banks. In the same way, all sterling deposits owned by non-UK investors appear as credits on the account of UK banks. All these dollars or pounds are termed Eurodollars or Eurosterling because their ownership and control is outside the USA or the UK. Eurocurrencies are never bought and sold; they are borrowed and lent.

The Eurocurrency market consists of all the currency deposits owned by non-residents of the countries of origin which are available to borrowers. The borrowers are principally governments and government agencies. The lenders are the international banks, who also act as intermediaries. Loans can be for varying periods depending on the state of the market and the quality of the borrower, occasionally going to twelve years or beyond. Interest rates are generally fixed for six months and then recalculated for a further period. The rates quoted are expressed as a percentage over LIBOR (London Inter Bank Offered Rate). It is this market which provides the 'front-end' financing demanded more and more by overseas buyers.

In any project where long-term finance will be required, it is essential for the exporter to enlist the aid of a bank at the earliest opportunity. In recent years — particularly since ECGD relaxed the rules about foreign currency credits — the merchant banks have been very active in their support of exporters. Different banks offer specialist help in different markets, which may even include advice on the negotiation of commercial contracts and the presence of a banker in the negotiating team. The credit manager's role in project financing is one of liaison. He should provide the link between his company and the banking world.

Barter

A form of business not touched on so far is barter. This is a loosely used term which may indicate either a straightforward exchange of goods between two traders or a compensation arrangement whereby the exporter commits himself to purchase from his customers goods of equal value to his own deliveries. Under this latter system, a third party is often involved who acts as intermediary. An example of compensation would be where a UK supplier of equipment has a potential buyer in Turkey. Turkey has no foreign exchange but wants to sell tobacco. A possible solution is for the UK company to find a non-Turkish buyer for Turkish tobacco of equivalent value to the equipment. In this situation there would actually be four principals — the UK equipment supplier, the Turkish equipment buyer, the Turkish tobacco supplier and the tobacco buyer. To bring all these parties together and conclude arrangements satisfactory to all of them requires the services of a specialist firm. There are a number of these in the City, generally belonging to merchant banking groups, who will undertake the task in return for a percentage of the UK exporter's contract. Experienced intermediaries are also to be found in other European centres, in particular Vienna and Zurich.

As was illustrated by the above example, the incentive for a barter deal is generally lack of hard currency. Eastern bloc countries and developing nations such as Brazil, Iran and other Middle Eastern markets are the most common seekers of barter contracts.

Another type of barter arrangement, sometimes referred to as 'cooperation', takes place when a UK exporter contracts to build a plant or install equipment in an Eastern European country and agrees to be paid in products from the completed plant or equipment. While this can be good business for a UK construction or engineering company, the problems of marketing the end product in the West can

281

be considerable, especially if Western markets are already suffering from over-capacity.

Help for the smaller company

Midland Bank Ltd introduced a scheme in 1979 designed to help customers who, because of their relatively small or occasional export business, do not make use of ECGD insurance or ECGD-backed finance. Initially the scheme was limited to firms exporting less than £100,000 p.a., dealing on bills of exchange or promissory notes on terms up to 180 days. Buyers have to be credit-approved by the bank and the maximum value of each bill or note is normally £10,000.

Midland Bank take out a policy with ECGD and give their customers 100 per cent without-recourse protection on accepted bills or issued promissory notes. The bank then finance the bills and notes at $1\frac{1}{2}$ per cent p.a. over their normal base rate, plus a flat 1 per cent (minimum £10) on each bill or note. This is to cover not only the ECGD premium but also the bank's normal collection and handling charges. Finance will also be provided on unaccepted bills or sight bills on a with-recourse basis. Bills or notes drawn in foreign currency will also be financed in sterling at the appropriate forward contract rate.

At the time of writing, this scheme had only just been launched. There is no doubt, however, that it represents a major step forward in the provision of short-term export finance.

Chapter 17

Contract risks and bonds

A number of market risks facing the exporter were examined in Chapter 11, principally the dangers of disruption of trade, the lack of foreign exchange and restrictive government regulations. Difficult as these problems can be, they only represent a part of the story as far as exporters of capital goods and contractors working overseas are concerned.

In this chapter an attempt will be made to summarise these additional hazards and to indicate how far protection can be obtained from ECGD and what facilities are available in the private market.

The private market concerned with protection against political risk consists of Lloyd's Underwriters supported by the leading British insurance companies. An alternative for some forms of insurance is American International Underwriters (AIU). Both Lloyds and AIU are approached through insurance brokers, such as those named at the end of Chapter 10.

Pre-contract signing problems

Nature of the market

The first task facing the UK exporter is the need to understand something of the market. Business methods and business ethics are not the same the world over, and the exporter who neglects to study his market and gain some understanding of its customs and traditions will suffer the inevitable fate of someone who has not done his homework. The Near and Middle East are the principal areas of problems at the moment, but business with any non-Western industrial market demands close attention to local practice and law. Sources of information include the British Overseas Trade Board.

Identity and status of the buyer

Unlike in the UK or Europe, the standing of the buyer is frequently not clear. The distinctions between sole traders, companies, consortiums and even local or central authorities are not always clear-cut, especially in the Middle East. It is most important to establish whether the other party is a 'public buyer', since ECGD bond support or cover does not extend to private buyers who require 'on-demand' bonds. This will be covered in more detail later in the chapter.

Reliable financial information on private buyers in the developing countries is very hard to obtain, but the exporter may be no better off dealing with a public buyer. It is not unknown for a government official — supposedly representing a ministry or department — to be dismissed and negotiations carried out in his name to be ignored or dishonoured.

The agent

It is often necessary for a UK firm to use a local agent. The extent of his authority should be clearly defined in writing. Commission will doubtless have to be paid, both as an agreed percentage of contract value to the agent and as part of his expenses. In many instances this will be pure and simple bribery, and the exporter must recognise that in many countries commerce could not exist without it. The only safeguard is to have enough in the price to cover it. With regard to commission which is directly related to contract value, the seller must be careful to avoid any commitment to pay it all at the front-end of the contract. An arrangement whereby commission is paid pro-rata to the receipt of stage payments is preferable; otherwise cash-flow can be seriously affected.

Taxation and profits

In a construction project — or any project that requires employees to be resident in the overseas country — liability to local taxation must be examined. Some countries impose withholding taxes on money remitted from them, and others have tight regulations about the remitting of locally earned profits back to the supplier country.

These matters may not appear to be relevant to the job of the credit manager, but all too often it falls to him to provide the answers because no one else in the company has thought of the questions.

Bid or tender bonds

The purpose of a bid bond is to give the buyer confidence that the seller is financially able to carry out the contract if it is awarded to him. Frivolous tenders are thus avoided. The bond is normally for 5 per cent or less of the bid and it has to accompany the bid. As for other types of bond, bid bonds may be issued either by banks or by surety companies. The main differences are:
1   Banks are less concerned with the underlying questions — can the bidding company be considered competent to do the work? They issue bid bonds against the counter-indemnity of the exporter, having first satisfied themselves that his balance sheet is strong enough.
2   Surety companies only issue bid bonds if they are satisfied that the bidder is technically and financially competent to undertake the contract.

A bid bond is normally returned for cancellation if the contract is not awarded or replaced by a performance bond (see below) if the tender is successful. Bid bonds are generally acknowledged to be justified and do not cause serious problems. Support from ECGD in the issue of a bond is examined below under the heading 'ECGD bond support'.

Contract problems

The content of a major contract with an overseas buyer gives rise to many problems, some of which are beyond the scope of this book. Those which the credit manager should be aware of are dealt with below. The exporter will very often be asked to submit a draft contract. It is most important that clauses with wording most favourable to the seller can be prepared quickly.

Payment terms

Contracts for capital goods are either on 'cash' terms, i.e. under Letter of Credit or short-term bills, or credit (supplier or buyer credit).

A typical cash contract might have the following payment terms, the *wording* of which is important:

> 15 per cent of contract value, paid in sterling within 30 days of contract signature by cable transfer to Exporter's Bank Ltd, High Street, Anytown, for the credit of UK Exporter Ltd A/C No.....
> 85 per cent of contract value to be covered by an Irrevocable Letter of Credit confirmed by a UK bank, to be opened and loged with the confirming bank within 30 days of contract signature. Payment to be made on presentation of the following documents (all in quadruplicate):
> Commercial invoice
> Certificate of origin
> Insurance certificate (on CIF or Franco terms)
> Full set clean Bills of Lading
>> *or*
> Forwarding agent's or warehouse receipt (for ex-works and FOB contracts)
> Packing note
> Seller's Inspection Certificate

The Letter of Credit will permit part-shipment to be made from any UK port and will permit documents to be presented up to 21 days from date of Bill of Lading.

In a credit contract, payment terms will be more complicated. Assuming that ECGD support is being provided, the wording for a supplier credit might be:

> 15 per cent of contract value paid within 30 days of contract signature by cable transfer to Exporter's Bank Ltd, High Street, Anytown, for the credit of UK Exporter Ltd A/C No. ....
> 10 per cent of contract value to be paid on shipment out of an Irrevocable Letter of Credit confirmed by a UK bank, to be opened and lodged with the confirming bank within 30 days of contract signature. Payment to be made on presentation of the following documents (all in quadruplicate):
> Commercial invoice for 10 per cent of each shipment value
> Certificate of origin
> Insurance Certificate (on CIF or Franco terms)
> Full set clean Bills of Lading
>> *or*

Forwarding agent's or warehouse receipt (for ex-works and
FOB contracts)
Packing note
Seller's Inspection Certificate

The Letter of credit will permit part-shipment to be made from any UK port and will permit documents to be presented up to 21 days from date of Bill of Lading.

The remaining 75 per cent of the total contract price will be paid by ten Bills of Exchange against each shipment, each of equal value, maturing at intervals of 6, 12, 18, 24, 30, 36, 42, 48, 54 and 60 months from the shipment date.

The cost of opening and confirmation of the Letter of Credit shall be for the account of the buyer.

Advance payment bonds and performance bonds

It is becoming normal practice for overseas buyers to require an advance payment bond to be provided as a condition of agreeing to any pre-shipment payment. The purpose is to ensure that, should the exporter fail to complete the contract, any such payment will be recovered. Performance bonds also insure the buyer against losses should the exporter fail to perform. While advance payment bonds are issued for the amount of any down-payment, varying from 5 to 30 per cent, the value of a performance bond is expressed as a percentage of contract value, usually 5 or 10 per cent.

Bonds are either 'on-demand' or conditional. A conditional bond requires the buyer to prove that the exporter is in default, and generally provides for payment up to the extent of the actual loss suffered. This type of bond may be issued either by a bank or a surety company. It does not present a problem because payment will not be made unless the buyer can prove default. Regrettably, overseas buyers are prone to insist on 'on-demand' bonds, under which the issuer is required to pay, the amount claimed on the buyer's first written demand — without having to show that default has occurred. This type of bond is rarely issued by a surety company. It is left to the banks who are generally much happier with 'on-demand' bonds than with conditional ones, since they wish to avoid having to exercise any form of judgement on contract performance. An example of a typical 'on-demand' bank bond is given in Exhibit 17.1. A bond issued by an American bank takes the form of a Standby Letter of Credit, which is illustrated in Exhibit 17.2. This latter example attempts to make the bond conditional, but in fact it is 'on-demand' since the bank promises to pay 'against your written statement'. Exhibit 17.3 shows a conditional

Exhibit 17.1 'On demand' bank bond

We understand that our customer ... has been awarded a Contract for the supply of....

We are informed that in this connection a Bank Guarantee for..., being...% of the Contract value, is required.

We, ... Bank Ltd, hereby guarantee to pay you an amount not exceeding ... upon receipt of your first written demand, certifying that in your absolute judgement... have failed to fulfil their obligations under the above-mentioned Contract.

This Guarantee expires on completion of the Contract or on..., whichever is the earlier. Any claim under this Guarantee must be submitted to us before the expiry date.

Any dispute over the interpretation of this Guarantee shall be subject to the laws of... (Buyer's country).

Exhibit 17.2 Standby Letter of Credit (Performance Bond)

Upon request of... (hereinafter referred to as the Seller), we hereby issue this irrevocable Standby Letter of Credit in your favour, for their account, up to.... This Performance Bond will be payable against your written statement that the Sellers have failed to perform subject to the Sellers having become liable to supply...to... (hereinafter referred to as the Buyer). Also subject to ..., being 15% of the total net contract price, having been paid to the Seller in accordance with the terms of an agreement made with the Buyer.

We hereby agree to repay to you in Sterling any amount for which the Seller shall be so liable under the above-mentioned agreement up to a total of .... The amount payable shall be calculated on a reducing basis pro-rata to the value of the goods supplied up to date if and when this Performance Bond is called. This Bond may be called if the Seller fails to meet his obligations under the agreement, except those obligations which are excluded or qualified under 'Force Majeure' of the agreement. This Bond will expire when the final delivery has been made, and in any event not later than....

We confirm this Letter of Credit and thereby undertake that all claims will be duly honoured by us, if presented to the negotiating bank not later than....

Exhibit 17.3

Credit & Guarantee Insurance Company Limited

Colonial House, Mincing Lane, London, EC3R 7PN
England

GUARANTEE

THIS GUARANTEE is issued by **Credit & Guarantee Insurance Company Limited** (the Guarantor) to the Indemnified Party stated in the Schedule.

WHEREAS the Supplier stated in the Schedule has paid to the Guarantor a premium as consideration for this Guarantee and whereas the Indemnified Party and the Supplier have entered into the Contract specifically described in the Schedule.

THE GUARANTOR hereby undertakes subject to the provisos stated overleaf and the terms conditions and endorsements contained herein to indemnify the Indemnified Party against loss not exceeding the amount stated in the Schedule in the event of the Supplier defaulting in the performance of the Contract.

THE GUARANTOR undertakes to settle liability under the terms of this Guarantee within thirty days of receipt of evidence that the Indemnified Party has exercised all legal rights and remedies against the Supplier and that the loss suffered is not recoverable from the Supplier.

THE LIABILITY of the Guarantor shall be paid in the currency stated in the Schedule through a Bank in the United Kingdom as nominated by the Indemnified Party whose receipt of such payment shall discharge the Guarantor from further liability.

Date:

....
Authorised Signatory

....
Underwriter for the Guarantor

Provisos *

1 This Guarantee shall only be valid provided it is delivered by the Guarantor to the Indemnified Party through a Bank in the United Kingdom as nominated by the Indemnified Party.

2 The Indemnified Party is not aware of the Supplier being in any financial difficulties at the date of acceptance of this Guarantee and has no reason to doubt that the Supplier will be able to perform the Contract.

3 The Indemnified Party shall not amend the Contract nor exercise any right to amend the Contract nor grant any indulgence thereunder without the prior written approval of the Guarantor.

4 The loss relating to this Guarantee shall have been directly and naturally suffered by the Indemnified Party as a result of a default by the Supplier during the validity period stated in the Schedule.

5 The Indemnified Party shall upon request of the Guarantor irrevocably assign to the Guarantor all rights in regard to any loss claimed under this Guarantee but such assignment shall only become effective on the date the Guarantor settles liability.

* *The Provisos incorporated in this Guarantee are conditions precedent to any liability of the Guarantor.*

Conditions

1 In the event of the Supplier defaulting in the performance of the Contract or any part thereof or the Indemnified Party having knowledge that the Supplier is unlikely to perform the Contract the Indemnified Party shall immediately take such action as is possible and prudent in the circumstances to require the Supplier to perform the Contract and immediately notify the Guarantor by telex or telegram and confirm such notification in writing. Thereafter the Indemnified Party shall in consultation with the Guarantor take all reasonable and prudent steps to mitigate any loss which may be suffered. The Indemnified Party shall if so required by the Guarantor allow the Guarantor to perform the Contract and shall credit and transfer to the Guarantor all monies and benefits due or to become due to the Supplier notwithstanding any terms of the Contract which entitles the Indemnified Party to retain such monies and benefits.

2 Evidence of loss suffered by the Indemnified Party shall include:—

    (a) an award of an Arbitrator in accordance with an arbitration provision incorporated in the Contract or

    (b) an unsatisfied Judgement Debt against the Supplier awarded in favour of the Indemnified Party by a Court in the United Kingdom or

    (c) written evidence from a Liquidator of the Supplier that the loss suffered by the Indemnified Party is a debt which will be admitted to rank against the insolvent estate of the Supplier or

    (d) written evidence in accordance with a procedure as detailed by the Guarantor in a special endorsement typed on this Guarantee.

3 The Indemnified Party shall at all times make available to the Guarantor and allow the Guarantor to examine or take copies of any letter accounts or other documents in the possession or control of the Indemnified Party relating to or connected with this Guarantee or any transactions between the Indemnified Party and the Supplier and the Indemnified Party shall at the request of the Guarantor supply the Guarantor with any information in the possession of the Indemnified Party or take any reasonable steps to obtain for the Guarantor any information or the sight of any documents in the possession of any third party relating to or connected with this Guarantee or any transaction between the Indemnified Party and the Supplier.

4 If the Indemnified Party makes any claim knowing it to be false or fraudulent as regards amount or otherwise this Guarantee shall become void and all claims under it shall be forfeited and any sums previously paid by the Guarantor under this Guarantee shall forthwith become repayable by the Indemnified Party.

5 The liability of the Guarantor shall cease at the expiry of the validity period stated in the Schedule except for any loss which directly relates to a default previously notified to the Guarantor under the terms of Condition 1 of this Guarantee.

6 This Guarantee shall be governed by the Laws of the United Kingdom whose Courts shall have exclusive jurisdiction in any dispute doubt or question arising hereunder.

Exclusions

1 The Guarantor shall not have any liability under this Guarantee in respect of loss directly or indirectly occasioned by happening through or in consequence of war invasion acts of foreign enemies hostilities (whether war be declared or not) civil war rebellion revolution insurrection military or usurped power or confiscation or nationalisation or requisition or destruction of or damage to property by or under the order of any government or public or local authority.

2 The Guarantor shall not have any liability under this Guarantee in the event of the Indemnified Party or any associated concern or subsidiary of the Indemnified Party obtaining any form of control or financial control of the Supplier or the Indemnified Party having failed to comply with the terms of any contract with the Supplier or any associated concern or subsidiary of the Supplier.

The Schedule

Guarantee Number:

(Please quote this number in all communications to the Guarantor)

The Indemnified Party:

The Supplier:

The Contract: Contract Value:

Terms of Payment:

**Maximum Liability
of the Guarantor:**

**Currency for payment
of liability:**

**Validity Period of this
Guarantee:**

Date:

Checked:

SPECIMEN

_____
Authorised Signatory

_____
Underwriter for the Guarantor

291

bond, drafted by Credit and Guarantee Insurance Co. Ltd, who introduced this service to exporters in 1977.

It is common practice to require bonds to be issued by a local bank in favour of the buyer. The exporter's bank consequently issues a counter-indemnity in favour of the local bank. This places the vital issue of calling and paying of bonds at arm's length from both buyer and seller. The validity of a demand turns entirely on the wording of the bond and the need for banks to be seen to be honouring their bonds one to another in accordance with international banking practice.

In considering the issue of a bond, a surety company has regard to the following:

1   How competent is the exporter/contractor to perform the contract satisfactorily?
2   Has he sufficient plant and equipment available to do the work?
3   Are the contract conditions reasonable?
4   Is the contractor financially strong enough to pay the bond?
5   If sub-contractors are involved, what protection does the contractor have against a possible failure?

Banks regard bonds issued as part of their customer's credit facilities. They are less concerned with the ability of their customer to perform his contract. Refusal to issue a bond will only result from the customer's reaching his overdraft limit or for some other reason directly related to the customer's financial position.

ECGD bond support

An exporter who cannot obtain a bond from his bank or from a surety company may be able to claim assistance from ECGD in the form of an indemnity to a bank or surety company to encourage the issue of a bond. Before ECGD will consider such support, the contract must be worth at least £250,000, basic ECGD insurance cover must be available and taken up, and the terms of payment must be cash or near-cash (thus ruling out any business under supplier or buyer credit). Support for on-demand bonds is only available for public sector buyers. If these criteria are satisfied, ECGD will thoroughly examine the exporter's finances and the proposed contract and the ability of both the exporter and any sub-contractors to perform it.

ECGD's premium rate is 1 per cent p.a. for bid bonds and $1\frac{1}{4}$ per cent p.a. for all others (with a minimum of one year's premium). If an ECGD-backed bond is called and paid, ECGD repay the surety within 30 days plus interest since the date of payment.

ECGD has the right of recourse to the exporter in the same way as a bank or surety company after paying an unsupported bond, although it is not usually exercised immediately.

This scheme was introduced in 1975 primarily to assist companies with large Middle East contracts who were having difficulty in raising bonds. Originally there was a minimum contract value of £20 million, reduced over the years to the present £250,000. The amount of information required by ECGD is generally not so great as that called for by banks or surety companies.

Unfair calling of bonds

The great risk of an on-demand bond is that it can be called without notice and without good cause. Underwriters will never forget the events of 1969 in Libya when the new Ghadaffi regime arbitrarily called guarantees given on behalf of contractors (notably Italian but also UK). This was a 'political' act and, therefore, not predictable according to ordinary commercial expectations.

Another instance of unfair calling occurred in 1977, also in Libya. An English exporter, Edward Owen Engineering Ltd, contracted to supply goods to a Libyan buyer against a Confirmed Letter of Credit. The buyer required an on-demand bond, which was issued by Barclays Bank International Ltd *before the Letter of Credit was opened*. The Letter of Credit was *not* opened, the exporter refused to ship and the bond was called. The bank paid and its action was upheld in the Court of Appeal. Lord Denning, Master of the Rolls, ruled that a bank's obligation on a performance bond is absolute and commented 'these performance guarantees are virtually promissory notes payable on demand'.

Protection against unfair calling may be sought either from ECGD or from Lloyd's Underwriters. The main points of these are shown in Exhibit 17.4.

It will be seen from this comparison that neither ECGD nor Lloyd's cover offers a clear-cut advantage over the other. At the risk of over-simplifying, the principal factors to be considered are as follows:

1 ECGD's premium rate is invariably cheaper than Lloyd's, but it is charged over the whole contract, whereas Lloyd's premium is calculated pro-rata to the risk according to contract performance.
2 As a last resort Lloyd's use of the London Court of Arbitration may be preferable to ECGD's requirement that the exporter should settle all disputes according to the terms of the contract. At the time of writing however, this form of arbitration has not been tested.

Exhibit 17.4 Comparison of unfair calling cover

	ECGD	LLOYDS
Basic credit insurance required?	YES	NO
Public sector buyers only?	YES	NO (but only substantial private buyers)
Minimum contract value?	NO	NO
Cash contracts only?	NO	NO
Must all bonds under the contract be offered?	YES	NO
Can all forms of bond be offered?	YES	YES
Principal exclusions to causes of loss (other than non-compliance with contract terms – unless caused by political reasons	NONE	(a) War between any of the five Great Powers (b) War between buyer's country and exporter's country (c) Insolvency and/or financial default (d) Failure or inability of the buyer or the exporter to obtain an import/export licence

Can bond be extended? Cost of cover?	*YES* *0.5% p.a.*	*YES* *Flat rates for contract period, according to market risk, generally 1 to 8%. Cost may be calculated pro-rata to a reducing risk (net of all recoveries and possible salvage).*
How are claims substantiated?	*All alleged defaults must first be settled by the exporter through the Courts in accordance with the conditions of the contract.*	*If the underwriters are not satisfied that the exporter is not in default, as a last resort the dispute is referred to the London Court of Arbitration whose decision is binding*
How much is paid?	*100% of the bond less any recoveries received by the time the loss is assessed.*	*90% (80% for bid bonds) of the ascertained net loss, i.e. the amount paid by the bank less any recoveries and salvage. This percentage may be reduced on particularly high-risk markets.*
How are foreign currency bonds covered?	*Policies are in sterling. Exporter can add a margin of cover to the bond value to guard against exchange losses.*	*Policies are issued in the same currency as the bond.*
Any limitations on bond value and period of cover?	*Depending on ECGD's view of the market risk.*	*Depending on Lloyd's view of the market risk.*

3   In some markets at times Lloyd's can offer better cover than ECGD. For example, in 1977 ECGD would only give protection for export to Libya against war risk. Lloyd's were able to give cover against contract repudiation (which was the chief worry of many exporters) and import/export embargo.

Another related problem with bonds is their validity period and the difficulties sometimes encountered in recovering the documents. Under Syrian law a bond remains valid until it is returned for cancellation by the buyer to the local bank of issue. Other markets where periods of validity extent to 10 or 15 years include Turkey, Thailand and Libya. UK banks are very reluctant to accept such terms,

Exhibit 17.5 Long form of 'force majeure'

(a) If either party is delayed or hindered in or prevented from performing any of its obligations under the Agreement by reason of Act of God, fire, flood, earthquake, epidemics, quarantine restrictions, accident, explosion, breakdown or failure of plant or machinery, war, riot, civil disturbance, strike, lockout, work slowdown, labour dispute, acts, orders or regulations of Governments, failure (whether partial or total) of or shortage in any of the Company's or its suppliers' existing or contemplated sources of material (including parts and components) or fuel or labour or transport whether such failure or shortage be existing or apprehended by the Company, failure of any supplier or sub-contractor of the Company to perform any contract with the Company or by reason of any cause whether or not of the same nature as the foregoing beyond its control, it shall be under no obligation but the time for performing the same shall be extended until the operation of the causes preventing hindering or delaying the performance thereof has ceased.

(b) Without prejudice to the generality of the foregoing, if manufacture or delivery by the Company is delayed hindered or prevented, or if the quality of the goods available for supply by the Company is reduced by reason of any of the causes described in paragraph (a) above the provisions of the said paragraph shall apply and the Company shall be entitled to suspend deliveries in whole or in part and shall not be obliged to purchase or other-wise acquire any goods from any third party or to arrange for any supply of goods by any third party.

---

which give them an indefinite exposure. Counter-indemnities from the exporter are naturally required, which can often cause difficulties. Not many exporters can present such a solid appearance as to warrant a 15-year risk!

Retention bonds are sometimes required when a buyer releases the final instalment of the contract price or the retention element of monthly progress payments. The bond is required to cover the period between such a payment and the final expiry date of the contractor's obligations.

To conclude this examination of the bond problem, there follows a shortlist of checkpoints for the exporter:

1   Allow for the cost of bonding in the contract price.
2   Try to persuade the buyer to accept a surety company bond.
3   If an 'on-demand' bond is unavoidable:
    a   Ensure there is an expiry date as close to contract completion as possible.
    b   Try to make the bond value reduce pro-rata to contract performance.
4   Obtain quotations from both Lloyd's and ECGD (providing the contract itself is ECGD-covered) against unfair calling.

Force majeure clauses

A strong force majeure clause is essential in a contract. Exhibit 17.5 illustrates a long form of force majeure which has an exhaustive list of reasons preventing the supplier from incurring any obligations or penalties.

Many clauses provide for termination of the contract after a specified period of force majeure interruption. Losses resulting from such termination can be insured with Lloyd's.

Contract ratification

A risk which cannot be covered by ECGD is the possibility of losses arising from work done or expenses incurred prior to the contract becoming operative, which are irrecoverable in the event of the contract collapsing. Under this heading also come losses arising from the enforced closing-out of a forward foreign exchange contract. (See Chapter 18 for further explanation.)

A Contract Ratification Indemnity policy may be obtained from Lloyd's.

Arbitration

One of the hazards of contracting abroad concerns the handling of disputes. It is normal to find overseas buyers insisting that a contract be subject to the laws of their own country. Even if a contract is made subject to the laws of England, enforcement of a favourable decision will often be impossible.

Exporters are strongly recommended to include the following arbitration clause (recommended by the International Chamber of Commerce):

> 'All disputes arising in connection with the present contract shall be finally settled under the Rules of Conciliation and Arbitration of the International Chamber of Commerce by one or more arbitrators appointed in accordance with the said Rules.'

This standard clause may be supported by stipulations as to the place of arbitration, the number of arbitrators and the national law applicable to the contract.

Further information on this subject may be obtained from the International Chamber of Commerce booklet, *ICC Arbitration: the international solution to international business disputes*, available from the British National Committee of the ICC, 6-14 Dean Farrar St, London SW1H 0DT. The ICC have also published *Uniform Rules for Contract Guarantees*, in an attempt to secure 'a uniformity of practice based upon an equitable balance between the interests of the parties concerned'.

Only surety bonds are covered by these guidelines, and it remains to be seen whether they gain any degree of general acceptance.

Post-contract problems

Apart from the unfair calling of a bond, most of the 'post-contract' problems are those which prevent one side or the other from fulfilling their obligations. These are as follows:
1   Import or export embargo.
2   Contract repudiation.
3   Exchange transfer delays.
4   War, civil war, etc.
5   Expropriation of assets.
Losses arising from these causes may be covered either with ECGD or with Lloyd's, depending on the view taken of the market in question. There are several important limitations however:
1   Contract repudiation cover from ECGD is only available for public sector buyers.

2   Exchange transfer losses can only be claimed under a Lloyd's policy if transfer of the required currency to the UK is prevented by law or government regulation. Many transfer delays occur without any such official announcement.

Other sources of protection

Exporters supplying countries in the Comecon block (USSR, Bulgaria, Czechoslovakia, East Germany, Hungary, Poland, Rumania and Yugoslavia), Mongolia, Vietnam or Cuba may obtain cover (100 per cent) against the risk of non-payment (for any reason, commercial or political) from the Black Sea and Baltic General Insurance Co. Ltd.

Separate policies are available for post-shipment risk only ('non-payment risk') or pre-shipment risks ('manufacturers' risks'). A minimum insured value of £20,000 is required, and cover is given on a specific contract basis rather than on whole turnover.

Black Sea and Baltic is controlled by the Russian state insurance company. This fact must raise doubts about the efficacy of the political risk cover in the event of a major claim.

The cost of protection

The costs of insurance cover, bank guarantees, etc., have all to be included in the contract price. The credit manager must be ready to provide these details to the commercial department as soon as they are available. Approximate costs should be obtained as far in advance of final negotiations as possible.

Exhibit 17.6 illustrates the costing of an actual contract quoted for Nigeria in late 1978. It is important to note that the rates quoted were only relevant to that particular contract at that time and are *not* intended as a guide to current rates.

The calculation of item 6, interest charges for the five-year loan, is based on the following formula:

$$\left(\frac{A}{B} \right) \div \left(\frac{CDE}{100} \right)$$

where A is the amount of loan, B the total number of repayment instalments, C the number of instalments per year, D the rate of interest and E the sum of instalment numbers, e.g. $10 + 9 + 8 + \ldots + 1 = 55$. In the example given, the calculation is

$$\left(\frac{4.25\text{M}}{10}\right) \div \left(2 \times \frac{7.5}{100} \times 55\right)$$

$$= £876,562.50$$

Exhibit 17.6

BASIC DATA

1 *Contract value: £5 million.*
2 *Terms wanted: 15% down, 85% over 5 years under Supplier Credit.*
3 *Repayment by ten equal six-monthly instalments.*
4 *Interest rate: 7.5% p.a.*
5 *Shipment period: 3-15 months from date of contract.*
6 *Advance payment bond required.*

COSTS	£
1 *ECGD premium (3% on £5 million)*	*150,000*
2 *ECGD premium for bank guarantee (0.32% on 85% of £5 million)*	*13,600*
3 *Bank fee (0.375% on 85% of £5 million)*	*15,937.50*
4 *Advance payment bond fee (1% on 15% of £5 million)*	*7,500*
5 *Premium for unfair calling cover (3% on 90% of 15% of £5 million)*	*20,250*
TOTAL	*£207,287.50*
(4.1% of contract value)	
6 *Interest charges*	*£876,562.50*

Chapter 18

Currency and foreign exchange problems

There is an exchange risk in virtually every export transaction. If the UK exporter invoices in sterling, the customer has to buy pounds in order to pay. If prices are in a foreign currency, the seller has to convert his receipts back into sterling. In both situations one party is at risk because the prices at which currencies are bought and sold fluctuate in a generally unpredictable manner.

The proportion of UK exports invoiced in currency (the word is used to denote any non-sterling currency) has grown to around 30 per cent in recent years, for two principal reasons. First, exporters became aware that in order to win orders — particularly in the USA — they had to quote in the buyer's currency. This is a very good reason. Secondly, the dramatic fall in the value of sterling in 1975-6 made many exporters realise (mostly belatedly) that extra profits could be made by selling in 'strong' currencies. This is not a good reason for moving out of sterling, as many exporters found in 1978 when they saw the collapse of the dollar. Once a customer has agreed to buy in, say, dollars, it is rarely possible to persuade him to change to sterling — particularly as the reason for changing is clearly to transfer the currency risk from seller to buyer.

The role of the credit manager in currency transactions is threefold:
1   To give advice on which currencies to favour or avoid, on exchange rates and on how to use exchange rates in preparing quotations.

2   To minimise the company's exposure to exchange risk — usually by selling forward.
3   To ensure that incoming currency payments are handled properly.

Exchange rates

Some basic knowledge of exchange control and the foreign exchange market is essential. What follows is not intended as a detailed explanation. The aim here is merely to sketch the framework, to give the credit manager some understanding of the market from the exporter's point of view. Further reading is suggested at the end of the book.

Exporters who receive currency payments are required, under the Exchange Control Act, to deliver them to an 'authorised dealer', i.e. a bank, within two days unless Bank of England permission has been obtained to retain a particular currency because it will be used to pay for imports. The exchange rate that the bank will use to change the offered currency into sterling is determined by the foreign exchange market. The London market consists of over 200 dealers (the clearing banks, merchant banks and foreign banks) who are in constant communication both with each other and with exchange brokers in the City and with banks in other financial centres. Currencies are bought and sold freely in the market and the price of one currency, say US dollars, in sterling is a reflection of the supply of and demand for those currencies. The majority of foreign exchange transactions are made 'spot', i.e. purchase and sale become effective in two working days. (This allows for time differences and local holidays in financial centres round the world.)

Spot rates

The exporter who receives $100,000 without having made any prior arrangements for its disposal has to offer it to a bank. He will be quoted the spot rate. Small variations in the spot rate can be found from bank to bank, and within one day each bank will have a 'spread' of rates, the movement depending partly on changing demand by the bank for the currency through the day and partly on political/economic factors which affect the market's overall view of its strength or weakness. Not all currencies can be readily exchanged in the market, and it is very important for the exporter to be aware of this. As an example, an exporter to Ghana in 1978 would have been extremely

302

foolish to agree to be paid in Ghanian cedis, because there was no market for them. Officially, a sterling-cedi exchange rate is quoted, but this does not help the exporter if no one in the London foreign exchange market wants to buy cedis.

Virtually all international trade is conducted in a small number of currencies which are immediately convertible on the London market. The value of these currencies against the pound is quoted daily in the financial press. The list is as follows:

US dollars	(New York)
Canadian dollars	(Montreal)
Austrian schillings	(Vienna)
Belgian francs	(Brussels)
Danish kroner	(Copenhagen)
Dutch guilders	(Amsterdam)
French francs	(Paris)
German marks	(Frankfurt)
Italian lire	(Milan)
Japanese yen	(Tokyo)
Norwegian kroner	(Oslo)
Portuguese escudos	(Lisbon)
Spanish pesetas	(Madrid)
Swedish kroner	(Stockholm)
Swiss francs	(Zurich)
Irish punt	(Dublin)

The UK exporter is usually only interested in the relationship between one of the above currencies and sterling, but in the market all rates are calculated through US dollars. Thus a bank asked to quote Deutschemarks in sterling will first obtain the Deutschmark/dollar rate and then convert to sterling. It is important to understand this because it means that DM-sterling rates cannot be forecast solely with reference to the relative strengths of the German and UK economies.

Forecasting of any kind is extremely difficult, and the exporter who arranges to be paid in currency and then does nothing to insure against the possibility of an exchange loss is a speculator. At times when sterling is losing value against, say, US dollars, it can seem entirely justifiable to anticipate that dollars arriving over the next 6-12 months will be worth more sterling than if they arrived today. Nonetheless, to rely on such a belief is speculation, and there are many exporters who did exactly this and were caught out in 1978. Against the forecasts of nearly all the 'experts', sterling had a period of prolonged strength against the dollar. Dollars were exchanged for less and less sterling, and exporters who had decided to sell their dollar income 'spot' lost money.

303

Forward rates

The alternative to speculating on the spot rate is to sell forward. In the foreign exchange market, banks quote forward rates as well as spot rates. The *Financial Times* each day gives a summary of the rates quoted on the previous business day, showing spot, one month forward and three months forward. In some currencies, notably US dollars, Deutschemarks, Swiss francs and Canadian dollars, forward rates can readily be obtained for the next 12 months or even further.

A forward rate of, say, three months is *not* the bank's forecast (or anyone else's) of what the spot rate will be in three months' time. It is the result of calculations done within the market using three known facts:

1   The spot rate.
2   The cost of the currency being sold in its country of origin.
3   The cost of the currency being purchased in its country of origin.
These last two factors are usually expressed as interest rates. The difference between interest rates in the two centres is the biggest factor in determining the difference between spot and forward rates. This difference is either a premium or a discount. (If there is no difference between spot and forward, the currencies are said to be 'at par'.)

A three-month forward premium in US dollars against sterling means that a contract to deliver dollars to the bank in three months' time will produce more sterling than if those dollars were delivered today. The amount of forward premium is expressed in hundreths of a cent, as in the following example taken from the *Financial Times*, 1 February 1979:

JAN. 31	CLOSE	THREE MONTHS	% P.A.
US $	1.9895—1.9905	1.55—1.45 c. pm	3.01

This tells us that at close of business on 31 January the banks were selling dollars spot at 1.9895 and buying them spot at 1.9905. If the banks were asked to buy dollars, i.e. to receive them from an exporter, on 30 April (three months' time), the cost would be 1.9905 less 1.45 cents = 1.9760. The letters 'pm' indicate a premium. When the bank is buying, the second or right-hand amount is deducted from the second or right-hand amount in the spot (or 'close') column. The final column indicates the annual percentage by which the dollar is appreciating against the pound. In this example, selling dollars three months forward is giving the exporter an exchange profit of 3.01 per cent p.a. Applying these rates to a payment of $10,000 which the exporter is expecting on April 30, gives the following result:

Selling $10,000 at spot (1.9905)   = £5,023.86

Selling $10,000 3 months forward (1.9760)   = £5,060.73

Benefit   = £36.87.

The opposite of a premium is a discount and selling currency at a forward discount means receiving less sterling than would be available today. For example, on 1 February appeared this entry:

JAN. 31	CLOSE	THREE MONTHS	% P.A.
PORT. ESC.	93.80—94.30	60—260 c. dis	—6.80

The calculation involved in selling forward Portuguese escudos is as follows:

Selling E.10,000 at spot (94.3)   = £106.04

Selling E.10,000 3 months forward
(94.3 *plus* 260 cents = 96.9)   = £103

Loss   = £2.84

The rules to remember in forward calculations are that premiums are deducted and discounts are added.

Currencies at a forward premium are often referred to as 'strong' currencies, those at a forward discount as 'weak' currencies. This classification often over-simplifies the relationships and is misleading. For several months up to the date in the example, the dollar was undoubtedly weak against sterling and most other major currencies largely because of a lack of confidence in the Carter administration. Yet it was still at a premium against sterling. The reason is that it is the difference between interest rates which produce premiums and discounts. At the end of January 1979, the UK minimum lending rate was 12.5 per cent compared to 9.5 per cent in the USA. This made the dollar at a premium against sterling.

It is a combination of forward rates and the movement of the spot rates which make currencies strong or weak.

The exporter expecting to receive $100,000 in three months' time has, therefore, a choice. He can either wait until the payment arrives and then sell it 'spot', or he can take out a forward contract now, under which he is committed to deliver those dollars to the bank in three months time *at a rate which is fixed today*. To wait and sell at spot is speculation, whereas to sell or cover forward is a form of insurance. A further alternative is to borrow the expected dollars and immediately sell them at 'spot' for sterling. When the payment arrives, it is used to repay the dollar loan.

Forward contracts

Bank of England regulations do not permit an exporter to make a forward sale unless he has a firm contractual commitment with an overseas buyer which will result in the currency entering the UK. The only exception is forward cover on tenders, for which a special ECGD scheme has been devised (see later in this chapter). Additionally, *Exchange Control Notice 54, Supplement No. 4*, dated 16 March 1972, permits UK exporters to apply to the Bank of England (through their own banks) for forward cover in respect of tenders submitted which will, if awarded, incur exchange risks.

It is not usually possible to predict the exact date of a payment. To overcome this difficulty, the exporter can make an 'option contract' (as opposed to a fixed contract). Under this, the bank will accept the payment between any two fixed dates. The agreed forward rate will apply whenever payment is made within the option period. If there is a forward premium, the bank will fix the rate on the earlier date, and on the later date if a discount exists. For example, an exporter selling in dollars on 60-day terms might make an option contract to deliver to the bank any time between 60 and 90 days from date of invoice. If the payment arrives *after* the beginning of the option period, the bank obtains the benefit. It follows that the exporter should fix the start of an option period as far ahead as possible, to try and gain the maximum benefit from the forward premium. Thus if he knows that his buyer habitually pays one month late, he might decide to sell forward 90 option 120 days from invoice date. If, however, the payment arrives before the option period, the exporter will suffer a penalty for delivering early. An alternative to an option contract is to sell at a fixed date and then 'roll-over' or extend it as necessary. This will cost more in bank fees besides entailing more work.

If an exporter is unable to deliver the currency, perhaps because the buyer cancelled the order or returned the goods for credit, the forward contract has to be 'closed out'. This means buying the currency at spot in order to fulfil the contract. Depending on how the exchange rate has moved, there will be either a loss or a gain.

Currency quotations

Apart from the very large corporations, most companies do not employ more than a handful of people conversant with foreign exchange. It will frequently fall to the credit manager to assume the role of adviser on currency. If he is responsible for arranging forward sales and controlling the receipt of currency payments, this is a logical move.

Before examining in detail how exchange rates can be used in quotations, there are two basic principles which should be observed:

1   The decision to quote in currency should always be because it will help win business — never because of the prospect of exchange profits.
2   The choice of a conversion rate should be dictated with a view to long-term business rather than an immediate killing. Thus exporters who won business in the USA by quoting at around 1.60 found within a relatively short time that they had to choose between drastic profit erosion (as the rate moved into the 1.80-1.90 range) and the risk of losing business if they increased prices to keep pace.

When a currency quotation is prepared, there are a number of alternative methods:

a   Use an agreed fixed rate.
b   Use the spot rate.
c   Use a fixed rate with an exchange variation clause.
d   Use the forward rate.

An agreed fixed rate

The price is agreed with the buyer in both currency and sterling. The buyer then undertakes to pay sufficient currency to produce the required sterling figures. All the exchange risk is thus passed back to the buyer, who might just as well be paying in sterling. This is most unlikely to be accepted and needs no further consideration.

Spot rate

The exporter converts into currency at spot (at the time of quotation). If an order is obtained, any forward premium is extra profit. This may be good practice in a period of stable prices and low inflation, providing the currency price is not too high for the buyer. Problems are likely to occur, however, when price increases are required, unless the currency has weakened against sterling, thus making the original spot rate more beneficial to the exporter.

A fixed rate with an exchange variation clause

This involves sharing the exchange risk with the buyer. It is usually complicated to set up and administer, but it can offer a reasonable compromise in periods of unstable exchange rates.

Example A dollar price is agreed, based on a rate of 1.90 to £. Providing the spot rate at date of shipment (or date of payment) remains within 5 per cent of 1.90, i.e. 1.805—1.995, no action is needed.

If the spot moves beyond that range, both parties may agree to share any profit or loss — measured either from the base point or from the edge of the range.

Forward rate

Using the forward rates is at once the most difficult and the most fruitful way of quoting. Difficulty arises because in the interval between quotation and receipt of order, both spot and forward rates may change significantly, and the exporter can do nothing about it because without a firm order he cannot sell forward. (For the moment, use of the ECGD Tender to Contract facility is ignored.)

The following example illustrates the use of forward rates:

Stage 1 British Widgets Ltd is seeking business in Germany. A potential buyer agrees to be quoted in Deutschemarks. Delivery will be wanted over a 12-month period on 60-day terms. Price competition is very fierce. The order at stake is 100,000 widgets.

Stage 2 The exporter must obtain a minimum unit price of £5 for the first six months, rising to £5.50 in the second half-year following labour and material price increases.

Stage 3 These facts are given to the credit manager. He telephones the bank and asks for 'indicated' rates for selling Deutschemarks at monthly intervals for 12 months beginning in three months' time. He should make it clear that the rates are only for indication.

Stage 4 The indicated rates are shown in Exhibit 18.1. Assuming an even spread of deliveries, the average rate is 3.4618.

Stage 5 The credit manager recommends that the Deutschemark price be based on 3.50. This is between spot and the average forward rate, thus building in a margin of safety in case the rates go against the exporter before an order arrives, i.e. in case the pound appreciates against the Deutschemark.

Exhibit 18.1 Indicated rates

Spot -			
Mid November 1978	3.7025	Quotation date	
28 February 1979	3.6110		
31 March	3.5808		
30 April	3.5507		
31 May	3.5205		
30 June	3.4925		
31 July	3.4645		
31 August	3.4365		
30 September	3.4148		
31 October	3.3932		
30 November	3.3715		
31 December	3.3590		
31 January 1980	3.3467		

Average rate = 3.4618

Stage 6 In order to hold prices firm for the whole period, the recommended rate of 3.50 is applied to £5.25 (the average sterling requirement), giving a price of DM18.375. This unit price of DM18.375 should be compared with the price based on spot at the date of quotation. This is calculated as:

a   £5.00 × 3.7025 = DM18.5125 for 6 months, and
b   £5.50 × 3.7025 = DM20.3637 for 6 months.
c   Average rate for 1 year = DM19.438.

The price reduction achieved by using the forward rates is 5.47 per cent. In this example it is, of course, assumed that British Widgets have to quote as low a price as possible to stand any chance of winning the business.

Operating forward contracts

If the order is obtained, the credit manager then has to make the forward sale. The procedure to adopt is as follows:

1   Check the *Financial Times* for a general idea of both spot and forward rates. If the rates have moved against him since the indications were obtained, he must decide whether to sell and obtain less sterling than anticipated, or to delay the sale in the hope that rates will improve. This is a dangerous practice, and the credit manager should not embark on this course without being very confident of the outcome

— and also being prepared to accept sharp criticism if things go wrong! This point is examined in more detail further on.

2   Assuming the decision is to sell, the credit manager should then contact those banks he regularly uses for Deutschemark transactions and obtain spot and forward rates from each of them. The bank which offers the best combination of spot and forward rates will be asked to buy the Deutschemarks.

Certain 'rules' should be noted in order to ensure good service from banks. First, it is not worth shopping around for rates on small amounts (say, under $100,000). To do so is likely to cause annoyance. Secondly, it is wrong to go back and forth between banks trying to 'run an auction'. It follows from this that several telephones must be used simultaneously if an immediate decision between offered rates has to be made. If no immediate decision is to be made, it should be made clear at the outset and the bank told that an 'indication' is required. Thirdly, it helps the dealer if calls are made when the market of the country of the required currency is open, e.g. New York and other Eastern cities of North America at around 14.30 London time. Fourthly, always be precise in speech. if dollars are to be sold to the bank, say 'I will sell you X dollars' *not* 'Please buy X dollars'.

If good relations are to be maintained, all the banks which are asked to quote must be offered business from time to time. This really limits the number to, say, three or four — which should be sufficient for the needs of most companies.

For the purpose of this illustration we will assume that British Widgets' credit manager is very fortunate and makes his forward contracts at the same rates used in the quotation. However, the production department have now said that instead of an even flow of shipments, delivery will start at 6,000 for the first two months, increasing to 8,000 for the next two and then remaining at 9,000 for the next eight months.

Exhibit 18.2 shows the forward contracts made with the bank. The date at the start of the option period is known as the value date.

In the event, deliveries do not take place as scheduled and Exhibit 18.3 shows how a careful record must be kept so that each invoice and payment is matched to the appropriate contract.

While the invoices to the customer will be in Deutschemarks, there have to be sterling entries to the ledger. The conversion rate can either be that used to obtain the Deutschemark price at the quotation stage, or it can be the actual forward rate. There is much to be said for using the forward rate, since when payments arrive they will be converted into sterling by the bank at exactly the figure shown on the ledger. A complication illustrated in Exhibit 18.3 concerns the need to 'split' an

310

Exhibit 18.2 Forward contracts

Contract number	DM value	Option period		Rates
1	110,250	28 Feb – 31 May		3.6110
2	110,250	31 Mar – 30 Jun		3.5808
3	147,000	30 Apr – 31 Jul		3.5507
4	147,000			
5	165,375			
6				
7				
8				
9				
10				
11				
12		31 Jan – 30 Apr		3.3467

NOTES
1 Delivery is due to start in December and payment will therefore arrive in February at the earliest.
2 Having fixed the beginning of the option period, there is nothing to be lost in arranging a three-month option to allow for late payments and/or late deliveries.

invoice between two forward contracts. This results in the conversion rate for such invoices having to be calculated.

For example, in Exhibit 18.3 DM20,250 is taken from Invoice 247 to complete Contract No. 1. The full value of Invoice 247 is DM30,000, so the balance of DM9,750 is carried forward to Contract No. 2. The rate of exchange on contract No. 2 is DM3.5808. The sterling value of Invoice 247 is therefore:

DM20,250 at 3.6110	= 5,607.86
DM9,750 at 3.5808	= 2,722.86
	£8,330.72

(Conversion rate = 3.6011)

As already stated, an exporter is not permitted to sell a currency forward unless he has a firm contract involving receipt of that currency. Once the order arrives, however, he can choose whether to sell forward immediately or whether to wait until a more favourable

Exhibit 18.3 Foreign exchange contract no. 1

Amount purchased	Rate	Value date
DM110,250	3.6110	28 Feb - 31 May

RECORD OF CONTRACT USAGE

Invoice number	Value, DM	Cumulative value, DM	Date paid
230	30,000	30,000	
239	30,000	60,000	
245	30,000	90,000	
247 (part)	20,250	110,250	

NOTE: In order to reach the exact contract value of DM110,250, the last invoice in the series has to be split. DM20,250 is used to complete this contract and the balance is carried forward to start Contract No. 2. This process is continued until all deliveries have been made and the last invoice will complete Contract No.12.

moment occurs. It is often tempting to delay making a forward sale, especially when the credit manager knows that the business was obtained by quoting at a rate better than he can immediately obtain on a forward sale and if 'expert opinion' in the City is expecting the rates to improve in the exporter's favour. But no matter how strong are the reasons for delaying a forward sale, to do so is just as speculative as is deciding not to cover forward at all. Such a policy should not be adopted without the credit manager consulting with the sales manager concerned. To have any chance of success, the credit manager or one of his staff must have a permanent 'hot line' to his bank or other contact in the City so that any favourable movement in exchange rates can be acted on immediately.

Currency accounts

If an exporter can satisfy the **Bank of England** that he needs to maintain an account in a foreign currency, because of the volume of payments for imports, he may be permitted to open an account in dollars or whatever the currency may be. This account is often referred to as a 'retained dollar account', and may be held in the UK or in the country of the currency. Thus a retained Deutschemark account could be held in London or in Frankfurt (or in both). Currency payments are credited to the retained account, enabling the holder to pay for his imports without having to buy currency in the market. Quite apart from the obvious savings in bank charges and commissions, there are other benefits of particular interest to the credit manager.

Bank of England regulations allow a payment received in a retained account to remain there until the end of the following month. Payments arriving early on a forward contract can, therefore, be retained *without penalty* until the value date arrives. This enables the credit manager to obtain an extra month's premium. Looking back to Exhibit 18.2, if a retained Deutschemark account were held, the option period in Contract No. 1 could run from 31 March to 30 June, because if payment arrives in February (as it should) it can be 'held' legitimately until 31 March. Retained currency accounts therefore allow considerably more flexibility in the planning of forward contracts.

It is very desirable to discuss the whole question of currency hold accounts in detail with specialist bankers before applying for permission to the Bank of England.

Currency problems

A frequent problem results from currency payments not matching forward contracts because of changes in invoice value or the deduction of debit notes by the customer. The only remedy is to buy the shortfall at spot from the bank in order to deliver it to the bank to fulfil the forward contract.

Another very frustrating problem can occur if the UK bank which first receives a currency payment decides to convert it into sterling without checking with the beneficiary. Some of the clearing banks only refer to the payee if the payment exceeds a certain minimum, and the result can be that the exporter receives sterling at spot and he is unable to meet his forward commitment. This is very difficult to overcome when payments are sent by many different buyers whose own banks may be routing transfers through different UK correspondents. A possible solution is to give all currency customers very precise instructions abou the disposal of their payments, and then to hope that these instructions are carefully noted and passed on by all the banks in the chain. Regrettably this does not always happen. A better solution, but not always practicable, is to arrange for currency payments to be made into a retained currency account in the country of the buyer. This was examined in Chapter 14.

Currency and credit terms

The fact that the cost of money varies from country to country is clearly important when credit terms are being considered.

When quoting in a currency with a high forward premium such as Deutschemarks, Swiss francs or Japanese yen (in early 1979), an exporter may be able to win business by offering extended credit because the cost of this can be offset by the forward premium. This could *not* be done in the example quoted of british Widgets, because the forward premium was used to reduce the price.

The alternative strategy — using the forward premium to offset the cost of credit — is illustrated in the following case study involving United Spares Ltd.

Foreign exchange/payment terms – case study

Your company is in the process of negotiating a contract for automotive spares with München Autopart GmbH, the value of which is £50,000 delivered to Munich. The buyer has indicated that the products are technically acceptable and he requires them to be delivered in one lot within 30 days of date of order.

You have calculated your price on the basis of being paid net cash within 30 days of shipment. This is due to the buyer having squeezed you on price, leaving very little profit margin for you. However, your company is very keen to get the business, as it will fit in very well with another order they have received and allow them to make some savings by economy of scale. The cost of credit is 1.5 per cent per month.

Shortly before the contract is about to be signed, the buyer states that 90 days credit is required. A possible solution is to quote in Deutschemarks. The buyer indicates he will accept this. Using the rates given below, calculate whether the business can be accepted on these terms without eroding the profit.

QUOTATION DAY	DAY'S SPREAD	CLOSE	THREE MONTHS	% P.A.
DMark	3.68-3.71	3.69-3.70	10-9 pf-pm	9.97%

The buyer also offers to pay in 30 days for 2 per cent discount, or in 60 days for 1 per cent. How do these alternatives compare? The answers are given in Exhibit 18.4.

Exhibit 18.4

(i) 90 days

    (a) Cost of credit = £50,000 x 1.5% x 3 = £2,250
         LESS 30 days credit built into
         price (= £750)   *= £1,500*

    (b) Proceeds from forward sale: cost in DM using
         spot will be £50,000 x 3.7 = DM185,000
         Proceeds from selling forward __4 months__

Spot =	*3.7000*
LESS 3-month forward premium	*(0.0900)*
	3.6100
LESS estimated premium for fourth month	*(0.0300)*
Forward rate	*3.5800*

         DM185,000 at 3.58   *= £51,676*
         Potential profit   *= £1,676*

    (c) Result
         Potential exchange profit =   *1,676*
         LESS Cost of credit   *= (1,500)*

               Net extra profit = £176

(ii) 30 days less 2%
    Payment will be DM181,300 (DM185,000 x 98%)
    This can be sold forward two months for a forward
    premium of 6pf, giving a forward rate of 3.64:

    181,300/3.64 = £49,808

    Net result = a loss of £192

(iii) 60 days less 1%
    Payment will be DM183,150 (DM185,000 x 99%)
    This can be sold forward three months for a
    premium of 9pf, giving a forward rate of 3.61:

    183,150/3.61 = £50,734

    Therefore exchange profit = £734
    LESS cost of one extra month's credit at 1.75
    per month = £750

    Result = Break even

(iv) Conclusion: the best alternative is net 90 days

ECGD Tender to Contract cover

In August 1977 ECGD introduced a new facility, aimed at reducing the exchange risk exporters are faced with when negotiating major contracts. It was revised in November 1978 and its main features are as follows:

Purpose To protect the exporter against exchange rate fluctuations between submission of a bid and signing of contract. Only US dollars or Deutschemarks may be covered.

Operation
1 Exporter gives ECGD a rough estimate of the total sterling return expected if the contract is won, and the total payment period.
2 ECGD then calculate how much currency the exporter would need to sell forward to produce the required sterling figure.
3 The forward rates used by ECGD become guaranteed rates up to the date of contract.
4 The exporter prices his contract in the amount of currency indicated by ECGD. He is free to negotiate whatever payment terms he wishes, providing they fall within the overall framework given to ECGD.
5 If the contract is won, the exporter sells forward immediately. If the rates have altered and the sterling obtainable is different from that guaranteed by ECGD, any shortfall or surplus is covered as follows:
   a The exporter bears the first $1\frac{1}{2}$ per cent of loss on the agreed sterling figure and ECGD pays the balance up to a maximum of 25 per cent.
   b ECGD retains the first 10 per cent of any gain and the exporter keeps anything beyond that.
6 Premiums are charged on the total sterling proceeds, at rates dependent on the period of cover chosen by the exporter:
   a Up to 3 months 0.3 per cent.
   b 4-6 months   0.1 per cent for each extra month.
   c 7-9 months   0.15 per cent for each extra month.
7 A deposit premium of £5,000 has to be paid on acceptance of ECGD's offer. This is non-returnable.
8 TTC cover is only available if the exporter applies for a Specific Guarantee.
9 At the end of nine months, if no contract has been signed, a further series of guaranteed rates will be issued by ECGD.

Costing currency contracts

In Chapter 17 an example was given of the calaculations needed to cover interest costs, ECGD premium, bank charges, etc., in a sterling contract.

When currency is involved, a further set of calculations is necessary which will indicate any additional profit (or loss) to be offset against (or added to) the other costs.

Case study

The case study has been prepared with the aid of ECGD, whose cooperation and help is gratefully acknowledged. The basic data is shown in Exhibit 18.5 and the contract costs in Exhibit 18.6.

Exhibit 18.5 Basic data

1	*Proposed Buyer*	*Acme Steel Co. Ltd*
	Country	*Nigeria*
2	*Currency of contract*	*US dollars*
3	*Maximum contract value*	*$12 million*
4	*Minimum required Sterling proceeds*	*£6 million*
5	*Payment terms*	*5% within 30 days of contract signature*
		10% on shipment
		85% over 5 years (10 equal 6-monthly instalments)
6	*Shipment*	*12 consignments at monthly intervals, commencing within 4 months of contract signature*
7	*Bond requirements*	*Advance payment bond (15%) Performance bond (10%)*
8	*Type of ECGD policy required*	*Supplier credit*
9	*Interest rate*	*7.5% p.a.*
10	*Estimated period to date of contract (from date of application to ECGD)*	*6 months*

Exhibit 18.6 Contract costs

		$
1	ECGD premium (3% on $12 million)	360,000
2	ECGD premium for bank guarantee (0.32% on 85% of $12 million)	32,640
3	Bank fee (0.375% on 85% of $12 million)	38,250
4	Advance payment bond fee (1% on 15% of $12 million)	18,000
5	Performance bond fee (1% on 10% of $12 million)	12,000
6	ECGD premium for unfair calling cover (0.5% p.a. on 25% of $12 million for 15 months)	18,750
		$479,640

(4% of contract value)

PLUS, if required)

7	ECGD Tender to Contract premium (0.6% of £6 million)	£36,000

PLUS (payable by the buyer)

8   Interest at 7.5% p.a. on Supplier credit $2,103,750

$\frac{1}{2}$(10.2 million/10) x (7.5/100) x 55)

Formula given in Chapter 17.

Currency income   If ECGD TTC cover were obtained on this contract (at a cost of £36,000, see No. 7 in Exhibit 18.6) the exporter would be given dollar values, calculated from forward exchange rates available at the date of offer, which would *guarantee* the minimum sterling value of £6 million provided a contract was signed within six months.

A specimen quotation for this case study has been specially prepared by ECGD and is shown in Exhibits 18.7 and 18.8.

Paragraph 4.13 shows the forward rates presently available for each month throughout the contract period. Section 1 shows the amount of currency needed to produce the required sterling outcome at those rates. The bottom line on this exhibit shows that to guarantee a total sterling outcome of £6 million, using the forward rates available at the date of offer, the total contract value would have to be $11,180,962. These figures give an average forward rate for the contract of 1.8635.

If the exporter decides to take out TTC cover, he must, therefore, quote at a minimum of $11,180,962 in order to obtain the ECGD guarantee of £6 million proceeds. If the exporter decides *not* to take up the TTC cover, he is gambling that exchange rates will not move against him, i.e. that the dollar will not weaken, *more* than will produce a shortfall equivalent to the cost of TTC cover (£36,000).

On the other hand, if he believes that a contract price of $12,000,000 will be acceptable to the buyer, there is no advantage in taking TTC cover.

With a price of $12,000,000 and the forward rates quoted by ECGD, the result would be a sterling figure of £6,439,495 — an extra 7.3 per cent profit. To obtain *less* than the minimum £6,000,000 with a contract price of $12,000,000, the average forward rate must be over $2 to £. On this example, expected to be signed within six months, this would be extremely unlikely. *(Written in March 1979)*.

A figure of $12,000,000 has been used in Exhibit 18.5 to calculate the contract costs.

Points arising from Exhibits 18.7 and 18.8

Exhibit 18.7, para. 5g 'Maximum period expressed in months . . . 69 months'. This is calculated by adding 5 years (60 months) to the ninth month after contract signature, which is the mean average delivery date.

Exhibit 18.8, para. 4.2 The rate of 0.6 per cent is calculated at 0.3 per cent for the first three months and 0.1 per cent for each subsequent month, making up the total estimated period from application to date of contract.

Exhibit 18.8, para. 4.5 The 'shortfall' and 'excess' margins refer to the percentage losses or profits born by the exporter or retained by ECGD, respectively.

Exhibit 18.8, para. 4.6 The minimum payment of £500 is a figure set by ECGD, relating to the 'shortfall' and 'excess' margins.

Exhibit 18.8, para. 4.8 The 'largest figure' of £7,500,000 is an amount fixed by ECGD, as being the maximum sterling outcome the exporter can enter when finalising his currency prices. (It represents a 25 per cent increase over the £6,000,000 minimum.)

Exhibit 18.8, para. 4.9 The figure of £1,762,500 is 23½ per cent of £7,500,000 and represents ECGD's maximum liability under this

Exhibit 18.8 Specimen proposal for ECGD Tender to Contract Agreement

1. We have read a specimen of your ECGD Tender to Contract Agreement (Revised October 1978) hereinafter called the "Agreement" and request you to inform us of the terms on which you are prepared to enter into such an Agreement in respect of the proposed contract (hereinafter called "the Supply Contract") specified in paragraph 5 below. We acknowledge that any such Agreement issued to us pursuant to this Proposal may only relate to the UK Element (as defined in the Agreement) of the Supply Contract and we certify that the details given in paragraph 5 herein refer only to such UK Element.

                              *full 100% of the

2. The form of this Proposal shall be incorporated as Schedule 1 to any Agreement subsequently issued in respect of this Proposal.

3. We have not entered into any contract of insurance or indemnity relative to the Supply Contract in respect of any cause of loss set out in the Agreement and we will not enter into any such contract of insurance or indemnity without your prior consent in writing.

4. All discussions and correspondance in connection with this Proposal and with any Agreement arising therefrom are to be treated by both sides as confidential and we undertake not to disclose without your prior consent in writing either the existence of the Agreement or any of the details thereof to our agents or to the Buyer or to any other person or firm other than in confidence to our bankers.

5. The Supply Contract details are as follows:

   a. Buyer   The Acme Steel Co Ltd

   b. Buyer's Country Nigeria

   c. Purpose of the Supply Contract   Supply of Engineering Equipment for new foundry

   d. Stage and date at which firm foreign currency price needs   16 May 1979

320

e. Maximum scoring requirement in respect
of 100% of the UK Element only
of the Supply Contract and for   £6,000,000
which cover is required under
the Agreement

f. **Validity Period of Agreement   6 months**
   required by us

g. Maximum period expressed in months from date of
   signature of the Supply Contract over which
   payments are to be received pursuant to the
   Supply Contract: 69   months

6. We certify that the representations made and facts stated by us are true,
and that we have not misrepresented or omitted any material fact which might have
a bearing on the Agreement and that the truth of such representations and facts
and due performance of each and every undertaking contained herein or in the
Agreement shall be a condition precedent to any liability on your part thereunder.

APPLICANT'S SIGNATURE(S)

SIGNED   CAPACITY OF SIGNATORY   DATE

NOTES

1.   In the case of incorporated companies this Proposal should be signed
by an authorised officer for and on behalf of the company and should state
the capacity in which the signatory acts (eg Managing Director, Secretary etc).

2.   In the case of partnership this Proposal should be signed by one or more
partners having authority to sign.

Exhibit 18.9 Specimen offer of ECGD Tender to Contract Agreement

---

OFFER OF TENDER TO CONTRACT AGREEMENT
  BUYER: THE ACME STEEL CO LTD
COUNTRY: NIGERIA

1   I have pleasure in informing you that ECGD has considered your Proposal for Tender to Contract cover and is prepared to offer you such cover in the form of the Tender to Contract Agreement (Revised October 1978) a specimen of which you have read and on the terms set out below. For the purposes of this Offer any expression defined in the Tender to Contract Agreement (Revised October 1978) shall have the same meaning when used in this Offer.

2   The form of this Offer shall be incorporated as Schedule 2 to any such Agreement subsequently issued in respect of this Offer.

3   This Offer can only be accepted by payment of the sum of £5,000 on account of the Premium mentioned in paragraph 4.2. below so that such sum is received by ECGD by the Expiry Date shown at paragraph 4.1. below. Such payment will not be refundable in any event. This Offer is subject to withdrawal at any time before acceptance and will in any event expire on the said Expiry Date.

4   Particulars of Offer

   4.1   Expiry Date   24th February 1979

   4.2   Premium shall be charged on the largest figure entered in Column 2 of Schedule 3 at a rate of 0.6 %.

   4.3   Declaration Date 14th day of each month

   4.4   First Declaration Date will be the 14th day of the month following date of signature of the Supply Contract.

   4.5   Margins   4.5.1   Shortfall Margin: 1½%

                   4.5.2   Excess Margin: 10%

   4.6   Minimum Payment   £500

   4.7   Validity Period 24th February 1979 to 21st August 1979

   4.8   The largest figure to be entered in Column 2 of Schedule 3 shall not exceed £7,500,000

   4.9   The figure to be entered in Section 2 of Schedule 3 shall not exceed £1,762,500

   4.10 The figure to be entered in Section 3 of Schedule 3 shall not exceed £750,000

   4.11 Last date for Payments 28th February 1986

   4.12 Date of the Tender to Contract Agreement (Revised October 1978) shall, on acceptance of this Offer, be 24th February 1979

322

4.13 Forward Exchange Rates to be used to complete Currency Payments Schedule

List 1: Exchange Rates (US Dollars)	List 2: Periods (Months)	List 1:	List 2:
2.0071	1	1.8866	31
2.0025	2	1.8820	32
1.9974	3	1.8774	33
1.9967	4	1.8728	34
1.9941	5	1.8682	35
1.9913	6	1.8636	36
1.9879	7	1.8591	37
1.9850	8	1.8545	38
1.9829	9	1.8499	39
1.9787	10	1.8453	40
1.9755	11	1.8407	41
1.9716	12	1.8361	42
1.9671	13	1.8316	43
1.9627	14	1.8270	44
1.9583	15	1.8224	45
1.9539	16	1.8178	46
1.9495	17	1.8132	47
1.9451	18	1.8086	48
1.9406	19	1.8041	49
1.9362	20	1.7995	50
1.9318	21	1.7949	51
1.9274	22	1.7903	52
1.9230	23	1.7857	53
1.9186	24	1.7811	54
1.9141	25	1.7766	55
1.9095	26	1.7720	56
1.9049	27	1.7674	57
1.9003	28	1.7628	58
1.8957	29	1.7582	59
1.8911	30	1.7536	60 (and for each subsequent month)

5.   It is a condition of any Agreement to be entered into as a result of your
acceptance of this Offer that not later than your delivery to ECGD of the
Currency Payments Schedule pursuant to Article 5.1 of the Agreement you shall
have applied for,received and accepted an offer from ECGD of an ECGD specific
guarantee or an ECGD buyer credit facility in respect of the business the subject
of this Offer. Failure by the Company to satisfy such condition shall,unless
ECGD at its sole discretion shall otherwise elect in writing, render the
Agreement null and void EXCEPT that ECGD shall retain any Premium paid. This Offer
should not be construed as any indication of ECGD's willingness to consider any
application or make any offer in respect of an ECGD specific guarantee or an
ECGD buyer credit facility in respect of the business the subject of this Offer.

Yours faithfully
for the EXPORT CREDITS GUARANTEE DEPARTMENT

(Continued)

CURRENCY PAYMENTS SCHEDULE
SECTION 1

Schedule of Currency and sterling cash flow position (becomes Schedule 3 when approved by ECGD and attached to Agreement)

Column 1	Column 2	Column 3	Column 4	Column 5
Sterling amounts corresponding to Currency amounts in Column 4	Accumulation of Column 1 amounts	Periods in Months for which Currency amounts in Column 4 will be sold forward in accordance with Article 5 of the Tender to Contract Agreement	Currency amounts which will be sold forward or which have been sold forward in accordance with Article 5 of the Tender to Contract Agreement *US $/~~Francs~~	Accumulation of Column 4 amounts
300,000	300,000	1	602,130	602,130
50,000	350,000	4	99,835	701,965
50,000	400,000	5	99,705	801,670
50,000	450,000	6	99,565	901,235
50,000	500,000	7	99,395	1,000,630
50,000	550,000	8	99,250	1,099,880
50,000	600,000	9	99,145	1,199,025
50,000	650,000	10	98,935	1,297,960
50,000	700,000	11	98,775	1,396,735
50,000	750,000	12	98,580	1,495,315
50,000	800,000	13	98,355	1,593,670
50,000	850,000	14	98,135	1,691,805
560,000	1,410,000	15	1,096,648	2,788,453
510,000	1,920,000	21	985,218	3,773,671
510,000	2,430,000	27	971,499	4,745,170
510,000	2,940,000	33	957,474	5,702,644
510,000	3,450,000	39	943,449	6,646,093
510,000	3,960,000	45	929,424	7,575,517
510,000	4,470,000	51	915,399	8,490,916
510,000	4,980,000	57	901,374	9,392,290
510,000	5,490,000	63	894,336	10,286,626
510,000	6,000,000	69	894,336	11,180,962

* Delete as applicable

SECTION 2

ECGD's Maximum Liability
to make Payments and
payments pursuant to
Articles 6.2 and
8.2 of the Agreement: 23½% of the largest figure entered in Column 2

£.1,762,500..........

SECTION 3

The Company's Maximum liability
to make Payments and
payments pursuant to Articles
6.2 and 8.2 of the Agreement: 10% of the largest figure entered in Column 2

£.750,000...........

COMPANY'S SIGNATURE(S)

                SIGNED

                DATE

 CAPACITY OF SIGNATORY

NOTES

1   In the case of incorporated companies this Proposal should be signed by an
authorised officer for and on behalf of the company and should state the capacity
in which the signatory acts (eg Managing Director, Secretary etc).

2   In the case of partnership this Proposal should be signed by one or more
partners having authority to sign.

325

offer, i.e. 25 per cent of loss on £7.5 million less 1½ per cent born by the exporter.

Exhibit 18.8, para 4.10   The figure of £750,000 is 10 per cent of £7,500,000, representing the maximum amount of exchange profit the exporter would have to pay ECGD.

Exhibit 18.8, Currency payments schedule   Column 3 identifies the period numbers (in months from contract signature), on which currency payments will be received according to the contract terms.

Chapter 19

Measuring and reporting credit performance

'A credit department is only as good as last month's results'. This comment is frequently applied to business operations of all kinds. It is perhaps not a bad motto to put on the wall, but the prudent credit manager will take care to establish a pattern of reporting which will put each month's results into context.

Reporting to management takes many forms, ranging from a simple note of how much cash has been collected, to a detailed analysis of movements on the sales ledger, the ageing of major customer balances and the computation of ratios. Given a 'green field' situation — or at least a climate amenable to change — the principal recommendations are as follows:

1 Report monthly.
2 Balance statistics with narrative.
3 Be as brief as possible.
4 Identify trends.
5 Highlight problems.
6 Indicate progress towards objectives.

Monthly reporting is normal practice and particularly sensible where payment terms are monthly or similar, i.e. net 30 days. There are three measurements basic to the credit function:

1 Debtor level.
2 Cash.
3 Overdues.

While the relationship between cash and debtor level is so close as to be termed 'cause and effect', these items should be reported separately.

Debtor measurement

There are many possible ways of measuring the level of receivables, most of which are unsatisfactory because a change in sales volume or the incidence of holidays or shut-down periods prevents true comparisons being made over a period of time.

The system recommended is usually called the 'working back' method, referred to in Chapter 8. It is illustrated in Exhibit 19.1. The use of whole months and percentages of months avoids distortions arising from fluctuating sales volume and months of unequal lengths.

There is little merit in quoting the current debtor level in a monthly report without putting it in context. This can be done in two different ways:

a   Showing a trend, and
b   Comparing with budget.

A trend in the debtor level can hardly be detected in under three months. To go beyond six months involves too many statistics.

Comparison with budget assumes a debtors budget is set. If there is

---

Exhibit 19.1 Debtor measurement

Total debtors - £10,000,000 at 30 June 1979

Information needed - Sales invoiced (including VAT) in June, May and April

CALCULATION

Debtors	10,000,000	
Less June sales	(4,500,000)	= 1 month
	5,500,000	
Less May sales	(4,850,000)	= 1 month
Balance	650,000	

The balance of £650,000 has to be expressed as a percentage of next month's sales, i.e. April's:

$$April\ sales = 4,250,000$$

$$Balance = \frac{650,000}{4,250,000} = 15.2\%$$

The debtor level is therefore 2.15 months

---

no debtor budget, the credit manager should himself be setting targets for at least three months ahead. It is important when establishing a budget or target level for debtors that ratios, i.e. so many months sales, as in Exhibit 19.1, be used rather than actual monetary figures. These depend on sales achieved whereas a ratio is not affected by actual sales volume.

If the monthly report shows a trend (either improving or deteriorating) the credit manager should explain why, perhaps by identifying some major customers whose payments are slowing up. Similarly variations from budget should be explained.

Where several divisions or product groups are involved, it is very desirable to report separate debtor ratios for each unit because a satisfactory overall performance may conceal serious credit problems in some of the units. another refinement is to show separate ratios for home and export debtors. This can logically be extended to the calculation of a ratio for every different payment term used by the company, since a ratio has limited significance unless it is compared to terms of payment.

Cash

Using the 'working-back' method means that the amount of cash collected is the key to the debtor level. It is not possible to set an annual 'cash budget' since the amount of cash collectable depends initially on the actual sales volume. Each month, therefore, the credit manager must calculate how much cash is needed to achieve the budget debtor ratio. The method of doing this is shown in Exhibit 19.2.

Exhibit 19.2 Cash target calculation

Using the same figures as in Exhibit 19.1:

A *Budget debtor ratio for 31 July 1979 = 1.95 months*
B *1.95 months at the end of July will mean the current month (July) plus 95% of June sales*
C *Therefore the cash target for July will be total debtors at 30 June (£10,000,000) less 95% of June sales (£4,500,000), which equals:*

$$\begin{array}{r} 10,000,000 \\ \underline{(4,275,000)} \\ \underline{\underline{£5,725,000}} \end{array}$$

Overdues

Measurement of debtor-level alone cannot give an adequate picture of the sales ledger. The ratio of 2.15 months given in Exhibit 19.1 gives no indication of the ageing of debtors, and indeed two totally different age analyses could produce the same ratio, as shown in Exhibit 19.3. The ageing of Column A is clearly far less satisfactory than Column B, but both represent 2.15 months.

In Chapter 7 an example was given of a computer age-analysis (Exhibit 7.2, page 84). This is intended for use within the credit department and is not suitable for inclusion in a monthly report. The credit manager must decide which overdue statistics to select. Two possible figures are:

a   Percentage overdue of total debtors.
b   Percentage over 90 days overdue of total debtors.

If these results (or other similar figures) are reported, they should be reported against a target or budget and shown with the figures for previous months so that trends can be identified. Just as total debtor ratios should be broken down into divisions and home and export, so should overdue figures. An alternative to the percentage over 90 days overdue is to quote the actual amounts. In contrast to total debtors and even total overdues, these are hardly affected by sales volume and it may be more useful to monitor the fitures themselves.

The drawback of the type of overdue measurement described is that no distinction is made between payments received, say on the 2nd of the month, and those arriving on the 30th of the same month. An account paid one day late is included under the same heading as one paid thirty days late. In Chapter 7, brief reference was made to an account history report which showed the number of days' credit taken against each month's sales (Exhibit 7.5, page 90). This is valuable as a reference on individual customers but of no use in any end-of-period measurement across the whole ledger.

There is another method of measurement which produces a total of 'overdue days' both for individual customers and for the total ledger. It is only practicable if operated by computer.

Stage 1 The computer must hold a record of the due date of every invoice.
Stage 2 The program compares the actual payment date of each invoice with the due date, and gives each item paid a weighting factor determined by the number of days overdue.
Stage 3 At the end of the period a calculation is made, giving the number of overdue days.

Exhibit 19.3

	A		B
		Percentage of	
Current month	45	Total debtors	45
1st overdue month	23		35
2nd overdue month	9		20
3rd overdue month	4		–
4th overdue month	4		–
5th overdue month	3		–
6 months overdue and prior	12		–
	100%		100%

Example Assume there are five customers on the ledger, named Brown, Jones, Smith, Black and Thomas. Their purchases in June (on net monthly terms) and payment record up to 30 August are as shown in Exhibit 19.4. Conventional debtor measurement would show that at the end of August, all the June accounts of these buyers having been paid, the debtor level would be two months (assuming no overdues exist prior to June and no July accounts are paid to terms), regardless of whether payments were received as shown or altogether on 30 August. The additional measurement tells us that June accounts were paid in an average period of 45.5 days (31 days in July being the allowed period plus 14.5 overdue days).

Exhibit 19.4

Name	June purchases	Date paid	Number of days overdue	Weighted value
Brown	2,000	5 Aug	5	10,000 (2,000 x 5)
Jones	8,000	8 Aug	8	64,000 (8,000 x 8)
Smith	5,000	13 Aug	13	65,000 (5,000 x 13)
Black	3,000	20 Aug	20	60,000 (3,000 x 20)
Thomas	4,000	30 Aug	30	120,000 (4,000 x 30)
TOTAL	22,000			319,000

Average overdue days for all five customers

$$= 319{,}000/22{,}000 = 14.5 \text{ days}$$

The same principle is applied whether there are five customers each with one payment (as above) or one customer making five payments or five customers each making five payments. Any payments arriving ahead of due date can be given a negative weighting.

The merit of this method is that it produces a precise measurement of credit taken. If targets are based on it, the problem of a month-end cash scramble is largely avoided because payments received one or two days late are given a much more favourable weighting than those arriving a whole month late. The disadvantage is that a special computer programme must be written, capable of matching every line item paid with the appropriate due date. Debit notes, credit notes and other adjustments must be ignored.

A further method of reporting overdues is given in Exhibit 19.5. By expressing the overdue balance at the end of month 2 as a percentage of the total account at the end of month 1, attention is focused on the slowest paying customers. Customers owing above an agreed minimum are listed individually, with a 'balancing' line for all those below the minimum. Other features can include the use of a target overdue percentage, the listing of customers in descending order of overdue percentage and the inclusion of the due date on items more than six months overdue.

Any measurement and reporting of overdues against a target is worthwhile if it prevents the efforts of the credit manager being concentrated too much on the achievement of a cash target, which might be reached solely by accelerating the flow of current and near-current money.

Beyond these three basic types of measurement — debtor level, cash and overdues — there are, of course, others which can be added. Some examples are as follows:

1 *Bad debts* Serious bad debts must be reported as they arise. It is wrong, however, to focus too much attention on the incidence of bad debts, unless an adverse trend is developing. On an annual basis, the amount written off must be reported but this should not be given undue importance. With most companies in most years, the amount of money tied up in overdue accounts is generally greater than that lost in bad debts.

2 *Disputes* If the level of items in query is a significant problem, the monthly volume should be reported. It can be helpful to turn the figure into a ratio. Thus, if 10 per cent of the debtors in Exhibit 19.1 are under dispute, this represents 0.215 month. If the queries had been resolved, the debtor ratio would be 1.935 months.

Exhibit 19.5 Home trade overdues as at 31 May 19.. (1979 budget ratio is 40%)

Account at 30 Apr £	Customer	Credit limit £	Total account at 31 May £	Amount overdue at 31 May £	Ratio – Col.4 as % of Col.1	Age analysis, months				Comments
						1 £	2 £	3 £	3+* £	
10,509	J.Bloggs	15,000	18,904	10,509	100.0	7,304	1,615	1,590		
43,682	ABC Co.	50,000	57,311	23,907	54.7	12,633	11,274			
45,799	British Widgets	50,000	42,988	14,610	31.9	14,610				
	All others		51,087	16,342	32.0	9,503	3,412	2,916	511	
TOTALS			170,290	65,368	45.4	44,050	16,301	4,506	511	

Note 1 – Overdue amounts in excess of £10,000 are to be shown separately together with a total for all other overdue amounts.

Note 2 – Customers would be ranked by ratio in descending order.

*If debt is more than six months overdue, the due date for payment should be noted.

3 Credit decisions A relatively small number of companies endeavour to highlight the more positive side of credit activities by reporting the number or value of favourable to unfavourable credit decisions. This can be limited to new accounts or applied to all referred orders, in which case it may be worth relating the percentage rejections to each risk category. Whilst the credit manager may derive some satisfaction from this type of report, unless it is used in some way outside his department there is little point in producing it.

4 Export ratios Companies exporting to many different countries will be interested to see a debtor ratio (or 'collection period') for each major market. While each must be related to the primary payment terms in the market, the result will show how credit costs and the consequent effects on profits vary from market to market.

No form of report should consist entirely of statistics, or else it becomes virtually unreadable. In addition to the selective measurements, the credit manager should include brief references to any problems such as the worsening payment behaviour of a key customer, a request for extended credit by a major buyer or the continued lack of settlement in a large dispute.

Budgets

The credit manager will generally be asked to prepare a debtor or receivables budget for the following year. As already indicated it is preferable to budget ratios only because the inevitable variations in actual sales compared to budget sales will swiftly make a debtor budget using money values quite useless.

In preparing a budget, attention must be paid to regular 'seasonal factors', such as a rise in the debtor ratio at the end of August because of the holiday period affecting the throughput of invoices in customers' accounts payables. Another factor that must be checked is any expected change in the 'mix' of sales, e.g. an increasing proportion of exports on longer terms than home sales, or a switch from distribution sales to direct outlets, which may lead to difficulties in cash collections. Finally, any 'external' factor considered likely to affect credit operations should also be allowed for, e.g. computerising the sales ledger.

It follows from the above that if debtor budgets are to be prepared as painlessly as possible, the credit manager must educate the sales office to provide him with certain information which would probably not otherwise be prepared — for example, sales forecasts by different payment terms.

With the increasing emphasis being placed on cash-flow, credit managers can expect to be under pressure to reduce debtor ratios. What is achievable will depend very much on the starting point, and every credit manager will be aware of 'the law of diminishing returns'. As the debtor ratio reduces, so a further reduction requires an even greater effort. There may come a point where the credit manager has to use his commercial judgement to temper the demands of his financial masters. It may seem logical (and entirely reasonable) to persuade all customers to pay to terms, and a debtor ratio goal of 1.0 month (if everyone is on net monthly terms) should therefore be attainable. Quite apart from the existence of disputes and those customers unable to pay, the major obstacle will usually be a number of big customers who refuse to release their cheques those few days (or possibly weeks) earlier. Assuming that all approaches have failed, the credit manager is left with the choice of trying to force an improvement, through the holding of orders, or accepting defeat (without admitting it to the customer, of course).

As in so many situations, the 'right' decision will depend partly on the size of the gap between the actual and the required payment dates and partly on the relative strengths of buyer and seller in the market. A delay of up to, say, ten days will probably have to be accepted unless the supplier is in a monopoly or near-monopoly situation. On the other hand, payments regularly arriving three weeks or more late can reasonably be regarded as unacceptable. These are only intended as broad guidelines, and every credit manager has to determine what he believes is the ultimate or best debtor ratio he can achieve in the context of his own industry.

Similarly any budgets or targets prepared for the reduction of overdues must be realistic. If overdues aged 90 days or more are £10,000 at the end of December 1979, it is not very sensible to fix a target of nil for December 1980. The right target can only be established by reference to how that overdue figure has moved over the previous twelve months, or by how long it has taken to reduce from £20,000 to £10,000. Targets of this nature can usually be broken down into smaller units within the department. It is most important to set targets which, while difficult to achieve, are not impossible. Quarterly reviews of progress may be helpful, and the credit manager should be ready to change year-end targets in the light of events through the year.

Expense budgets

Credit department costs are subject to the same controls as those of any other department. In times of declining demand and rising unit costs, every area of the company must expect close scrutiny, which may result in expense cuts or even reductions in staff.

In this environment, the credit manager needs to be able to demonstrate the cost-effectiveness of his operation. A simple method is to calculate the cost of collecting every £1,000 of sales. This takes no account of how efficiently collections are being made. An alternative is to produce a kind of productivity ratio, using the following formula:

$$100 \ (SH/MAD) \ / \ R$$

where SH is the sales per head (in credit department) in the previous year, MAD the mean average debtor level in the previous year and R the ratio in the base year. This is illustrated in Exhibit 19.6. (Acknowledgement and thanks to Mr H. Edwards, Treasurer of ITT Components Group Europe, who originated the basis of this ratio.)

In this example, within two years the credit department has succeeded in reducing the debtor ratio by 13.6 per cent, while sales have increased by 40 per cent. Credit staff has actually decreased by 20 per cent. Using the formula, this indicates that credit department productivity has more than doubled. Had the number of staff

Exhibit 19.6

	Year 1 (base year)	Year 2	Year 3
Number of credit department staff	10	9	8
Annual sales, £million	50	60	70
Sales/head, £million	5.0	6.66	8.75
Mean average debtor level, months	2.2	2.0	1.9

Base year ratio = 5.0/2.2 = 2.27

Since this is the base year, 2.27 is treated as 100.

Year 2 ratio = (6.66/2.0) ÷ 2.27 x 100

= (3.33/2.27) x 100 = 1.466 x 100

= <u>147</u>

Year 3 ratio = (8.75/1.9) ÷ 2.27 x 100

= (4.65/2.27) x 100 = 2.048 x 100

= <u>205</u>

remained constant (at 10), productivity would have increased by only 62 per cent.

The main weakness in this formula is that it assumes that increased sales result in a proportionate volume of work in the credit department. This is not always true.

Bad debt provisions

In the absence of firm rules laid down by a company's auditors or accountants, the credit manager should draw up his own disciplines for determining the level of bad debt provisions.

Both the age and the 'quality' of a debt should be considered. Under the first heading, every item aged over a certain period should be examined with a view to reserving unless there is a valid reason to exclude it. Valid reasons would include a recent promise of payment (the customer being regarded as solvent), or an existing reserve for credit (goods having been rejected or returned). Quite apart from items selected on an age basis, there may well be other items of more recent date which must be regarded as doubtful quality. These will include customers under Receivership or in liquidation, customers in the hands of solicitors and possibly those in the hands of collection agents. A further category may include export debts 'frozen' by transfer delays.

Listings of this nature may only be required annually, but it is a good discipline to review quarterly. Where credit insurance polices (home or export) are held, a reduction in bad debt reserve may be possible. Credit insurance, however, is intended to protect against the unexpected failure, i.e. those which would probably not be identified in a bad debt provision exercise.

337

References and further reading

General

Credit Control and Debt Collection, British Institute of Management Guide No. 5 (1974).
Credit Management Handbook, Gower Press (1976).
Industrial Performance Analysis, Inter Company Comparisons Ltd.
Benz, G., *International Trade Credit Management*, Gower Press (1975).
Grandjean, G., 'A proposal to develop better credit information in Europe', Thesis, Credit Research Foundation, New York (1976).
Kirkman, P.R.A., *Modern Credit Management*. George Allen & Unwin (1977).
Parker, R.H., *Understanding Company Financial Statements*, Penguin (1972).

Insolvency

Thompson, J.H., *'Sales' Law Relating to Bankruptcy, Liquidations and Receiverships*, MacDonald & Evans (Sixth edition, 1976).

Computer aids

Whiteside, C.D., *EDP Systems for Credit Management*, Wiley-Interscience (1971).

Credit insurance

Carson, P.J.B., *Credit Insurance: An Appreciation,* Chartered Insurance Institute, 20 Aldermanbury, London EC2Y 7HY.

Export credit and finance: books

Accounting Principles & Practice in European Countries, Institute of Chartered Accountants in England and Wales.
Butterworth, J., *Debt Collection Letters in Ten Languages*, Gower Press (1978).
Lafferty, M., *Accounting in Europe*, Woodhead-Faulkner Ltd in association with National Westminster Bank Ltd.
Oldham, K.M., *Accounting Systems and Practice in Europe*, Gower Press.
Schmitthof, C., *The Export Trade*, Stevens & Sons Ltd (Sixth edition).
Syrett, W.W., *Finance of Overseas Trade*, Pitman (1971).
Syrett and Pither, *Sources and Management of Export Finance*, Gower Press (1971).
Watson, A., *Finance of International Trade*, Institute of Bankers, 10 Lombard St, London EC3 (1976).

Export credit and finance: other publications

Croner's Reference Book for Exporters, Croner Publications, New Malden, Surrey.

The following publications are available on request from the Swiss Bank Corporation, 99 Gresham St, London EC2:
British Exports & Exchange Restrictions Abroad
Documentary Operations
Bid & Performance Guarantees

The International Chamber of Commerce, 6-14 Dean Farrer St, London SW1H 0DT, publish the following:
Uniform Rules for a Combined Transport Document
Uniform Rules for Contract Guarantees
The Problem of Clean Bills of Lading
Guide to Documentary Credit Operations
ICC Arbitration: the International Solution to International Business Disputes

Documentary Letters of Credit and *An Introduction to Exporting*,
Barclays Bank International Ltd, 54 Lombard St, London EC3P
3AH.

Services for Exporters, Midland Bank Ltd, International Division,
60 Gracechurch St, London EC3P 3BN.

International Trade, Hambross Bank Ltd, 41 Bishopgate, London
EC2P 2AA.

Exports: Credit Insurance & Finance, Report of the proceedings of the
ECGD/NEDO seminars, National Economic Development Office.

The Forfaiting Manual, Finanz AG London Ltd.

Export Handbook (annually), British Overseas Trade Board.

Exporters Handbook (annually) and *Export Times* (monthly), Export
Times Publishing Ltd, 60 Fleet St, London EC4Y 1LA.

Trade & Industry (weekly), HMSO.

Export Direction (monthly), IDG Publishing Ltd, 140-146 Camden St,
London NW1 9PP.

Foreign exchange

Foreign Exchange & the Corporate Treasurer, Heywood, J., A & C
Black (1978).

Foreign Exchange and Your Business and *Forward Foreign Exchange
Contracts*, Barclays Bank International Ltd.

Foreign Exchange & Money Market Operations, Swiss Bank
Corporation.

References to other publications, etc.

Trade & Industry (various statistics).

British Institute of Management survey on Credit Management (1974)
— quoted from (Chapter 2).

Credit & Financial Newsletter, published by National Association of
Credit Management, 475 Park Avenue South, New York 10016 —
statistics taken from (Chapter 2).

'The Exeter Survey', published in *Modern Credit Management* by
P.R.A. Kirkman (George Allen & Unwin), information taken from
(Chapter 2).

Lloyd's Law Reports, and *Journal of Business Law* — both referred to
(Chapter 3).

Conditions of Sale – Retention of Title by D. Roberts, published by Institute of Chartered Secretaries & Administrators — referred to (Chapter 3).

Credit Management Databook, Gower Press, referred to (Chapter 4).

Industrial Performance Analysis, published by Inter Company Comparisons Ltd, referred to (Chapter 5).

'Business Failures in England & Wales', R. Brough, published in *Business Ratios* Issue 2 (1967) — quoted from (Chapter 5).

Survey by J.C. Drury, Huddersfield Polytechnic — information taken from (Chapter 5).

Article on factoring by Anthony Thorncroft in *Financial Times* (16 January 1978) — information taken from (Chapter 9).

'A Proposal to Develop better Credit Information in Europe' by G. Grandjean (Thesis published by the Credit Research Foundation, New York 1977) — quoted from and information taken from (Chapter 11).

British Exports & Exchange Restrictions Abroad, Swiss Bank Corporation — referred to (Chapter 13).

Debt Collection Letters in Ten Languages by J. Butterworth, Gower Press — referred to (Chapter 14).

'ECGD Facilities at a Glance' — chart reproduced with permission of ECGD (Chapter 15).

'Credit Limit Check for ECGD Guarantees' — chart reproduced with permission of Stewart Wrightson (Credit Management) Ltd. (Chapter 15).

'Guide to ECGD-backed Supplier Credit Finance' & 'Guide to establishing a Single Project Buyer Credit Facility' — diagrams reproduced with permission of Midland Bank Ltd (Chapter 16).

Pre-shipment finance illustration — based on a paper issued by Barclays Bank International Ltd with their approval (Chapter 16).

342

Facilities offered by Export Finance Houses — extract from a quotation given by Grindlay Brandts Export Finance Ltd (Chapter 16).

The Forfaiting Manual by Finanz AG London Ltd, referred to (Chapter 16).

Help for the smaller exporter — description of scheme operated by Midland Bank Ltd. (Chapter 16).

Conditional performance bond — specimen supplied by Credit & Guarantee Insurance Co. Ltd (Chapter 17).

ICC Arbitration and *Uniform Rules for Contract Guarantees*, published by International Chamber of Commerce — referred to Chapter 17.

Case study on ECGD Tender to Contract cover, produced with help of ECGD (Chapter 18).

Index

The letter-by-letter system has been adopted. The letter (E) after an entry indicates Export matters, unless already obvious. The so-called Third World is indexed under Lesser Developed Countries.

345

347

Earnings, attachment of, 129
ETGs (E), 254
Evaluation of Credit Performance (E), *see*
Credit Performance
Exchange, problems relating to foreign, *see*
Currency and foreign exchange
problems
Exeter Survey, 1975, 11
Expense budgets (E), 334-5
Expenses and collection (E), 227-8
Export Credit Guarantee Department:
assistance from, and decision to allow
credit, 230-1
circular of (Jan. 1978), 250
Comprehensive Short-term Guarantee,
254-9
deciding when to call in aid from, 259-60
diagrammatic explanation of, 251
Extended Terms Guarantee, 254
finance facilities, 274-82
acceptance credits, 275
barter, 281
confirming houses, 275-8
export merchants, 278
forfaiting, 279-81
instalment method, 279
leasing, 278-9
LIBOR, 276, 280
small firms, special aid for, 282
ways and means, list of, 274
insurance policy, value of, 236
use of, for legal action to recover debts,
247
what makes value for money for,
261
maintenance of contact with, 273-4
problems that can be encountered, 261-2
roles of accountant and sales department,
inter-relationship of, 143-4
services provided, 249-51
specific guarantees, 263-73
buyer credit, 264
specialised facilities, 272-3
supplier credit, 263-4
subsidiaries guarantee, 259
supplementary stocks guarantee, 259
see also Bonds and Contract Risks
Export merchants, 278
Export Trade, The (journal), 182
Extended credit, effect of, 5-6
Extended Terms Guarantee (E), 254

Factoring as means to collect debts, 133
Federal Democratic Republic of West
Germany, *see* Germany (West)
Filing system, must be essentially good, 95
Finance, Credit and International New
York (FCIB), 157

Finance for export, *see* Export Credit
Guarantee Department
Finland:
accounts and exports to, 154
equivalent terminology used in, 181
specimen letters of collection in local
language, 245
see also Currency and foreign exchange
problems
Firms, stability of, *see* Risk assessment
Flemish:
equivalent terminology used in, 167-8
specimen letters of collection in local
language, 245
see also Currency and foreign exchange
problems
FOB (E), 183, 196
Force majeure clauses in export contracts,
296-7
Foreign exchange, *see* Currency and foreign
exchange problems; Export credit
guarantees
Foreign terminology, English equivalents of,
159-81
Forfaiting system for financing exports,
279-81
Forward contracts, operating, 309-12
Forward premiums, 314
Forward rate (of foreign exchange), 308-9
Forwarding agent, receipts from (E), 187
France:
accounts and exports to, 148-9
equivalent terminology used in, 159-61
practical problem illustrated, 234-5
specimen letters of collection in local
language, 245
see also Currency and foreign exchange
problems
Free On Board (E), 183, 196
Freight, *see* Shipping

Garnishee, order of, 129
Germany (West):
accounts and exports to, 149-50
equivalent terminology used in, 162-4
specimen letters of collection in local
language, 245
see also Currency and foreign exchange
problems
Glossary of foreign equivalents in
terminology, 159-81
Goods, seizure of, 129
Government-controlled business, assessment
of credit risk and, 56-7
Grace, allowing, 25
Greece, accounts and exports to, 154
Group consignments, documentation for,
187

349

351